VIA Folios 72

Pino Aprile

Terroni

All That Has Been Done To Ensure That The Italians of The South Became "Southerners"

Translated from the Italian by
Ilaria Marra Rosiglioni

Library of Congress Control Number: 2011939913

Terroni first appeared in Italian in 2010
published by
Edizioni PIEMME Spa
www.edizpiemme.it

Cover image used with the kind permission of Edizioni Piemme.

Printed in the United States.

Published by
BORDIGHERA PRESS
John D. Calandra Italian American Institute
25 West 43rd Street, 17th Floor
New York, NY 10036

VIA FOLIOS 72
ISBN 978-1-59954-031-3

"We do not have the right to be lazy."
— *Gaetano Salvemini*

"The place where one would like to live without humiliating anyone and without being humiliated."
— *Emmanuel Roblès*
definition of "homeland"

"Someday, this land will be beautiful."
— *Paolo Borsellino*

Publisher's Note

The word "terrone" is an offensive term used by people in northern Italy in order to describe those from southern Italy. With an etymology tied to the term "terra" (dirt, land), an English equivalent would be almost impossible to conjure up. "Dirtball" might be close to an appropriate term in English, but it does not possess the derogatory socio-cultural foundation that "terrone" has in Italian. Not dissimilar to the various, negative epithets launched at Italian immigrants a century or so ago in this country ("dago," "wop," "guinea," "grease-ball," spaghetti-bender," and the like), "terrone" is often associated with that type of person who is ignorant, uneducated, lazy, unwilling to work, rude, and of poor hygiene.

For this reason, we decided, together with the author, Pino Aprile, and the translator, Ilaria Marra Rosiglioni, to maintain the original Italian title, *Terroni*, for the English translation.

Also, it should be known, that Italy's Corte di Cassazione (Supreme Court) had in fact upheld a lower court's decision that the term "terrone" is indeed a derogatory and offensive term. As a result, the guilty party, a high school student, had to pay his classmate of southern origin €1,000 in reparations (http://www.corriere.it/Primo_Piano/Cronache/2005/04_Aprile/19/terrone.shtml).

Finally, Bordighera Press acknowledges the kind generosity of the Italian Language Inter-Cultural Alliance (ILICA) for providing the necessary funds for the publication of this book.

TABLE OF CONTENTS

CHAPTER 1

Becoming a Southerner

I did not know that the Piedmontese did to the South what the Nazis did to Marzabotto. Many times. For years.

They effaced many towns forever, in "anti-terrorist" operations, much like the U.S. military did in Iraq.

I did not know that, in acts of reprisal, they allowed themselves the liberty to rape women from the South, much like in the Balkans during their ethnic conflict or like the Moroccans with the French troops. These acts were performed in the Ciociaria region during an invasion of the South performed in order to free Italy from Fascism. (Anytime the South is "freed," they lose something of value)

I was ignorant of the fact that, in the name of the Unification, the "*fratelli d'Italia*," our Italian brothers, also retained the right to sack the cities of the South like the *Landsknecht* soldiers in Rome. I was also ignorant of the fact that they employed torture like the Americans at Abu Ghraib, the French in Algeria, and Pinochet in Chile.

I did not know that in Parliament, in Turin, a representative (an ex-Garibaldi supporter) compared the ferociousness of the Piedmontese massacres of the South to those of "Tamerlane, Genghis Khan, and Attila the Hun." Another representative preferred to be silent about such matters, stating, "These are revelations which would certainly horrify the rest of Europe." Garibaldi himself spoke of "things that are pertinent to cesspools."

I was also unaware that Southerners were often incarcerated without formal accusations, without trials, and without convictions, as was the case with the Muslims at Guantànamo. There, the prisoners numbered in the hundreds and were considered terrorists because they were Muslims. In Italy, the prisoners numbered in the hundreds of thousands and were considered brigands by definition because they were from the South. If they happened to be children, they were considered precocious brigands. If they were women, they were either considered brigands themselves or wives and daughters of brigands or in some manner associated with brigands (up until the third recognizable degree of ancestry). They were considered brigands even if they were from the same town as other presumed brigands. Often, a mere suspicion was enough for imprisonment. All of this was naturally in accordance with the law, like in South Africa under apartheid rule.

I believed that brigands were actually brigands, and not former Bourbon soldiers and guerrilla patriots who defended their invaded homeland.

I did not know that the Southern countryside became like that of Kosovo, complete with mass executions and respective graves as well as burning hillside towns dotted with tens of thousands of refugees marching away.

I did not want to believe that the first-ever concentration camps in Europe were actually put into operation by the Northern Italians to torture and kill Southern Italians by the thousand, perhaps even by the tens of thousands (we are not certain of the exact number because the bodies were dissolved in caustic lime) as in the Soviet Union under Stalin.

I was ignorant of the fact that the Italian Ministry of Foreign Affairs searched for years for a "desolate land" somewhere between Patagonia, Borneo and other distant shores, in order to deport Southerners and annihilate them far from prying eyes.

I did not know that our Northern Italian brothers emptied the wealthy Southern banks, palaces, museums, and even private homes (even stealing eating utensils) in order to pay off Piedmont's debts and to establish their enormous private fortunes.

I could never have imagined that Garibaldi's famous "*Mille*" soldiers had robbed both public and private funds.

I did not know that, in such a unified Italy, there was an additional tax imposed upon the Southerners to pay for the war expenses incurred during the war to conquer the South. This war was never even officially declared.

I was ignorant of the fact that the occupation of the Kingdom of the Two Sicilies was decided upon, planned by, and protected by the English and the French and partially funded by the freemasons (as stated by Garibaldi and all freemason leaders through to Grand Master Armando Corona, in 1988).

I did not know that the Kingdom of the Two Sicilies was, up until the moment of the aggression, one of the most industrialized countries in the world. It stood in third place behind England and France prior to the invasion.

There was no "Bourbon bureaucracy," meaning a situation of chaos and inefficiency: an expert sent by Cavour to the Two Sicilies, with the intent to give some order to the scene, reported that he found an "admirable financial structure." He then proposed to copy this structure, as stated in a report that is "a sincere and continuous praise" of the system. Meanwhile, "the model that governs our administration," from 1861, "is Franco-Napoleonic, whose Savoy version was formulated since the unification while under a myriad local and corporative pressures." (Marco Meriggi, *Breve Storia dell'Italia Settentrionale*)

I was ignorant of the fact that the newly unified state ferociously taxed millions of desperate Southerners who emigrated to America to financially support the owners of the ships that carried them and of the Northerners, who vacationed for a few months of the year in Switzerland.

I could not imagine that the unified state of Italy placed higher taxes on those dying of malaria in the caves of the *Sassi* in Matera than on the owners of the villas on Lake Como.

I have had prior experience with the railroad system being worse in the South than in the North, but not at the turn of the 21st century: the rest of Italy has railways fit for use by high speed trains while the *Mezzogiorno* (the South) has thousands fewer kilometers than prior to World War II (7,598 kilometers versus 8,871 kilometers). Furthermore, these railways almost always have a single track and a large portion of the network does not have electricity.

Pino Aprile

How could I have imagined that we could be in such poor conditions when during the "Bourbon Inferno," in order to oblige us to enter the "paradise" brought to us by the Piedmontese, reprisals, massacres, a dozen years of combat, special laws, states of siege and concentration camps would be necessary? How could I have imagined that when we were finally able to quit preferring death to their version of "paradise" that millions of us would choose to emigrate (when this had never happened before in our history)?

I was ignorant of the fact that I should have studied French to truly understand that I am Italian: "*Le Royaume d'Italie est aujourd' hui un fait,*" Cavour announced to the Senate, "*Le Roi notre auguste Souverain prend pour lui-même et pour ses successeurs le titre du Roi d'Italie.*"

I believed in Giosue Carducci's words in *Letture del Risorgimento italiano*: "Never has the unification of a nation been made by more grand aspirations and pure intelligence nor with more noble sacrifice of holy souls nor with more broad consensus of all the population." This affirmation was printed as the opening of the book (*Il Risorgimento italiano*) distributed for free by the Centers of Reading and Information curated by the Ministry of Public Education's Popular Education Department from 1964. The curator, Alberto M. Ghisalberti states that "after a century (...) the critical revision undertaken by historians could possibly suggest different interpretations than those originally intended (...) regarding the complex reality surrounding the "broad consensus" to which the poet refers." Those who know, understand. Those who do not know, continue not to understand. I later discovered that Carducci, privately wrote, "Does this Italy really seem to be a beautiful thing?" For him, to avoid speaking of Italy "could also be considered a charitable act" (*Storia d'Italia*, Einaudi).

I had always believed in the history books and in the legend of Garibaldi.

I had no idea that I was a Southerner, in the sense that I had never attributed any value, negative or positive, to the fact that I was born more to the South or North of someone else. I only believed myself to be lucky because I was born an Italian, and among the luckiest of Italians because I lived by the sea.

As I learned these things, I spoke of them. I was stupefied. My listeners were incredulous. Then, I became furious and my readers became annoyed. They believed what I said to be exaggerations or purely inventions and if they were to be true, that these facts were too old to be important.

I noticed that I became "Southern" because I stupidly nurtured a sort of pride towards the geography that Bossi and his accomplices, also stupidly, wanted me to be ashamed of. They use the word "Italian" as an insult and yet they live on the part of the peninsula that was named "Italy" when Rome reorganized the empire (the Southern part was named "Apulia," from the name of my region. However, the first "Italy" in history was actually a piece of Calabria on the Tyrrhenian Sea).

Much has been written about the South, but it does not appear to have served much of a purpose because "any battle fought against widely-held prejudices is a lost battle," according to Nicholas Humphrey (*A History of the Mind*). "Why don't you reprint one of those Southern publications from twenty or thirty years ago? Who would notice that time has passed, uselessly?", suggested Piero Gobetti eighty years ago to Tommaso Fiore, who fortunately wrote *Un popolo di formiche*. Today, an indomitable economist named Gianfranco Viesti (*Abolire il Mezzogiorno*) throws up his arms and states, "To speak of the South means to speak of that which has already been said and that which has already failed."

The situation does not change because the current state of things is useful to the stronger part of the country, even if the country presents itself with two different sets of problems: "Southern Issues" pertaining to the aspiration of the South to come out of imposed subordination and "Northern Issues," recently coined, pertaining to the willingness of the North to maintain the South's subordination and the profitable advantage of power conquered with weapons and unequal legislation. After 150 years, this system risks splitting the country. All of this information is well known; people pretend to be unaware of it because there are too many interests at stake. In this manner, it happens that the truth is written, but not read. If it is read, it is not believed. If it is believed, it is not taken into consideration. If it is taken into consideration, it is not enough to change one's behavior and to compel one to act "out of consequence." Southerners always complain and convicts always proclaim their innocence. This comparison is not casual; in the book *Sull'identità meridionale,* Mario Alcaro writes: "One could say that it is like preparing a case for a defendant, of a Southerner who seeks an answer to the criticism and accusations which have rained down upon him." Prejudice (*pre* means "before") is a conviction without a trial. I suspect that its persistence avoids, to those who hold it, an admission of guilt. "Man is an animal that is moved in a decisive manner by guilt," according to Luigi Zoja in *Storia dell'arroganza.* "A feeling of guilt may be moved, but not canceled." The North, the aggressor, accuses the victim of the consequences of the aggression, all while removing any trace of remorse, if there ever was any.

We Southerners know this all very well: it no longer even shocks us, rather it tires us. "You feel that the people do not understand you, and that you must speak louder, yelling," Chekov explains. "The shouting becomes repugnant. You are forced to speak lower, and perhaps in a little while you will cease to speak altogether." We find ourselves amongst each other's shouting and by now we are no longer held back by the shame which once rendered this discussion civil.

Today, new turmoil fuels a search for historical truth, not only from the South, but from further down in the university halls, politics, and the institutions. It is not easy to understand where this search could take us; whether it be to an equal and opposite revanchist movement in response to the racist pro-North policies of the *Lega* and its respective associates or to a common growth in understanding and acknowledgment: a new "Southern" mentality that wouldn't only be "Southern." It would be a return to one's origins for those born in the North, especially the Lombards, in order to restore a decent soul to an Italy that has lost it, in the failure of its politics that are prey to personal and territorial egotism.

I fear, due to the pessimism of reason and because I see signs that
indicate that outcome, that the worst will prevail because "of" and
not "in spite of" its defects (it is the law of Greg and Galton, as I
discuss in *Elogio dell'imbecille*) But for optimism's sake, I hope the
opposite will come true (not even the worst things last forever,
they die as well).

The North, from the point of view of the South, is Cain: from
there came those who, claiming to be our brothers, carried out the
largest massacre ever in this region, which is saying a great deal,
since we have seen our fair share of Barbarians. They accomplished this with the sole intent to rob us. The majority of the museums documenting the *Risorgimento* are found in the Center and
the North of the country, according to Mario Isnenghi in his *Breve
storia dell'Italia unita a uso dei perplessi*.

The North is where I worked for many years, where I have
many friends and the place I also considered home. This is much
like the South, where I was born, and the Center, where I currently reside. Italians move North in search of money and South
in search of their souls. Abroad, they cease to be Northerners or
Southerners, and are only Italians (considered by others to be,
without distinction between North or South, either geniuses or
scoundrels).

The South, from the point of view of the North, is Hell, like
L'inferno, the title of Giorgio Bocca's book. In 2008, Bocca wrote in
the *Venerdì* magazine published by the *Repubblica* newspaper, although I am unsure of how provocative the tone may have been:
"Yes, it is true, I am an Anti-Southerner.... I may come off as a racist, and perhaps I am." No one objected to this statement. After all,
is the South not, according to its geographical and moral position,
a place of evil? Is it not the type of evil that cannot be redeemed
because it is Hell? Hell is defined by Alexandre Dumas as "Heav-
en inhabited by devils." This was stated by the same Dumas that
accompanied Garibaldi in his conquests and plundering missions.

"Cain" on the other hand, is a more appropriate nickname that
is closer to the truth. Cain is not lost forever, like those who fall
down to Hell. He is given a chance to redeem himself in another

land, even if he does not take this opportunity. It seems as though they do not want to take this opportunity either because they still benefit from the advantages that they inherited from those who came to efface us. When I write "Northerners" and "Piedmontese," I don't intend to generalize (which happens when "Southerners" are mentioned). Some of the greatest pro-South advocates were from the North; and the "*askari*" who in Parliament vote against equality (since 1861) for the regions that elected them, are from the South.

The South has been deprived of its institutions; it has been deprived of its industries, its riches and of its ability to react. It has also been deprived of its people (with an emigration that was induced or forced unlike any other group in Europe). Lastly, through a cultural lobotomy, the South was deprived of its self-awareness; its memory.

We no longer know who we were. It happened similarly to the Jews in the Holocaust (the comparison is not exaggerated: hundreds of thousands, or perhaps even a million, Southerners were killed by the Savoy troops; thirteen to twenty million people, according to records, were forced to abandon their land over the course of a century). Many who were able to survive the concentration camps began to wonder whether the evil that was inflicted upon them was perhaps deserved. When the damage becomes intolerable one seeks a cause to blame it on, even if the cause is inexistent or absurd, in order not to lose one's mind. The historian Ettore Ciccotti spoke of "a sort of Italian anti-Semitism" referring to the treatment of Southern Italians. The *Lega*, an expression of local comical nationalism, were it not so tragic, is the most sincere example of this.

It has happened that the Southerners have made those prejudices, of which they were the object, their own. It is by some odd phenomenon of inversion of blame that the victim has turned into the executioner. This happens when the pain of the blame that one takes on becomes more tolerable than the evil that has been inflicted.

It is in this manner that the resistance against the invaders, rapes as well as the loss of wealth, life, identity, and of one's own country becomes "shame." It is only now, after a century and a half, that Southern families are beginning to recuperate their pride in their ancestors, who had previously been labeled as brigands by their aggressors (Naturally this phenomenon has also caused the moral redemption of those who effectively were brigands as well. There were other criminals: those mafia members that were enlisted by Garibaldi and the Piedmontese, but they were considered "good Italians." To be deemed a criminal it does not matter what you do, but for whom).

One day I calculated how many of my family members emigrated, from both my mother and father's sides. The people from Puglia were amongst the last to emigrate from the country. I determined that one out of every two family members emigrated.

One of my cousins, after having spent six months in the North, returned for her summer vacation (This is much like what happens with birds. The periodic reappearance of emigrants announces the seasons. They call them "birds of passage" in North America and "*golondrinas*," or swallows, in Southern Italy). She had changed considerably: she dressed with a flashier style and spoke with an accent that was not hers. She acquired the habit of squeezing her shoulders in a gesture of annoyance and held her chin high. She began to speak badly of the Southerners with a tone of fiery resentment and ridicule. My mother, out of curiosity, asked her, "But what do they do that is so terrible?" My cousin was quiet out of evident stupor and proceeded to look around as if seeking an answer. It seemed as though she were surprised by the stupidity of the question: was a reason necessary in order to speak badly of Southerners? In this manner, she, a Northerner for a mere six months, uttered a phrase which forever tainted her in the eyes of our family: "They dirty our monuments."

Just like the pigeons, though fortunately not from above.

I understood much later what had happened to her. One of my best friends was amongst the first to arrive from the *Lega Nord*. We discovered that we shared the same passion for sailing and that we had purchased (prior to our meeting) the same boats. We discovered that our wives share the same very rare first name and that we had married on the same day.

My friend is named Remo and his grandparents are from Benevento and Matera. He lived for a long time in Argentina and returned to Italy. His wife is Venetian and emigrated from the Polesine area of the Veneto region to France (her family's island, located at the Po River delta, actually sank along with the family farm and orchards and they went from being landowners to being "shipwrecked"). She then returned to Italy and settled between Piedmont and Lombardy.

They were both fervent members of the *Lega* party, up until the party began demonstrating separatist tendencies. "The *Lega* is full of Southerners and sons/daughters of Southerners," Remo explained to me. "They are the most convinced members." My cousin had become a *Lega* member.

But why does this happen? Those who emigrate abandon a community and a land they believe to be weak. They aim to take root somewhere that appears to be strong: the emigrant no longer belongs to his/her people and yet they do not belong to this new group either (or at least this is what they think). While searching for their identity, they cannot help but choose the stronger of the two. This new sense of belonging is stronger in proportion to the distance that exists between what one was and what one wants to become. In *La lingua degli emigranti*, it states that in the newly acquired land, those emigrants relive their status as a "dominated" people in an even more dramatic fashion than in their native land, and that they would like to emerge from this situation. They educate themselves and learn to be different from how they are. When a persecutor takes everything away from you, the only reference point you have left is the persecutor himself. Therefore, you imitate him. The Northerner does not need to be a member of the *Lega*. The Southerner, who emigrates to the North, if his roots are not strong, cannot do without becoming a member of the *Lega*. This emigrant is most active in supporting a policy of exclusion that no longer excludes him, but those who are like he once was. The next *Lega* members will surely be the grand-children of today's non-European immigrants. "But I doubt," states Piero Bocchiaro, professor of psycho-social behavior at the Vrije University in Amsterdam, "that that which is demonstrated corresponds to that which one actually is." In other words, the emigrant who acquires new customs does not do so in accordance with whom he really is. It is like living a double life, and the emigrant is not always aware that this is happening.

Is it really necessary to dig up old stories? They are not so old that they have ceased to hurt and have consequences: today's history is the same as yesterday's. Our history was interrupted and we can only rewind it up to the point where it was broken. We cannot choose the departure point that would be most convenient.

What the Northern Italians did to us was so horrifying that still today, the history books do not speak of it. As far as official "truths" are concerned, many important documents that recount these details are kept hidden. A part of Italy in full bloom was condemned to regress and was plundered by the other. With the spoils from their conquests, the North financed their own growth and proceeded to defend their newly acquired position with every means possible, including the law.

The issue of the South, the delay of progress with respect to its Northern counterpart, does not persist "despite" the unification of Italy, but rather emerged from the unification and lasts up until this day because the South continues to be the motor behind the North's economy. Not even a substantial return of the ill-gotten gains in question would restore things to the way they were: it is the loss of trust and cultural progress that was caused in the South by the removal of its brightest members, through the massacres and mass emigration that is not immediately recoverable. Certain historical and social processes cannot be reversed upon command. Perhaps the financial situation can, if it were so desired.

But no one desires this. Do I want to even begin to mention the defects of the Southerners? No. At least I will not mention them here because it seems as though only the South's defects are ever listed anywhere. My colleague Lino Patruno (*Alla riscossa terroni*) lists thirty-two of them. I believe they are all correct and that the list can be expanded to include sixty-four. Patruno's intention is an honest one: he wants Southerners to take up their responsibilities. However, I begin to fear that on this subject all of those in question have agreed to not act, while the Northerners feel that they are exempt from the same duty. It is for this reason that I have established a personal moratorium: one hundred and fifty years have been quite enough. For the next nineteen months, or perhaps even twenty-one months, I only want to hear about the defects of the Northerners. Why does every defect of the Southerners have to justify the discrimination of the South? Why is every claim, even the most blatantly racist one, considered to be the North's right to make? Why is it that every time that this dichotomy of Italy is mentioned, the best aspects of the South and the worst aspects of the North are omitted? Why do people say that the best of the South is not credible and that to mention the worst of the North is an insult? "Memory is biased, just as the glance upon which it is founded is partial," Walter Barberis (*Il bisogno di patria*) reminds us. "But the Parmalat Fraud Case alone is worth more than all of the similar cases in Naples put together," states Michele Emiliano, the mayor who renovated the city of Bari. Instead, the milk fraud cases defended by the *Lega* seem to be mere setbacks, along with the colossal health frauds in Lombardy ranging from the Poggi Longostrevi Case to the euthanasia death clinics and the intricate web of affairs of *Comunione e Liberazione…* "Our political corruption is neither an evil of the South nor of the North. The true distinctive character of these opposing parts of Italy should not be sought by looking at this corruption" (Ettore Ciccotti, *Mezzogiorno e Settentrione d'Italia*, 1898).

West Germany, already in the first years following the reunification with the poorer East Germany, spent "an estimated figure five times superior to that which was spent in the last fifty years for the much reviled *Cassa per il Mezzogiorno*"[1] according to Agazio Loiero in *Se il Nord*. The United States did as much with the

---

[1] TRANSLATOR'S NOTE: "Fund for the South."

Marshall Plan for the reconstruction of all of Europe after WWII. This was the only way to ensure that the wealth of the West could reach the East in order to make things equal over the course of twenty years. In this case, the redistribution of the wealth was desired, and the extra wealth had not been robbed from the East.

When such a difference exists for so long, one risks to no longer correctly attribute the reasons to the causes of the current situation, but rather to the inadequacy of those who continue to tolerate the status quo. So the ignorant are blamed for being ignorant. The learned man is blamed for having a bad conscience. The racist is blamed for being ignorant and having a bad conscience. All of this leads to the ease with which one can conclude that the economic underdevelopment of black people is due to the inferiority of their race. The same thing was said of the Lombards when their region was controlled by the Austro-Hungarians merely as an area of consumption for goods produced elsewhere. The North was subjected to the same conditions as a colony to which the South was condemned after it was annexed and subsequently sacked. Ciccotti states that "this is what capitalist economies do to the losers in a competitive struggle." Even then, the effects were studied, in order that the causes might not be acknowledged. People tried to understand why the Lombards were so incapable and inefficient, "in other words, null," according to the sociologist Cristina Belgioioso, the author of the investigation of the "narrow-mindedness" of the residents of the Padania region. Cesare Lombroso conducted the research to find the example of "perfect cretinism." Therefore, our politicians from the North, Bossi, Calderoli, and Gentilini were not born from nothing. The "Lombards," as all Italians from the North were called, were judged to be "inept cowards."

Lombardy "was too small to supply a sufficient internal market and too weak to construct a campaign to expand to markets outside of its borders, despite any assistance from the state," writes Luigi De Rosa *in La rivoluzione industriale in Italia.* "The industrial conditions of the regions of Veneto and Liguria did not fare better."

The South was united by force and was emptied of its riches and subjugated in order to allow for the development of the North. It was at this moment that the federalist Lombards began to emerge. Ciccotti warns that "They are those who speak of a "state of Milan" in contrast to the rest of Italy." They commit the error of believing "that Milan would have come into existence without the unification of Italy" and that "it is necessary to conceal the true reasons for this Evil so that we might live off of the fruits of the "illness of everyone" using our different language and dialect as well as our diverse latitude to create many causes for dispute." *To live off the fruits of the "illness of everyone"*: in other words, to ensure that everyone is worse off so that only they might prosper, with the excuse of federalism.

This is called stealing. It happened a century ago.

I remember a conversation I had with a colleague whom I admire. He is from Milan and he is a practical man who has been successful in life. The subject, as seen from the Northern perspective (his) was reduced to "Instead of always complaining, perhaps the Southerners should get a move on." The subject, as seen from the South (me) became "Instead of continuously trying to explain the inadequacies of the Southerners, perhaps the North should try to question their causes and try not to create any further ones."

Mark Twain once said that "We are all human beings. It is not possible to be anything worse." We did our part to try and prove him wrong on several counts. Salimbene from Parma, Barberis reminds us *in Il bisogno di patria*, attributes the vileness of the Southerners to be congenital because he considered them "*homines caccarelli et merdacoli.*"[2] According to one of the founders of the Socialist Party, a man from Bologna named Camillo Prampolini, the Italians can be divided into "*nordici e sudici.*"[3] A "scientist" would then proceed to confirm the correctness of the definition by con-

---

[2] TRANSLATOR'S NOTE: "men of excrement."

[3] TRANSLATOR'S NOTE: "northerners and filthy people": the first three letters of the word "sudicio" (filthy), "sud," means "south," and some Italians engage in this play-on-words.

sidering Southerners "those degenerates who abhor water both on the earth and in the sea so much that they cannot justify their immense filth with the immense misery in which destiny chose for them to be born." It is understood that if he had been the hand of destiny, they should not have been born at all.

Destiny cannot be changed and can be deserved (or not?).

The suspicion emerged that, after having formed Italy with thievery and bloodshed, the means needed justification. "In those years," we read in *La razza maledetta. Alle origini del pregiudizio antimeridionale* by Vito Teti, "the debate on race and the inferiority of the Southerners was held in a myriad of essays, books, and articles almost as proof that it was not a mere fad. The debate met with intellectual needs that were filled with political, social, and cultural urgency." "Lombrosian Science," (which was the result of the founder's three month stay in Calabria: he was the type of genius who would have made Darwin go pale) would provide the much sought after answers.

In this manner, I came to understand that I was part of a "damned race" and that the "racial, physical, psychological, social and moral inferiority of the Southerners with respect to Northerners" had been demonstrated with "facts." I realized this information late, as my father had not told me anything: either he had not noticed or he wanted to spare me my family's shame. I was really disgusting and I had to discover this by myself. It was better when, with everyone's tax money, they only opened schools in the North (someone else prior to the current Minister of Public Education Mariastella Gelmini had done this). This was done because if the Southerners learned to read, they could hurt themselves. How was I supposed to know that since I was a Southerner I was part of a subspecies composed of "degenerates, barbarians, and retards"? I learned while I emigrated abroad that only "delinquents" (from where else but the South?) emigrated. Even if one were to be considered a genius, it would be considered "diseased or sterile genius," according to Pasquale Rossi. How was I to know that an entire region, Calabria, could be considered a place of "degenerate epileptics, filled with superstitious people who have a tendency, due to their ethnicity, to be criminals"? How would you feel, you from the Euganei hills, the Aosta valley, the Brianza area, the Marche, and Molise if you were to discover, after having already married her, that your wife was from Calabria? Of course you would have been completely unaware of such revelatory clues as to their "sloping forehead and the accentuated diameter of their jaw." How could you have placed a member of the "most hated region of Italy" into your home? Would my poor wife have avoided me if she had known of the "study" that "certified" ("scientifically," you understand) the laziness, indolence, apathy, and sloth of those people from Puglia? For a considerable portion of my life I traveled around this country unaware that cranial classification dictated that the dolichocephalic skulls from the South were a clear indication of inferiority in comparison to the brachycephalic skulls of the superior North. Have you heard of Borghezio or Renzo Bossi (who looks exactly like his father)? Renzo Bossi is the sort of intellectual who manages to get his diploma after only four attempts. In an attempt to halt the "Flight of Geniuses" from Italy, the North employed him to watch over the Lombard conference and trade show system.

For Massimo D'Azeglio, the Southerners were "meat that stinks" (the history books do not mention anything about his own breath). One is always someone else's Southerner. This is troublesome because it means that those who classify others eventually are also classified themselves by others.

Why are these classifications drawn up? What purpose do they serve?

An experiment was conducted using some student volunteers. They were asked to put down certain living things by merely pressing a button. The living things were selected and placed in order according to their biological proximity to the species *homo sapiens sapiens*. Everything was fictitious and nothing actually died, but the students were unaware of this detail and were convinced they were killing living things. The experiment continued in a murderous crescendo, beginning with germs, insects, invertebrates, fish, birds, snakes, rats, cats, dogs, and monkeys. Some stopped when they reached the birds while others found it intol-erable to kill dogs or cats for the sake of an experiment. Other stu-dents refused to kill the monkeys, although there were also those who continued to press the button and follow orders. A similar experiment was conducted using humans as the "victims." In that experiment, the students were asked to push a button that admin-istered a progressively stronger electrical shock. Again, the button had no real effect, but the students remained unaware of this until the final round of the experiment. Science, progress, and civiliza-tion require some sacrifices, and it is always possible to find someone willing to ensure that others make them.

Classifications have also been used amongst humans: slaves, servants, masters; rich and poor; blacks, mixed, and whites; South-erners, northern-influenced Southerners, and Northerners…

I ask again, what purpose do classifications serve? The afore-mentioned students have offered us an answer: to establish who must suffer or die first, "for the good of all" (in other words, for the good of those people who have done the choosing). Classifica-tions are the necessary justification to ensure that this act occurs without remorse, "for a good reason." Napoleone Colajanni re-members those "anthropo-sociologists who, in order to see hu-manity progress and improve, would destroy a good half of the population."

Hitler tried. However, when he gave the order to begin the de-struction of the mentally handicapped, the German people re-belled and even the ferocious Nazis were forced to pull back due to the protests. The victims were to be mentally handicapped, but nonetheless Aryan. When the same acts were proposed against the Jews and the Gypsies, Germany fell silent.

In the civil city of Treviso, the mayor can propose armored freight cars to be used for the removal of non-European immi-grants. He can also propose that the immigrants be used as prey for local hunters and call for the removal of benches from the city center so as to avoid their contamination, and still be re-elected. However, when he calls for the same park to be closed off to dogs (and their detritus), the population protests. On the scale of defendable rights (or at least civil sensibility) Treviso places dogs (and even their feces, if I may be so frank to state) higher than non-European immigrants. This is not an opinion, this is a fact: for Fido, they feel offended; for Abdul, not as much.

Classifications are small steps that indicate the level of violence that generates them: from high to low. The amount of violence is inversely proportionate to the importance given to the principles of civic duty. If these weaken, we have seen how easily one can go from the racially charged comic quips of Balkan intellectuals (not all that different from the statements of Bossi, Salvini, Calderoli, Gentilini, and the like...) to adopting policies of ethnic cleansing. Fulvio Moliari, a writer and journalist, is afraid of this: "Those of us from Trieste have seen this happen at our doorstep: those who abuse words are overcome by the facts, though they do not realize it." Imagine if they did realize it...Trieste understands these things better than anyone due to their proximity to the border. Paolo Rumiz left from there to embark on his journey through the anxiety-ridden North; in his work *La secessione leggera*, he recounts the words of his friend from Sarajevo: "It was not the noise of the cannons that killed Yugoslavia. It was the silence. The silence regarding the language of violence before the violence struck."

The phrases *"Forza Etna"* and *"Forza terremoto"*[4] appeared in the North (and their memory evokes a sense of pride amongst the *Lega* members who are reminded of their heroic beginnings) hiding, under a clearly exaggerated tone, a true wish. A criminal wish: to those people whose homes/businesses the volcano destroyed or whose families were killed, an even worse fate was desired. It is for this criminal wish that further votes were obtained as well as a general consensus. Shame on them and to all those who agreed to this thought, and to those who continue to agree.

That sort of violence is only verbal, but can be considered a "classification" because when the Po River overflowed its banks destroying homes and lives or when a stroke paralyzed Bossi, no one in the South wrote on their roadways and bridges *"Forza Po"*

---

[4] TRANSLATOR'S NOTE: "Power to Etna"; "Power to the Earthquake."

or "*Forza Ictus.*"[5] The difference between the writings of the *Leghisti* and the absence of similar writings in the South can be attributed either to the tolerance acquired in a couple of more millennia worth of history (I wish!) or to the South's acceptance of their role as the vanquished enemy (the more likely reason).

This aggression by the *Leghisti* has induced many to feel "Southern" and to rediscover the history that the Northerners prefer to ignore. They ignore this history because they feel as though they already know what they need to know and they are not interested in knowing about the South because they associate it with a notion of culture that is uselessly contorted, too elaborate, unproductive, pretentious, and all in all, a "defeated" culture. Perhaps this is a mixture of petty envy and disdain towards those intellectuals from the *Magna Grecia* that know a great deal of useless things. Maybe it is because in their search for distant roots, rather than nurturing and appreciating the richness of their own, that they continue to entertain themselves with the notion of belonging to the Celtic culture. The desire for the past is comprehensible, but why force an aspect of it in order to adapt it to a desire in the present? One risks becoming a laughingstock through the adoption of the kilt, which is a recent folkloristic invention, or through the "alpine sun," the flower with six petals chosen by the *Leghisti* as their symbol, when it is in fact rather common throughout the Mediterranean. The flower was previously utilized as a symbol on the shields of the *Pugliese* (a true region of the north, eh?) warriors over three thousand years ago. *Sciur Asterix de la Briansa,* that is the sun of the Plateau! *Ch'el vaga schisc anca* (Go slowly) with the Barbarian ancestry: they left behind the name of a region in the North, and in the South and its states, they left behind a series of laws that lasted for almost three centuries. The Barbarians enforced these laws with such force (and over a widespread territory that included the regions of Campania, Basilicata, Puglia, and Calabria) that on the maps of the time, the capital of "*Longobardia*" (Lombardy) was Bari. *Terun!* (Southerner!) Since this book speaks

---

[5] TRANSLATOR'S NOTE: "Power to the Po"; "Power to the Stroke."

of how the South came to be considered inferior, I will come out and say that the longest lasting state in the South established by the Barbarians, that came to be "civilized" in our country, was called *Langobardia Minor*.

"When we do not want something to be understood," writes Marco Paolini, "we transform history into geography." Can we accept, against the facts, that the geography would be considered victorious in drawing up the North, and would be "defeated" in drawing up the South? Can we accept that latitude would become the means to measure the value of men and their actions and of their rights? Is this not the true essence of racism? Is it not within the simplicity of its promise that lies its success, amongst stupid and egotistical people?

"Multiple identities are perceived by nationalism as threats," writes Predrag Matvejevic in *Mondo ex e tempo del dopo*. He proceeds to explain that in those nations that "came about later," such as Italy, that "these illnesses of identity" are more easily contracted.

The North suffers from these "multiple identities" because wicked political and financial decisions have brought several million Southerners to the North, along with their dialects, diets, and habits. For as much as they tried to acquire new accents and customs, their own influenced those of others. Tastes and loves fused and generated a hybrid perceived as a threat to the Northern identity. The *Lega* invented the Celtic-Padania Region-Venetian rites. They are political devices used to transform the need to discover one's roots into votes and to arm them with racism. "We decided to take advantage of the anti-Southern feelings that are common throughout Lombardy and other regions of the North," writes the shameless Umberto Bossi in the *Lega*'s version of *Mein Kampf, Vento dal Nord*.

The South also suffers, but has managed to conserve its roots better (though they have been weakened by the exodus, they have not been blunted by different traditions). The Southerners have been led to deny them through their behavior. They have been led to believe that their roots have been defeated, just as the Jews were forcibly converted: they felt one way and were forced to act in another. This feeling, with the passage of time and throughout the generations, managed to become feeble, only to be reanimated by offense, prompting some to oppose it.

The belated discovery of being a Southerner revealed to me something absurd: Southerners acquire their name from the one thing that they are missing: the South. Yet when geography offered them one (such as in the misadventures of those Sicilian farmers in Libya and Tunisia) history denied it to them. The world of the Southerners has one less direction available: it is not possible for them to go further South, and they are forced to stay "home." The South carries with itself an idea of joy and nostalgia: if the first is due to the climate and nature, the second is due to (as is often the case after an amputation) the pain of the "phantom limb." That which is no longer present, hurts: the South. This negation is serious.

The farthest point of many regions, the area in which one truly perceives to be "at land's end" is referred to in Galizia, Cornwall, and Brettany in the same manner: *Finisterrae*. In Italy, a place that fits this description can be found in Puglia, more precisely in Santa Maria di Leuca. There the sea rises like a wall, as if to put an end to the discussion. Puglia is a finger of land that is nearly four hundred kilometers long, but only thirty meters wide around the town of Leuca. This means that not only are we missing the South (*Finisterrae)* but another two directions as well: East and West. Something else can be perceived in this place, of which one would never think of should they have a completely practicable horizon surrounding them. This could be the direction denied in life.

A Northerner can turn his gaze and seek the future in any direction. Southerners cannot. They are obliged to look only towards the North: through its history, through the economy that is the fruit of that history, and even through the geography. In reality, the North does not really have a choice either; if they were to give up the South, like some would like, they would become victims of the same situation in which we find ourselves (but in an unnatural manner, and therefore it would be sterile): the condition of an amputee. While for us the South is a phantom limb that ren-

Pino Aprile

ders us fertile (because it was not our volition to deprive ourselves of it) at the cost of a necessary pain; those who do not reach and comprehend *Finisterrae* (the part that is missing) do not know their limits. They do not know what they are worth. And it shows.

CHAPTER 2

Brigands in the Family

There were brigands in the South and the Piedmontese eliminated them. This is what I always believed. This is what I had
been taught in school, though hastily and with reluctance, as
though it were inappropriate to renew an ancient feeling of shame.
I was not troubled by this approach: I had seen the old photographs of the bodies of those brigands and their wives. They were
naked just like savages (but their clothes were removed by those
trying to render them civil). I saw the photographs of the heads
that had been chopped off in order to send them to those researchers following in Lombroso's footsteps, who studied the
physiological characteristics of the human skull. In this manner
they could have perfect examples of delinquents (that by nature
would be from the South, that much is obvious). In the movies, we
were assigned the role of the villain. We students from the South
were aware of the annoyance we had provoked in responding to
the glorious epic of story of Garibaldi with our gang of thieves
and pickpockets. We annoyed people with our pointy, witchlike
hats and shotguns hanging from our shoulders. We were troglo-
dytes that were only one hundred and fifty centimeters tall and
had heads full of thick, black hair, low foreheads and our eyes
were blank with grim expressions. This is of course the gaze that
appears when you photograph dead people: we looked a little like
Barabbas and a little like Judas. Thirty-one pieces of silver, one
more than what Judas paid, was the amount that Italy gave to
those Southern soldiers who aided Garibaldi when they chose to
let them go because their services were no longer needed. Do we
even want to compare this image with the one that was attributed
to Garibaldi? He resembled Jesus Christ Himself, with his blonde

hair flowing in the breeze and his eccentric white poncho. He gazed over the horizon, with his blue eyes and golden beard, towards our flag that was illuminated by the light of his sword (the weapon of knights) which was aimed at the sun. Now that is a man! So you understand that when your history book asks you what side you are on, would you respond that you are a Southerner, and therefore a brigand, or that you are "Italian" like Garibaldi?

And yet I could have understood much sooner how things really were, because there was neither shame nor disapproval in my father's voice when he showed me where the body of Sergeant Romano (who was from our town) was exposed in the town of Gioia del Colle. It seemed as though he spoke of a hero, and not of a brigand: at that time I did not understand the meaning of that discrepancy. I did not ask questions because of the idea that there might be something to add or to correct with respect to what had been passed off to us as "truth." My father said nothing further because he was reluctant to speak of such grim subjects. In fact, he revealed some details about the War and the concentration camps only a few years prior to his death.

He was not wrong about Sergeant Romano. I discovered this during my non-scholastic research. It was here that I learned that the Unification of Italy, at the expense of the South, did not overcome the crime attributed to the brigands, but rather generated it. It was a great opportunity for delinquents to take advantage of such a state of confusion as generated during a civil war. Amidst the boors who were robbed of state-owned land that was freely farmable and the gentlemen who had usurped it and those Neapolitan ex-soldiers, patriots, and citizens who refused to accept the end of their freedom, wealth, and rights (which were questionable with respect to quantity and quality, as is always the case anywhere). These people had appreciated these benefits under the Bourbon regime of the Kingdom of the Two Sicilies and they saw this rule substituted by a reign of terror filled with plundering and abuse. According to Nino Bixio, Garibaldi's second-in-command, this "system of blood was inaugurated in the *Mezzogiorno* " by occupants that spoke French or other dialects that had never been heard before in those areas.

Soldiers of the Neapolitan king, legitimist subjects, poor peasants, and true brigands wound up together and this, in the eyes of the invader, rendered them all brigands by association. Therefore anyone who was friendly towards, had knowledge of, or was a blood relative of any of these people was automatically considered a brigand. Why were there no distinctions made between distinguished soldiers and thieves? In 1979, for a news report, I caught up with some of the Khmer Rouge warriors in the jungle. At the official "luncheon" with the recently overthrown Cambodian government (the Vietnamese had invaded the country) I sat near the Minister of Science and Technology. He was a former entrepreneur equivalent to Italy's Agnelli or Moratti. His entire family had been killed and he had lost his position in the government. "How can you stay?" I asked him. He replied, in perfect Italian, "The alternative is that those same Vietnamese, who massacred my family, should do the same to the rest of my people."

"Up until now we have had thieves," wrote Vincenzo Padula, a liberal reporter of the time, who was favorable to the Unification project in his work *Calabria. Prima e dopo l'unità*, "now we have thievery: there is a great difference between the two. There are thieves when the population does not help them, when one robs to live, or at least to die, on a full stomach. " (but this did not only occur in the South), "There is thievery when the cause of the thief matches the cause of the people." If it is not this way, then the rebellion does not last, according to a legitimist in 1865 named Tommaso Cava de Gueva (as referenced by Francesco Mario Agnoli in *Dossier Brigantaggio*). In 1849, in a single month, Garibaldi remained alone and was forced to flee to the Papal States. Pisacane and his three hundred strong, young men were destroyed by farmers with their pruning shears and pitchforks. The *Bandiera* brothers and company were set before a firing squad in four days time. As far as the caliber of such brigands is concerned, the Marquis of Villamarina warned Cavour that the "masses" were being led by former Bourbon "officials." The *Squadra Ciccone* alone was composed of two hundred former Napoleonic soldiers. They were only captured after eight years of pursuit when, finally in 1868, a large group of Piedmontese soldiers surrounded them and killed them off.

Sergeant Romano was only a few steps away from becoming a Garibaldi-like figure, but in reverse. He was welcomed as a liberator in the towns he conquered, defeating the National Guard, the *carabinieri*, and the Piedmontese soldiers. He was able to place the major irregular military formations under his control, particularly those in the area of Puglia. He was also able to conduct various operations with those soldiers from other regions. Michele Clericuzio (speaking of brigands) was also under his command. For years, Clericuzio had been an instructor for the Bourbon regiments as well as for many other Neapolitan soldiers including: foot-soldiers, hunters, grenadiers, royal gendarmes, dragoons and lancers. In the beginning, Romano only enrolled fellow soldiers, but he knew that he could not continue to choose his own men. He attempted to transform, and almost succeeded, this large-scale robbery into a real, legitimistic civil war. In his diary, he recounts that "one day thirteen bandits presented themselves before me" as self-proclaimed "defenders of *Francis II* and of the Church." Except of course that he discovered that they "allowed themselves to commit robberies without my knowing, even after having been given specific orders to proceed in an orderly, well-mannered fashion." To this they grumbled, "We are considered robbers, and therefore we must steal." In order to flee, Sergeant Romano spent all of his savings: one thousand coins.

The occupying forces had to employ thousands of soldiers, *carabineri*, and the National Guard to succeed in surrounding Sergeant Romano in order to capture and kill him.

A reporter for the *Gazette de France*, recounted several months later, "At Gioia del Colle, a local farmer pointed me towards the location where the victors proudly placed his quartered body on display for eight days. All of the inhabitants of the village wanted to see the remains of their now unrecognizable brigand-hero. The men removed their hats, the women kneeled before his body and nearly everyone was in tears. He carried the grief and admiration of his townspeople with him to the grave."

The general population did not believe in his death. There were those who swore they saw him in the woods: "He is alive. He will come back." They believed he would come back, just as King Arthur did. Legend has it that another man died in his place; he was invulnerable and immortal due to a special medal given to him by the pope, according to a letter Carlo Gastaldi wrote to his parents. Gastaldi deserted the Piedmontese army to join Sergeant Romano (he wasn't the only "Soldier blue" to switch over to the side of the Cheyenne) and he became the Sergeant's best friend and secretary/lieutenant. According to legal records of the time, one comes to understand that "in the vivid imagination of the general population," Sergeant Romano "would live for many more years hiding in solitude and wandering."

My father must have heard about Sergeant Romano in this light: as a "messiah" not a delinquent. People who were witnesses of this historic event spoke to my father about the courage of one man. My history books, instead, spoke of the dishonor of many scoundrels and of the people they came from. The story evolved from one of pride to one of shame. There is an ever-growing number of Southerners who are tracing back their history in order to find out the truth regarding their roots and, consequently, a reason to be proud of them. They hope to emerge from their inferior position.

Naples, 2009: Franceschiello's army marched on the royal palace during the changing of the guards. It happened on May 23rd, on the 150th anniversary of the death of King Ferdinand II of Bourbon. "We are back!" stated Alessandro Romano, a fifty-four year-old government official with the Ministry of Internal Affairs (he was in charge of emergencies and civil defense) who, with uniforms and historic weapons, reconstructed the armed forces of the Kingdom of the Two Sicilies. In historical re-enactments, he marches at the head of the army. The firepower, despite the temporary, pretentious second conquest of the former capital, is not a cause for worry: "There are thirty-five members from the Regiment of Lucano, from Potenza, armed with muzzle loading rifles and bayonets, two bass drums and one rolling drummer and horn; twenty from the Navy: twelve from Sicily, with six rifles, a small naval cannon, a drummer, two sutlers and ten from Savona (Southerners from out of town); the First Foreign Regiment, from Cassino ("foreign" refers to the Swiss Bourbon divisions): six with rifles.

Alessandro, who was made a captain by the Princess Urraca of Bourbon, brandished a relic: "The sword of Pietro Quandel, heroic defender of the city of Gaeta, placed under siege by the Piedmontese. I am its custodian; when the time comes, I will entrust it to someone worthy. The army of the Two Siciles was Catholic and had double sovereignty: over weapons and over the spirit. There are no more weapons, the spirit embodies the ideals of chivalry. Against your enemy you are obliged to use violence, not cruelty: when your enemy is thrown from his horse, you must come to his aid." Alessandro is a mild, honest man, but he had one doubt that plagued him, "Perhaps this is why we lost...." In the decisive Battle of Volturno, dozens of Bourbon soldiers dove into the river to save those followers of Garibaldi who during their flight, found themselves drowning in the river's whirlpools. For this, " Corporal Gianfrancesco Agostino of the sixth regiment of hunters, was promoted and decorated as a sergeant," recounts Gigi Di Fiore in *I vinti del Risorgimento*. A suspicion arose, or at least it was noted by Vincenzo Gulì (*Il saccheggio del Sud*), that "Francis II wanted to lose his throne." If this were the truth, then he did so with dignity and courage; this is the type of humanity that is prohibited to those who rule a country. He did this because he was a good Christian. But he did it anyway. While he was on his way to exile, he wrote in his manifesto *Ai popoli delle Due Sicilie* that "from the moment I knew that the ruin of my enemy was certain, I ordered my generals to halt."

Captain Romano had other relics as well, which were re-purchased by a distant relative in 1930 in Turin at an auction of criminal evidence. These relics belonged to the legendary Sergeant Romano, his ancestor: a ribbon, a pair of binoculars, and a dagger. (He keeps them in a case that almost seems like a sort of tabernacle. His home is like an infinite archive filled with documents, photographs, legal papers, and reproductions of images of the time.)

As the ensign for the Fifth Bourbon Regiment, Pasquale Domenico Romano, after the Savoy invasion of the Kingdom of the Two Sicilies, guided his comrades and "brigands" on to conquer half of the region of Puglia before finally being captured. "Finish me like a soldier," he requested when he was alone and surrounded by the enemy. "No, you will die as a brigand," replied Michele Cantù, also a sergeant, but for Lombardy. He was gored with a saber and "was miserably disrobed of his Bourbon uniform, impaled, as though he were a trophy, and his body was placed on a cart," according to *Briganti e partigiani*. He wound up rotting in the center of his hometown, Gioia del Colle. It was January 9th, 1863. After a little over a century and lengthy reacquisition of memory, a commemorative pilgrimage can now be made that honors that date, in the forest (at one time it was truly a forest) of Vallata. There one can find an obelisk.

Any residual wooded area in the South is the "Forest of the Brigands"; any cave is called the "Cave of the Brigands" and any unexplored ravine or abandoned farm, abbey, or castle ruin might conceal the never recovered "Brigand Treasure" (even if some sudden improvements of wealth have often been explained in a different manner).

"When I was nine years old," remembers Chiara Curione, descendent and biographer of Sergeant Romano (*Un eroe dalla parte sbagliata*), "my grandmother told me that the Sergeant was her uncle. 'He was not a brigand, but a hero who fought for his king,' she told me. Over the years, I researched this information. It turned out to be true."

Romano was twenty-seven years old when his town was invaded: a portrait of him depicts him as an attractive man who proudly wore his uniform. He had a well-trimmed beard and thick hair. He was the son of a wealthy farmer from the Murgia area. While in the army, he became an educated man and grew in both style and rank. He was a respectable man and was recognized as such by the writers of war bulletins during the war with Piedmont. His behavior in the Bourbon army was as exemplary as it was as an "Italian" citizen after Piedmont's conquest of the South. He had no criminal record in a time when even a weak enthusiasm for the new king was sufficient for incarceration, even without formal accusations. The historian, Antonio Lucarelli, his main biographer, wrote that amidst the mob of those armed invaders, the Sergeant distinguished himself for his "natural talent, tenacious will, and his resourceful nature" but most of all "for a certain rugged knowledge and for a clean criminal record" (*Il sergente Romano. Brigantaggio politico in Puglia dopo il 1860*).

As a partisan, he was elusive, courageous and ruthless, if the situation required. In 1862, in the Brindisi area, two National Guard squadrons from the *Cellino San Marco* and *San Pietro Vernotico* along with a platoon of *carabinieri* intercepted the "brigands" and moved to attack them. They fled once they realized Sergeant Romano was their leader. A dozen were taken and "tried" by the former Bourbon official, who had an extremely efficient web of informants ("Giuseppe Mauro, you earned four carlins per day as a spy, under Francesco, and now you earn three under Victor Emanuel." Shot.) A soldier, Vitantonio Donadeo, invoked the Madonna of Carmine and the weapon that was to kill him jammed. "Stand. You have been spared." Romano spared him, as he too was a devout follower of the Virgin of Carmine and often wrote prayers dedicated to her.

He was skilled in open field combat, but even more so in commando actions. The civil guards in Alberobello, "while observing the neighboring forest," discovered a gunpowder repository. They seized it and captured the guard. He came with thirty men, attacked the army barracks, freed the prisoner, seized the stolen ammunition, and took flags, a drum, and the weapons of the guards. He also seized the guards and freed them once outside of town. The prefect, our of stupor, exclaimed in his report, all "in a quarter of an hour!"

But the undertaking that truly revealed his capabilities and audacity was the regaining of Gioia del Colle, which has twenty thousand inhabitants. A town, his (and mine), that brooded over rage (today, it fortunately seems sedated). Approximately every sixty years, political passions give birth to massacres. Lucarelli, who was born in a nearby town, writes that the inhabitants of Gioia reached such level of slaughter for "resoluteness of character, intolerance towards abuse of power (...) the instinct of an impetuous and rebellious spirit. They sustain their principles and their faith with fierce strength." In 1799, the clash was between the Jacobins and the Army of Holy Faith: the heads of the opposing parties were two brothers, Pasquale (a cultured jurist) and Cesare Soria. They were adversaries that were sought from house to house and the hunt ultimately resulted in plundering, killings, people being burned alive, and assassins running amok. It was truly a bloody Sunday. In 1861, the conflict arose between legitimist Bourbon supporters and those in favor of the Unification, along with all of the implied nuances of the situation. For example, many of those in favor of a unified Italy were disgusted when the saw that it came down to the oppression and plundering of the South ("The Unification is a beautiful thing," the docile Baron Gianantonio Molignani, a jurist, had the great misfortune of pronouncing aloud, "but we shall be the beggars of this unified Italy." In this manner, he landed himself in jail).

After a corporal of the National Guard was killed, the Security Committee of Gioia del Colle decided to do away with Romano and his men once and for all. In accordance with the prefect, his forces (soldiers and armed citizens) joined those of four other neighboring towns and attacked the forest of Vallata. The Sergeant knew of the attack right away, thanks to his network of spies. Under pressure by his own men, Romano attacked Gioia del Colle, rather than flee. He did so by outflanking the troops that sought him. The town was well defended: they even had a cannon that functioned similarly to a machine gun. His undertaking was however successful and the people followed their liberator, shouting, "Long live Francis II! Down with Vittorio!" On the other side were professionals, landowners, artisans, and even priests wielding rifles. The battle was fought in the streets, more or less: the bourgeois against the boorish peasants.

The worst things happened in the back alleys: those who had been previously oppressed sought out their oppressors, or at least those whom they presumed to be such. Up until the day before, they were their equals: their neighbors. Young followers of Garibaldi and the National Guard were dragged from their homes and into the streets where they were lynched. It was a true orgy of violence, and even though the injury toll was low, what happened later was worse: seven people were murdered by the frenzied mob. Hundreds of men came from nearby towns and the capital of the province to the aid of those under siege: *carabinieri*, soldiers, local militia, as well as good willed citizens that were handy with rifles. The Sergeant was able to flee with his men from the tight grip the troops had placed on the town.

Not much is known about what truly happened afterwards. The chronicles narrate very little because the victors would do so subsequently. Perhaps the numbers paint a clearer picture: the orgy began once again, with the aggressors and victims inverting their roles; the soldiers fired upon direct orders from citizens or groups of citizens. Other civilians took care of matters themselves (while in the Kingdom of the Two Sicilies not only was the defendant's right to defend himself sacred, but also for the past one hundred years it was obligatory for the magistrates to justify their verdicts). Those seven that were lynched by the townspeople were avenged by the rest of the population, give or take a few extra, and at the end of this massacre there were over one hundred and fifty bodies. A reprisal won on a scale of twenty men to one: not even the Nazis at the *Fosse Ardeatine* did quite so much damage.

Another sixty years pass, and it is 1920. My town continued to respect its turbulent tradition: forty landowners laid an ambush for several farmhands that solicited payment for a job done that was not requested ("Who sent you?" asked the judge, addressing one of the farmhands. "Our appetites," replied the farmhand). The landowners proceeded to fire upon the crowd and managed to kill six farmhands and injuring fifty. That evening, the survivors and some other farmers dragged five landowners from their homes and lynched them in the town square; two died and three survived. At the time, my father was a nine-year-old, who, for four years, assisted his father, the blacksmith. He saw what happened. He told me about a woman who delivered a blow to the head of a farmhand she presumed to be dead. He gave himself away when he moaned in pain. "She proceeded to crush his head with a stone from the sidewalk and exclaimed, 'Damn you, you are still alive?'" 1980 passed by without a problem (1920 + 60). No one was lynched in Gioia del Colle. Sometimes losing one's traditions can be a positive thing....

Cruelty is the principal weapon during a civil war: the families of rebels were incarcerated, kidnapped, and killed, like Sergeant Romano's fiancée: Lauretta D'Onghia (we were waiting to hear the "news that our king was on the train," he wrote, so that we would once again be "free" and be able to marry). The guerrilla fighters/brigands conducted their battles with brutal methods, "however not more so than those practiced by the Piedmontese soldiers. They had a political objective, exactly like their adversaries, but with the better motive as they were not the aggressors, but the victims," Agnoli from Bologna writes in his *Dossier Brigantaggio*. He was a member of the Superior Council of Magistrates and president of the division of the Court of Appeals.

In the report compiled by the investigation committee on brigand activity, that was read aloud during a secret session of the Chamber of Deputies on May3rd, 1863, a section dedicated to Sergeant Romano stated that "he was not as despicable as the others; he was brave and he died fighting; (...) not even acknowledgment of his crime was able to suffocate his sense of honesty;" he wrote well and "often , found no money or jewelry, but "poems and prayers for the Virgin (for whom he had a special devotion towards), his famous diary, and the even more famous oath he made his associates swear to uphold." ("We promise and swear to defend the standards of our King Francis II (...) and to see that our Roman Catholic Church is not defeated.")

"In my family," narrates the Sergeant's great-great-grandne-phew Alessandro, "it was seen as something to be ashamed of to merely mention 'Uncle Domenico, the Sergeant.' Still today, the majority of my relatives prefer to not have anything to do with the 'brigand.' The Romano family was forced to uproot itself out of Gioia del Colle and we ended up in between the regions of Campania and Calabria. The branch of the family that I am from has lived on the island of Ponza for three generations. I knew nothing of the Sergeant. It was my grandfather's brother, Salvatore, who said to me one day, 'Hey boy, I gotta tell ya something.' He was a sailor and had seen the world. He knew more things than the others. What they have written in the history books are lies. The Piedmontese did not unify Italy, they simply enlarged Piedmont and in the process they ruined the Romano family.'"

He explained that we were subjected to the dispossession of our wealth, but that our relative had died as a partisan hero. I was a boy, and did not understand what he said very well; I thought he was referring to World War II. When I finally understood, I asked myself why he told me stories that took place so long ago and in such a mysterious tone of voice ("I have told you these things, but don't go around mentioning them, not even to our family"). "It is not true that the Bourbon kings were tyrants. It is not true that the South was riddled with hunger and misery. No one left the South: at least not back then." And why must we not mention them? "It is not time, yet. The important thing is that you know how things really are." I thought he was exaggerating, so I mentioned something to my father. He became very angry: "Forget Uncle Salvatore. He says lots of foolish things." But his other brother, Uncle Luigi, confirmed to me that Uncle Salvatore spoke the truth, and that it was disgraceful.

This is how I came to know that my family concealed an obscure secret. It caused some family members shame, while it caused others great pride. While I was in high school I read *La conquista del Sud* by Carlo Alianello. Then I read an article by Denis Mack Smith, which was written in such a typically British snobby manner towards the Italians, but it recounted exactly what my Uncle Salvatore had told me. He was right when he suggested not to mention these stories, as "it is not yet time." At school, I distributed hundreds of photocopies of Mack Smith's article, amidst the incredulity and derision of my fellow students. By now I wanted to know the truth: I live for collecting documents, books, and conducting investigations. When I was hired by the Ministry of Internal Affairs, I had facilitated access to the State archives and libraries. I remember the first trial record that I found: a Piedmontese official asked a seventeen year-old farm boy from the Lucano region how he came upon the shoes he now wore. The boy did not understand, because he spoke another language. The official announced that he found him guilty of theft, because he wore the shoes given exclusively to soldiers of the "Italian" army. The poor boy still did not understand that he had to explain that he acquired these shoes without killing anyone. I imagined how lost he felt, along with his fear and rage towards the fact that he did not even understand what these people wanted from him or why they were treating him so badly. Then, he understood. They motioned to him to turn and face the firing squad. He heard that they loaded their weapons. He was shot in the back. I began to cry."

This anxiousness to recuperate memories that were lost became a reason for Alessandro Romano to live: "The little smiles and derisions that I elicited when I told my classmates what my Uncle Salvatore told me were enough to make me decide to seek the proof that the story was true."

In this manner, the ancestor of a "brigand" began his quest to retrace a forgotten saga beginning with his own name and his own blood relations.

"Since 1979 I've been visiting towns in the South and searching their town and church records as well as their libraries. I have also encountered others like me. We have divided up the tasks: I concern myself mainly with the 'brigands' and the resistance movement; Argentino d'Arpino tries to recover messages between the Kingdom of the Two Sicilies and the Vatican State; Antonio Ciano concerns himself with the political intrigues of the time as well as the massacres the Savoys conducted in the South; Gennaro

De Crescenzio is concerned with the innovations in art, science, industry, and commerce during the Kingdom of the Two Sicilies; Lorenzo Terzi tries to find lost documents: he has a superhuman ability to know where exactly in the enormous stacks of papers, covered with centuries of dust, to search; Luca Esposito tries to find the names of the fallen in the last strongholds of the resistance, Gaeta and Civitella, and of their final resting places. Gaeta was attacked while the surrendering papers where being signed. In Civitella, the prisoners were shot after they had surrendered!

We are all for a united and indivisible Italy. It was built with the money that was stolen from us and with our blood. The federacy was something that should have been made before, and not after, everything was stolen from us.

But I want the truth: the respect for our history and for our symbols, I feel, is owed to us. In the United States, the Southern States are honored: the soldiers that died in the civil war are considered heroes. Uncle Salvatore said that it was not yet time. I think that the time of deception, insults, and lies is over. It has lasted for far too long. How we once were and how we became must become widely known. If I deny my history, I deny myself.

I remember the stupor on the faces of my colleagues at the Ministry when I showed them the documents I had found. I remember their incredulity, their rage and their shame ('They shot children! They raped women! They destroyed the country! They closed the factories!'). It is the same confused expression that I see in the eyes of those students when they invite me to talk about my research in their schools. It is for this reason that I want documents for everything, so no one can have any doubts: things are so very different from what we have been told that you cannot ask your listeners to believe you without proof. Proof must be given for every detail, even the smallest detail. Sometimes, this is not even sufficient. Sometimes, even in front of incontrovertible evidence, one obtains silence or skepticism. One may elicit the inability to communicate, which amounts to a refusal."

Alessandro Romano drives thirty-five thousand kilometers per year in his car. He holds conferences and exhibitions on the effect "brigands'" have had on the economy prior to the Unification. Sometimes his hosts pay for his gasoline and other times they pay for his hotel. Occasionally he is a guest of his "compatriots." He spends many of his weekends and vacations in this endeavor. In 2003, he launched his website: *Rete di informazione delle Due Sicilie* (comitato @legittimisti.it). He boasts eight collaborators and thousands of subscribers. He hosts the editorial office in his home: four desktop computers and two laptops. His one daughter, Alessia, sorts through and answers the mail (she is the technology expert). His other daughter, Francesca, who holds a degree in historical sciences ("I may be unemployed, but at least I like what I do") resides in France and studies the Anjou dynasty. His wife, Rosanna, a teacher, proofreads everything. "Don Paolo Capobianco, son of the last person born in the Kingdom of the Two Sicilies, role model, and author of many books, who was mentally acute right up until his death at ninety-nine years of age, used to say: 'We are many, and we don't even know it.'"

In 1983, Alessandro Romano's research on his genealogical roots brought him to his native town, Gioia del Colle. "I was the first person in three generations of my family to return. I looked for Sergeant Romano's house with a map dating back to that time: the intersection of the roads had remained the same. Something, however, was not quite right because I could not find the house. Finally, I discovered that where the courtyard should have been, someone had built another home and had blocked the original passage. I was able to identify the tiny door and I trembled with excitement."

He knocked. "An old lady answered, and I asked, 'And you are...?' 'Maria Carolina Savoia,' she answered. 'Sa...?' I asked again. '...voia,' she answered. She only shared her last name with the royal family, but she was not a relative. 'No way!' I thought, and then I left."

That last name (my relatives, who still live in Gioia del Colle, explained to me) indicates only the place from which the family originates. Therefore, when one mentions Margherita di Savoia, they are referring to the town on the Adriatic Sea with the largest salt mines in Italy, "my crown jewel," as Ferdinand II of Bourbon used to refer to it. This was the king who proceeded to steal the throne and country from his son, Francesco, and wanted to further deprive him of these salt mines as well. In this manner, the salt mines of Barletta, as they were originally called, were dedicated to the first queen after the Italian Unification. Dogs mark their territory with their urine, while victors do so with their last names.

The house that belonged to the Romano family is only meters away from the house in which I was born. I could have known the history of my country and town right away. However, we were taught to be ashamed of it and therefore to hide it. The defeated often strive to meet the demands of the victors. The defeated do so in order to cancel their defeat. The victors do so to hide their crime. It does not matter how deep the sea of time is: sooner or later the bodies will rise to the surface.

When the knowledge of one's history resurfaces, it shouts to be heard. It wants to assert itself. It wants to even the score.

"There are already some people who want to capitalize off of this notion in politics. They want votes. Can you imagine this?" comments Romano. He believes that the moment is far from being ripe. "First, we must establish the truth, in other words, we must recuperate our memory and transform it into an identity. Then we must make this identity evolve into pride. From pride, it must then turn into politics, votes, and power. It is only at this time that history can be put back into balance." He is a hopeless romantic. He will be disappointed.

There are many people who are trying to speed this process up. In the past few years, new cultural and political movements have been formed in order to act as a catalyst for this rising Southern feeling (although some do resent this emotion, as well). The *Partito del Sud* was among the first to be formed by the initiative of Antonio Ciano from the city of Gaeta. He was a former officer in the merchant navy as well as the author of *I Savoia e il massacro del Sud* and *Le stragi e gli eccidi dei Savoia*. The party is present in the regions of Lazio, Campania, and Sicily. In Lombardy, *Per il Sud* was formed and in Naples, the *Lega Sud* party was formed and was actually affiliated with Bossi's party in the North. *Io Sud* took hold in Puglia, by the initiative of the former minister from the *Alleanza Nazionale* party, Adriana Poli Bortone. Meanwhile, the *Movimento autonomista siciliano*, created by Raffaele Lombardo, has conquered the presidency of the region and a sizeable portion of Berlusconi's party in Sicily plans to become more "locally" oriented.

It still came as a surprise when, in 2008, in the city of Gaeta, a symbol of the resistance against the Piedmontese invasion, Ciano's *Partito del Sud* along with a local electoral ticket won the mayoral election. The city became the only one of its kind, with over twenty thousand inhabitants, which was not run by one of the two major parties. "After one hundred and forty-seven years, we have taken back the fortress," proclaimed Ciano.

What he intended was immediately understood.

"For the one hundred and fiftieth anniversary of the Unification of Italy, the city of Gaeta has begun the legal proceedings to ask the Savoy family for compensation for the damage caused by the 1861 siege, in the amount of two hundred and seventy million euros (which is equivalent to two million lira at the time). Vittorio Emanuele and Emanuele Filiberto had requested this amount to compensate for the fifty-four years of exile to which they had been subjected. "Considering the thousands of people that died and the fact that our city had been destroyed, we figured that we would not ask for an exaggerated amount," explains Ciano (the Councilor for Toponymy, as per his choice). He is supported by the opinions of local lawyers and jurists. "Gaeta never adhered to the Kingdom of Italy. Therefore, it could claim its autonomy, and not apply the laws passed during the Savoy's reign. It could also reclaim the state-owned property that was annexed during that period. If our legal endeavors were to be successful, we would share the compensation received with the other cities that were subjected to the same "massacre" by the Savoy reign: there would be dozens of cities.

From 1861 to 1914, the city of Gaeta requested numerous times to be compensated for damages incurred during the four months of bombing. After a century and half, a large part of the city is still considered property of the state, and therefore does not belong to us," Ciano protests, "In order to walk along the boardwalk that is on the seafront, one must pay a duty to the state, as only a quarter of the passage belongs to the local municipality. In order to send our children to school, we have to pay an additional fee. In 2001, we rebelled. We refuse to pay one million euros in back taxes."

Technically, Gaeta's requests for compensation for war damages cannot be satisfied because Piedmont never officially declared war upon the Kingdom of the Two Sicilies. They invaded without declarations. "We are asking for those who called for the invasion and consequently benefitted from it: the Savoy family." But what do the descendants have to do with all of this? "They never renounced their claim to the inheritance. If they held onto the benefits, they should accept that the inheritance also includes debts. One could demand the confiscation of the crown jewels, which are held in the *Banca d'Italia* and therefore focus on their personal assets."

What do you mean when you say the city did not adhere to the part of Italy under the Savoy reign? "General Cialdini summoned the administrators in order to do so," Ciano explains, revealing the relevant documents. "Five town councilors presented themselves at the meeting out of twenty-five. By law, a majority composed of two thirds of the administrators was necessary. Cavour noticed this, and requested a list of the most important citizens. The *Gazzetta Ufficiale* published the deed with those names: a historically fake deed approved with an official seal."

In order to place the fortress under siege, Cialdini ordered "all of the inhabitants of Gaeta that reside outside of the fortress, which constitutes four fifths of the population, to vacate the city within ten hours," according to a document from 1866, signed by the mayor and the town council, in order to request damages. When the ten hours were up, "neither people nor objects can be carried out and the people remaining behind will be treated as though they were secret agents for the enemy." "One citizen out of every five was a target for the cannons," explains Ciano. "The remaining four became propertyless beggars."

"It is best not to speak of what happened," continues the document.

Ciano, however, speaks of what happened: "In the town of Terracina, a black market came into existence for the objects that "our brothers from the North" stole from Gaeta" (even in 1849, when the Piedmontese troops punished rebellious Genoa, the damage inflicted by the bombs was ten times inferior to the damage caused by the thefts committed by the soldiers). "In order to set up their camp, they destroyed nearly half of all the cultivated land including age-old gardens. The winter reached Siberian proportions that year and in order to heat themselves, they burned one hundred thousand olive trees. Of the original three hundred oil mills that once stood, not one remains standing. They were dismantled and moved elsewhere. I have discovered that several ended up on Lake Garda."

"The thriving fields remained barren and the houses defaced," states the 1866 document.

"The city was divided into three military zones," continues Ciano, "and the sea trade came to an abrupt halt: three hundred merchant ships, centuries–old shipyards with two thousand employees, sixty-four fishing boats. It all came to an end. After such violence came the emigration. After this martyrdom inflicted under the Savoy reign, the city never recovered. All of its sources of income dried up and the city emptied itself. For centuries, Gaeta was one of the most important cities in the world, a true capital of the sea. It was reduced to a little sea town. Since they were obliged to leave, my relatives, and many others, enlisted in the Austrian army, against the Italians, in the battles of Vis and Custoza: eighty years later, they would side with the United States. To the statement, "You will have to kill Italians," one of my American relatives replied, "I hope that I will kill many of them." "They drove us out," he later explained to me, "and we came back to kill them!" My grandfather, who was born in 1874, told me that when he was a boy, "the Piedmontese shot at least one citizen of Gaeta in the main square every morning." I am the only member of the Ciano family left here. There are more citizens of Gaeta in the state of Massachusetts than here. There are fifty-five thousand alone in Sommerville (where our mayor, Anthony Raimondi, was born). There are thirty thousand in Rochester. There are tens of thousands in Puerto de la Cruz in Venezuela, and in California, Michigan, Uruguay (one of its presidents was originally from Gaeta). Gaeta had never known of emigration until the massacre in 1860-61. Those who left, like Admiral John Cabot, (from whom the influential Cabot-Lodge family originates) did so because they were invited to share their knowledge of the sea with other nations."

The first to emigrate from the Kingdom of the Two Sicilies "freely" was the last of the Bourbon dynasty, Francis II, the defeated sovereign of Gaeta. Sometimes history is ironic: a little over eighty years later, the last member of the reigning Savoy dynasty, Umberto I, exiled as well, left from Naples from the same boarding dock as Francis II.

"Locally, we swear by saying 'Damn Garibaldi'; the children's game 'cops and robbers' here is called 'the brigand and the one-hundred Piedmontese,'" says Ciano.

Never mind Bossi being against the unification of Italy! "No way! Italy was united with our blood and our stolen money that was carried to the North. Now we are going to keep this unified Italy: we paid for it! We are republicans and Unitarians. We are not against the Savoy dynasty and for the Bourbons. However, our country treats us like a defeated enemy. In 1999, Piedmont was given six hundred and five billion lira in order to restore some former Savoy assets for public use. They gave us nothing. Only through the region will we receive the state-owned property we requested be returned to us. Nothing was given to us out of the one hundred and fifty million euros allotted to celebrate the anniversary of the Italian Unification, in 2011. We presented numerous projects. They did not even dignify us with a response.

To make matters worse, during the previous Berlusconi administration, the Minister of the Economy, Giulio Tremonti, actually wanted to sell our "state-owned" property. But, besides the private homes and Piazza Commestibili, the main square, every-thing is state-owned in the old historic quarter of Gaeta! Prodi's administration was able to avoid this with the Financial Act of 2007. In our opinion, the only things our country has set aside for us are bombs. In 1943, the Germans and the Fascists, fearing the Allied Forces would land here, destroyed seventy percent of the city. This was done to prepare for a defense that was never neces-sary."

Gaeta has been quite unlucky when it comes to anniversaries. "For the centennial celebrations in 1961, the President was sup-posed to visit. They made us understand that we would not have received any funding if we did not name our streets after the he-roes of the *Risorgimento*. For us, they were war criminals: they bombarded us while we were negotiating our surrender. Do they have a "Reder Street" in Marzabotto? Is there a "Kappler Road" in Rome, by the Ardeatine Trenches? In the end, we were forced to rename some of our roads after Garibaldi, Cavour, Mazzini, Bixio, and Mameli: these roads all lead outside of the city to the Bourbon cemetery."

Ciano, in his role as Councilor for Toponymy, has made it his mission to "reclaim" those streets and to rename them after the heroes of Gaeta's resistance to the siege. "*Via Battaglione Alpini di Piemonte* has gone back to being called *Viale di Montesecca* (we ac-tually never referred to it by any other name); *Corso Cavour* will be called *Viale dei Due Mari*; *Via Garibaldi* will be named after *Don Ca-pobianco*.

With the money received for the centennial celebrations in 1961, the Carducci middle school was built. When digging was be-gun to lay the foundation, a mass grave was unearthed. It meas-ured twenty four meters by twelve (today, the school covers this) filled with bodies: they were Bourbon soldiers and civilians that had been shot by the Piedmontese (when we were children we used to steal the buttons from their uniforms and trade them along with soccer figurines: we had no idea they were made of silver). When they exhumed two thousand bodies, the issue at hand began to fuel feelings of resentment. The matter was quickly closed: the grave was covered and the construction for the school began."

This story is so rich with metaphorical significance that it almost seems made up. If one had tried to invent such a story, they would have been unsuccessful. The school hides, in its foundation, the truth that emerged after one hundred years. The history from the victors' viewpoint is taught to the heirs of those defeated. They "tread" upon the truth every day as they walk to class (not for free, mind you: the municipality must pay a tax in their own city, as the school is built upon state-owned land).

"For us, left and right are merely driving directions. The right defends the economy of the Lombard and Venetian regions; the left protects the economy of Tuscany, Reggio Emilia, and the Marche region. The South has been abandoned to the likes of the *'ndrangheta,* the *mafia,* and the *camorra.* They are pawns in the economic system whereby only the North can produce goods and the South is merely the North's market. It was this way during the *Risorgimento,* continued through Fascism as well as through the administrations of the Christian Democrats (Dc) and the Italian Communist Party (Pci) established by Togliatti. They all sacrificed the South to the Turin-Milan-Genoa industrial triangle," continues Ciano.

"In the name of Victor Emannuel, King of Italy," immediately after the destruction of the city, the claim for compensation was recognized by Giorgio Pallavicino and the Minister of Internal Affairs, Raffaele Conforti ("Each person who has suffered losses will receive compensation in proportion to their loss"). The representative, Prince of Carignano, donated one thousand lira of his own money and commissioned Cialdini, the one who caused all of the damage, to pay out this compensation. The general wrote and guaranteed that after the war ended, "the Government of His Majesty would see to it that the highest possible compensation would be distributed equally." But the new representative, Luigi Carlo Farini, refused to acknowledge the importance of the matter and advised us to seek charity from the state," as reported in an incredibly sad document from 1866 that was drawn up by the local government of Gaeta.

"All that could have reminded us of our identity was destroyed," concludes Ciano. "Yet the only statue of Ferdinand II that the Piedmontese did not remove is in Gaeta. It is in the Church of San Francesco. Perhaps they thought he was a saint. The sovereign's name can be clearly read on the pedestal, but it is written in Latin. The invaders, however, only spoke French...."

CHAPTER 3

The Massacre

"I would have lived an honest life, if they had just left me in peace": I propose to hang plaques with this phrase on all of the town halls of all of the most notoriously *mafia* operated towns of the South, from Corleone to Platì, from San Luca to Casoria. The phrase was uttered by Pasquale Cavalcante, a "brigand" from Corleto Perticara shortly before he was executed. "I was a sergeant under Francis II," he explained, "when I came home looking like a drifter, my *bonetto* (military beret) was removed and my uniform was slashed. My face was spat upon. From that moment onward, I no longer had a moment of peace because, while constantly subjecting me to injustices and abuse, someone also tried to dishonor one of my sisters. "

One may wonder why people choose to live as outlaws.

Gianni de Vita, the representative of Carmine Crocco, the cleverest and most feared of the "brigands" (he led two thousand men) stated, at his trial: "We were trampled and we avenged ourselves" (this almost sounds like a direct quotation from Mameli's national anthem, "trampled and derided").

The invasion and subsequent plundering left the Southerners few choices. They could choose to react violently, with the notion that the use and abuse of others was permissible given how the conditions in which the "occupants" had left them. They could also choose to flee elsewhere. The violence, however, was fought with other violence, which was encouraged within the communities because it was useful to those in power. The roots remained, as in the Balkans, Iraq, and Africa, and they continued to generate *mafias*, or develop them where they were still in the early formative stages. "This is the destiny that all of the "Souths" of the world share," explains Franco Cassano, professor of sociology and sociology of knowledge at the University of Bari. He stated this thought in his book, *Il pensiero meridiano*: one of the deepest and most beautiful books I have read. That copious sowing of the seeds of savagery, which would be reduced to plain and simple crime, adhered and became the way out offered to the defeated in the newly rerouted course of history. Whores and *Mafiosi* arrived and continue to arrive on our shores from those nearby countries that have been broken by civil wars. They are the ones who determine how the land will be re-established, basing the foundation on a criminal economy that seeks legitimacy. This is much like the *camorra*. "Everything has become modernized, making just about everything marketable and rendering obscenity methodical. The territory and the environment are like prostitutes, as are public places and institutions. Social mobility becomes perverted through the growth of criminal activities that have already put forth their emerging elite class," writes Cassano. "This of course also includes the 'sale' of the new managerial class, in other words, their methodical corruptibility," and to this we also add the emergence of those who corrupt this emerging class.

The first tear in the *Risorgimento* mythology I had created for myself occurred when I read *La conquista del Sud* by Carlo Alianello. I read that "a woman was raped, under the eyes of her young son (they had already killed her husband), by eighteen Piedmontese soldiers. They left her there, dying and gasping for air. She died shortly after. Later on, this son, upon reaching adolescence, went on to boast that he had sought vengeance by killing eighteen of Victor Emanuel's soldiers in the Battle of Custoza."

There are places that are symbols of what happened all over the South at that time: two cities in the Campania region, Pontelandolfo and Casalduni, where, in response to their resistance against the Piedmontese soldiers, the situation evolved into one of the most savage reprisals ever to occur on Italian soil, including those during the time of the Nazis. Another example is Rionero in Vulture, located in the province of Lucano, which generated both the foremost pro-Unification thinker of the South and the best anti-Unification leader in Italy. The town of Patù, located in the

Salento area of Puglia, was the area from which the man, who ne-
gotiated the passage of power from the Bourbon dynasty to the
Savoys, both left from and retired to. These are all stops on my
personal pilgrimage chronicling the defeat of the South.

When Garibaldi arrived, he found a decade long socio-economic clash between the lower class and the bourgeois together
with the landowners. The latter, assisted by their farmers, took
over the "public land," which was the South's insurance policy
against poverty. Everyone, or at least nearly everyone, from the
hovel through to the castle, owned their own home. The same goes
for land ownership: everyone owned a piece of land, whether it
was a vegetable garden or a large estate. If the land was not substantial enough to render its owners self-reliant, the person could
cultivate the "public land," in proportion to what they sowed. "How
is it possible that Garibaldi's troops were greeted with such good
will on the part of both the upper and lower classes in 1860, thus
facilitating the fall of the Bourbon monarchy, and only a year later
that good will turned into dissatisfaction that echoed throughout
the social classes?" asks Franco Molfese in his book *Storia del brigantaggio dopo l'Unità*.

Justice was promised to the poor, who had had their land confiscated. The rich were promised a number of privileges. Both the
rich and the poor lost, in this case. When the "liberators" came
down from the North, they were obliged to choose an ally. They
chose to ally themselves with the *mafia* and usurpers rather than
with the poor and honest people of the land. In exchange for their
political support, the Northerners granted the usurpers the right
to steal: they could keep the land they stole, as long as they proclaimed "Long live Victor Emanuel!" The crook and the oppressor
legitimized each other's existence. That was the first lesson they
taught us. The second was when they called us delinquents. Poverty spread and the reasons for conflict multiplied: the resistance
against the invaders was further complicated by the civil war between peasants and lords (some even created their own private
militias). Even a regretful Garibaldi noticed this situation: "That

was a social issue that could not be resolved with iron and fire."
But that is exactly what they used: iron and fire.

Do you recall the embarrassing incident (if only it were limited
to one!) wherein George Bush Jr. announced, "The war is over!,"
because the U.S. military had just entered the city of Baghdad?
The same thing happened to us: Gaeta fell and the phrase "Italy
has been made!" was uttered at the end of the war. Well, that was
when the war actually began, and it lasted longer than in Iraq.
D'Azeglio stated that now that Italy had been made, the Italians
had to be made too. They made them … die.

Hardly any of the things I am going to talk about are unpublished, with the exception of a few details. If you do not know the
towns where these atrocities took place, imagine that they happened in your town, to your family, and to not have known it.
Imagine that your homes were treated in this fashion (can you envision your home burning, with a lifetime's worth of memories in
it?) along with the church's bell tower (which was torn down
amidst the screams of all those who had deceived themselves into
thinking that they would be safe in a church). Imagine all the people you know. Imagine your relatives tortured. Imagine the women in your family, raped. Then imagine you were told that this
was all your fault and that it happened for your own good, and
that you did not even deserve your own "good" because you were
the worst part of the country: filled with thieves and filth. If you
can imagine all of these things, and you begin to suspect that behind your shame, which has lasted for so long, hides someone
else's crime, you now understand what I mean. You understand
how it feels to continue to be insulted still today. The atrocities
that I have grouped together here are in no particular chronologi-
cal order and I did not write them to make a spiteful historic
point; it is merely a collection of bouts of rage that I have accumulated by reading, throughout the years, about the things that they
did to us. This rage is constantly renewed by the brazenly unpunished profusion of the worst aspects of the "Northern" mentality
(derision, disdain, and contempt) that still today pollute the language and actions of too many Northerners. There is a certain

man named Renato Brunetta, whom I am told is even a minister, who wants to solve the South's problems by sending them "another" thousand Northerners (have they not stolen everything already?). Does this mean, if Brambilla and Bragadin come to the South that the Salerno-Reggio Calabria stretch of the highway will sprout a third lane? If they dirty their hands will the Catania-Palermo one hundred and ninety kilometer-long train route cut its travel time from six hours down to three? Do you think that if we said, "Don't you dare!" that the Minister of Economy and Finance will cease to steal the funds for the South and stop rerouting them to the North? Are we dealing with a nobler race? And Brunetta would be an example of said race?

What I have written did not happen everywhere in the South. But, nonetheless, everything I have written did happen in the South. There is so much more that I have not included. There is so much more that is yet to be discovered, despite there being already hundreds of books written on the subject. There are books written by those who were touched directly by the facts in question. There are recent books that were born from the revival of interest in the matter, which prompted further research. It is thanks to these books that these hidden crimes have become known and act as proof to those actions that had previously been denied.

In the first works published that documented the atrocities committed in the South and the cross-eyed administration of the newly unified state, one perceives that the injustice may have been the fruit of misinformation; of facts that were not reported correctly (for personal convenience or prejudice) to those who base their decisions from afar, on hearsay. Perhaps it would be sufficient to shed some light on the truth in order to stir the conscience of others in order to make amends. In the works published more recently, this perception disappears. Instead, one perceives an awareness of the notion that the authors are gathering information on truths for people who do not want to know about them. Perhaps the people deride their efforts as being of inferior quality: an exercise in finding information that is not from the "victorious" side, and therefore dated, not credible, and "biased." The notion of the good faith of those people who benefitted from the imbalance of two areas of the same country, was lost. The first authors were disappointed. The more recent ones were disenchanted.

The Piedmontese count, Alessandro Bianco di Saint Jorioz, was a captain in the Italian army. He actively participated in the destruction of the Kingdom of the Two Sicilies and the massacre of the Southerners. He did this (according to what he wrote in his book *Il brigantaggio alla frontiera pontifica dal 1860 al 1863*) because he was convinced that he was fighting against "the poverty in the farmlands, the greed and arrogance of the nobles, and shameful ignorance." He believed he was fighting against superstition, fanaticism, idolatry, dissolute lifestyles, immorality, corruption of employees, magistrates, and public officials, robbery, and embezzlement. In a word: evil. Someone told him that this is what the South was.

He admitted that he understood, too late, that those people "in 1859 wore clothes and shoes, were industrialized, and had financial reserves. The average farmer had money. He bought and sold animals and this corresponded to the exact amount he needed to pay his rent. With what was left over, he fed his family. Everyone lived happily in their financial situation. Now it is the opposite." Because, after the Piedmontese invasion, "after a few years the majority of the property fell into the hands of the rich, speculators, usurers, and manipulators…. Men of merit faded away. The studies on the part of the youth were wasted." The wealth of the families were drained due to the inheritance tax that was so high that "within three generations of a family (which can even occur in one year's time) one could find themselves from a position of financial comfort to one of poverty."

This was after the massacre, which was so terrifying that even Nino Bixio, "who alone was responsible for seven hundred executions in the South," writes Ciano, was affected by it. He appeared like a dove amongst a sea of vultures when he appeared in the Parliament in Turin, in a failed attempt to stop the massacre. "Italy is out there, gentlemen, and if you want Italy to be united, we must do so with justice and not with bloodshed." Garibaldi himself wrote, eight years after his mission, that "the abuse the South-erners were subjected to is incommensurable. I am convinced that I did nothing wrong, however I would not return to Southern Italy. I fear I would be stoned, having given rise to such squalor and hatred."

There are myriad events that beg to be narrated, to recount the pain and the injustices that caused this state. With the passing of the years, I have accumulated so many emotions and, with them, the awareness of my inadequacy to render them justice. Someone once said that "human suffering cannot be summarized."

What does it take to kill our fellowman? For Giuseppe San-topietro and his newborn son, not much: a rifle shot was enough for him and his newborn was killed with a bayonet stab. For those thirty women who gathered around the cross in the square where the market stands, a burst of shots from the *bersaglieri*'s rifles was enough. They proceeded to take their newly acquired position by storm. Apparently the women's rosary beads were inefficient against their blades. Those who sought shelter in the church, cling-ing to the altar, were undressed and abused right there. One of those women had her hands chopped off because she scratched one of the *bersaglieri*'s faces. They proceeded to kill her. Gigi di Fiore chose to recount these events in a somewhat narrative form in his book *1861*, but he used names he came upon in documents that he lists in his appendix. Antonio Ciano, in order to chronicle this massacre in his work *I Savoia e il massacro del Sud* primarily consulted trial records. Other events were discovered through oral declarations and these often gave rise to disputes. As a result, the emphasis was placed on specific details (sometimes these are nec-essary) and thus the slaughter was forgotten. I report some of these anecdotes here, without expecting to solve anything. I only want to give an idea of what happened all over the South.

Perhaps Maria Izzo was the most beautiful girl in town, be-cause many men, those of our Italian brothers with the liberty to commit rape freely, desired her. However, there was much work to be done in that town ("No stone should remain standing," was the precise order given). So to save time they tied her, naked, to a tree with her legs raised. She remained this way until the last soldier pierced her stomach with a bayonet.

Concetta Biondi instead, after the rape, was killed with a bullet to the head: she was an adolescent. Her mother Rosa was raped and stabbed before her eyes. Even the Moroccans following the French troops raped women during the last world war (have you seen Sophia Loren and her "daughter" in the film *La Ciociara*?). They were also liberators, but they were foreigners. Perhaps this is why they did not kill the women after using them.

They say that Maria Ciaburri was in bed next to her husband Giuseppe when she was attacked. They killed them both. They killed him first. They killed her after they grew tired of her.

That town, Pontelandolfo, had five thousand inhabitants. The *bersaglieri* marksmen however, had excellent tactics (they were in the South to "train for Africa," as a pre-colonial experience). They searched homes and pushed their inhabitants out into the streets with their bayonets. They led the people, like a herd, down the streets until they met up with their other colleagues, who proceeded to fire shots into the crowd. This town was destined to disappear. In this manner, in order to avoid wasting anything, our plumed brothers went from house to house plundering money ("Coins, coins!" they shouted, one of them reported) jewelry, valuables, and even provisions (wine, salami, cheese, bread). A Garibaldi supporter tried to save some of his fellow citizens: "Staggering and bloody, a young girl dragged herself towards him. She had been shot in the shoulder because she wanted to safeguard her honor. When she finally found a place she deemed secure, she fell to the ground, never to rise again." A deputy from Milan named Giuseppe Ferrari, recorded this story. He wanted to personally see what had happened. He was scarred for life ("There are two old women who will perish amidst the flames. Over there are some people who have been shot, justly, but nonetheless shot. Earrings were torn from the ears of women..."). In other places, fingers were chopped off in order to remove rings.

It would seem easy to destroy a town in merely one day. There were five hundred *bersaglieri* marksmen against five thousand townspeople. Each of them had to kill ten civilians. However those officers who were actually "functional" were far fewer than those who did other things. One had to take into consideration the higher ranking officials, their assistants, those who were there to facilitate the troops' movement, the supporting troops, and those who were placed at the city gates to ensure no one could escape from the massacre. How many were there in all? Were they 20% less? Or 30%? More? To give a low estimate, let us say that each assassin had to take out around fifteen people. Would a day be enough? Wouldn't you have to find the people hiding in their homes, churches, and various dark corners? How about those who manage to flee? In that chaos, many manage to flee. Precious time is lost. Fifteen is an average figure, because amongst those soldiers you will find those that are incapable, faint of heart, and those dishonest soldiers who only think of stealing and raping. This leaves all of the hard work to the most scrupulous soldiers....

One of them, Carlo Margolfo, from the province of Sondrio, wrote in his diary, that was discovered fourteen years later: " We entered the town and immediately began shooting as many priests and men as we could. Then the soldiers plundered the town. Finally, we set the town on fire."

With the people in their homes, prayers and laments were heard coming from one of the burning homes, prompting several officers to enter. They found five women kneeling before a crucifix that had been placed on a table. Fearing further torture, they all retreated to a corner. The floor gave out, and they all wound up in the flames. According to our orders women, children, and the sick were to have been spared, according to Margolfo. But you know how these things go once you are there.... "There was such desolation," at the end of the massacre, one can read in the diary, "that you could not stay near the town due to the great heat and the noise that those poor devils made. Their destiny was to die roasting in the flames, underneath the ruins of their homes. Instead, during the fire we had everything. We had chickens, bread, wine, and capons. Nothing was missing." After all, the townspeople no longer had any use for those things, so why let them go to waste....

After such a hard day, they had earned it, didn't they? This "nest of brigands," as our *bersagliere* writes, "this town of Pandolfo," with techniques of force, "has now been domesticated quite well." Do you think the townspeople understood this?

The punishment came as the result of the deaths of forty-one "Italian" soldiers, who had been misled by their commander, according to the three survivors, within shooting distance of a guerrilla troop. These guerrilla fighters were supported by a good part of the population, and were loyal to their king. The commander of those soldiers, Lieutenant Bracci, was said to have been killed by his own men for his incompetence.

How many were killed during the reprisal in Pontelandolfo and Casalduni, in the province of Benevento? Were as many killed as those in Marzabotto by the Nazi troops led by Walter Reder? The *"Popolo d'Italia,"* a pro-unification newspaper of the time, stated that "only" one hundred and sixty four people were killed. They complained that the "real brigands" had been able to flee. Yes, this was a massacre, but of innocent people! The collaboration efforts between the media reached sublime heights: the *"Gazzetta del Popolo"* of Turin suggested that the soldiers "not only execute the people with rifles, but hang them instead with ropes, as the ropes can be reused for many others." Even the Khmer Rouge, in Cambodia, who killed one or two million of their countrymen, cracked the skulls of their enemies with pick axes in order to save bullets. This is the same newspaper that reports that should the Neapolitans invade the Savoy Kingdom, the Piedmontese should act as though they were "brigands."

A precise calculation of the number of victims is difficult. It is constantly changing and it always results in higher and higher numbers. According to the registers of the local church, there were only thirteen "deaths and burials." However, a study conducted by Father Davide Fernando Panella on the mortality rates in the five years preceding and following the massacre, the registries of Pontelandolfo (Casalduni's documents were destroyed in the fires) reveal that between August and September of 1861 there were one hundred and twelve deaths versus the twenty-nine from the previous year. Between 1861 to 1862, despite the fact that the population had diminished, there were four hundred and sixty-two deaths as compared to two hundred and eighty-five from two years before (not all of the injured and burn victims perished right away). This is not even the whole story. Those who fled were often followed to nearby towns where they were executed. Those who survived declared the deaths of their relatives, but if entire families were killed then who would report their deaths for the records? The town re-populated itself, but there still has not been a comparison conducted between the number of inhabitants and their last names before and after the massacre. Antonio Ciano estimates over nine hundred victims however, in the light of new stories recounted by witnesses, others suspect the death toll to be higher. In the book *Due Sicilie, 1830-1880*, the author estimates that the "death toll was certainly over one thousand." The deputy Giuseppe Ferrari (as well as others) speak of three thousand refugees, after the massacre (tales are told of mothers driven to madness for having witnessed the deaths of their children in their own arms). If we count only the people from Pontelandolfo, where did the other two thousand come from? The majority of the refugees were from Casalduni, who had approximately three thousand inhabitants. This is because they received news that the reprisal was imminent and more people were able to flee the town in time. So what happened? In the following days, there were four hundred arrests and many convictions. There were at least thirty executions in the records, and the same was registered a month later, in the town of Cerreto Sannita (where many citizens fled to from their burning towns) and again in Casalduni and Pontelandolfo. Two months later, thirty-seven people were executed.

Those five hundred assassins were only half of the expedition; the other four or five hundred (one thousand in all: a number that is bad luck, in the area where I am from) happened upon the nearby Casalduni with the same mission because it was there, under the castle and below the cliff, that those Piedmontese soldiers were killed while fleeing from Pontelandolfo. How many died in Casalduni?

The *bersagliere* Margolfo implied that few managed to survive from the town of Pontelandolfo. They had sealed them in their burning homes to "roast." Only three homes were left standing in the entire town. None were left in Casalduni. The day after the mass killing, August 15th, 1861, the *bersaglieri* set up a market in the town of Fragneto Monforte in order to sell the goods they had stolen. A priest managed to redeem the chalice that held the consecrated hosts in the tabernacle of the church of Pontelandolfo. In the meantime, their headquarters was informed of the positive outcome of the mission: "Yesterday, at dawn, justice was served in the towns of Pontelandolfo and Casalduni. They are still burning." A true specialist in massacres, General Maurizio de Sonnaz, led the slaughter. He was nicknamed *"Requiescant."*

"When the sun peeked over the shoulders of night, there were only dogs and smoke and overturned tents." I was only a young boy when I first read about the massacre of the sleeping Cheyenne by the blue soldiers on the banks of Sand Creek. It was my first real encounter with evil. Our education is one of consoling and reassurance. We grow up believing that it is guaranteed (as is offered by fables, the Gospel, our parents' wisdom, the law and by Perry Mason on television) that good deeds will be repaid with good deeds and evil will be repaid with evil. No one can live without this belief in the notion that justice (whatever it is you might intend by this word) will have the last word. There is a period between infancy and adolescence during which this need is agonizing: we would kill ourselves over an "unfair" grade in school. If you perceive the infamy behind the murder of a tribe that trusted the peace pact with the white man ("our boys," "the good guys") then you are marked for life. Later on, Fabrizio De Andrè touched our souls by telling this story in his song *"Fiume Sand Creek."* The question remained: How can someone dare to do this? This is just like what happened in Casalduni and Pontelandolfo.

If you don't mind, if you are not from the South, could you please imagine that you are? How do you feel?

So the dead amounted to less than one hundred, a few hundred, or over nine hundred? Or do we risk that those who estimate the dead to be in the thousands are correct? Perhaps some documents on the massacred were brought to Benevento, which was a stronghold of the Vatican State in the Kingdom of the Two Sicilies. Some years later, Piedmont-Italy annexed that town as well and if there were documents in the archives, they disappeared. If these records do not surface (like the diary of *bersagliere* Margolfo) then the truth about the size of the massacre will never be known.

If the victims of the reprisal were truly one hundred and sixty four, four Southerners would have been killed by each Savoy soldier. This amounts to approximately half of what the Nazis accomplished in the *Via Rasella* attack, where ten Italians were killed for every German. If the victims were nine hundred, the proportion would double: twenty Southerners for each Piedmontese or Lombard. If the worst estimates were to be true, then dozens of Southerners would have been killed for each "Italian" soldier. In Rome, the Nazis (besides the massacre of the Ardeatine Trenches) did not have the courage to destroy the neighborhood (including the Quirinale Palace) where the attack had taken place. Pontelandolfo and Casalduni, on the other hand, were destroyed.

The representative Ferrari attempted to express his disgust while in Parliament, but his efforts were futile. In the end, one gets the feeling that he grasps the justice system's powerlessness: "If your consciences do not tell you that you are wallowing in blood, then I no longer know how to express myself." This had a more significant impact upon the Chamber of Commons, in London, where a discussion ensued.

I felt that I was still missing something with respect to this event. Evil exceeds: when its plans go awry, it is because its goals have been surpassed. This excess becomes the drool dangling from the mouth of ferociousness. In the Ardeatine Trenches five extra hostages were executed because of an error. Then I read that Lieutenant William Calley, the author of the massacre that horrified the world in 1968 and that had accelerated the end of the Vietnam War, regretted his actions. The world never knew how many defenseless Vietnamese women and children were slaughtered in My Lai. The number oscillates around three hundred and forty-seven and five hundred and four. The reprisal actually involved three villages: My Lai, Binh Tai and My Khe. I then remembered that the Marzabotto massacre also extended to include two neighboring towns: Grizzana and Vado di Monzuno (of the one thousand eight hundred and thirty deaths, one thousand of them died in these two towns). It was only in this manner that I noticed what had been staring me in the face the entire time: the town of Campolattaro. Pontelandolfo and Casalduni supported the doomed reaction to the Piedmontese troops. But what about Campolattaro? It is located in between the two other towns, although slightly to the east, and is only a few kilometers from each town. If evil exceeds then savagery is blind. Campolattaro was located in the wrong place. It had one thousand five hundred inhabitants and was technically included in the retaliation even though no Piedmontese soldier was killed there. The worst thing to happen were a few violent slaps because the town archive had been violated and the basement had been raided. This was nothing compared to the butchery that happened in the rest of the South. The *bersagliere* Margolfo, along with his troops, arrived here after the massacres of Pontelandolfo, wearied by the long march.

But something boosted his morale: "Listen to how beautiful this is. Upon our entrance to the town," he writes, "all of the inhabitants came to greet us with olive branches, crying and praying." Had they heard about Pontelandolfo and Casalduni? Perhaps they had: they asked the soldiers "not to burn their town down ... that they would have showed them who the "brigand" was." In fact, only a few executions took place in that town." You know. Only a few took place, in passing through.

Haven't you heard how beautiful that is?

The executioner of Marzabotto, Walter Reder, lived nearly the rest of his life in prison, in Gaeta. The same goes for the commander of the Nazi troops in Rome, Herbert Kappler who was responsible for the massacre of the Ardeatine Trenches. Erich Priebke was finally found in South America in 1994, and was extradited to Italy and subsequently condemned.

The massacre of Sand Creek occurred three years after that of the Piedmontese in the Benevento area and it "officially" had the same number of victims (between one hundred and fifty and one hundred and eighty-four). But after twelve years, in 1876, the Native Americans evened the score: they caught up to the Seventh Cavalry at Little Big Horn and destroyed it. Even for them, the need for justice, in the end was satisfied.

Liutenant Calley was given a life sentence for My Lai, but was freed after three years of house arrest. He reappeared forty-one years later, in August 2009, saying, "Not a day passes that I don't feel remorse for what happened." Today, there is a museum dedicated to the My Lai Massacre. Many American tourists burst into tears when they visit. There is no place in Italy dedicated to what was done to the Southerners. It is not our custom to account for our history.

Every year, in the towns of Pontelandolfo and Casalduni, the battle between the "Piedmontese" and the "brigands" is re-enacted on the anniversary of the massacre. Nicola Bove, the President of the Pro Loco Society of Casalduni, who has dedicated all of his time to recovering evidence of lost history for the past twenty years, says, "The old townsfolk see the actors portraying the Bourbon guerrilla soldiers and shout at them, 'Don't go that way! The soldiers are there!'" as if the battle were real and as though history could be rectified.

"Around a thousand people come every year from the regions of Campania, Basilicata, and Calabria," says Bove. He assumes a more diplomatic tone when he says that each of the two towns celebrates this day of remembrance individually. (Someone from Pontelandolfo asked Casalduni to pay for damages because although the reprisal involved both towns, the Piedmontese soldiers that fled from Pontelandolfo were killed in Casalduni.) Bove was a furniture salesman. He had heard of the massacre while attending several conventions in 1990. He wanted to know more. The old townspeople remembered that "something bad had happened," but these were only bits and pieces of stories. These fragments along with his discovery of many incomplete documents pieced together a horrifying tale. "We search in the town's municipal and parochial archives as well those of neighboring towns," Bove explains, assisted by civil servants, "because here in Casalduni, everything was destroyed." Three houses were left standing in Pontelandolfo, while nothing was left in Casalduni. No one knows exactly how many were killed either. Today, the town has one thousand five hundred inhabitants; before the massacre it had three thousand. Following Bove's example, neighboring towns also organize conventions and events in order to remember the massacre.

We go to lunch in Pontelandolfo in a traditional restaurant of the area. As soon as one walks inside, there is a large bookcase that occupies the entire wall. It is filled with historical books and documents and some appear to be unpublished works. "They must be translated," says our host, Gaudenzio Di Mella, a former truck driver. He collects these documents and studies them with the help of experts. There are flags and coats of arms in his collection. "The time to be ashamed is over. Or at least it is for us," mumbles the restaurateur. I state my observation that a town can be reborn if it reacquires its memory. He shakes his head and slips a piece of paper into my view. It is an essay that a middle school student wrote in 1961 for the one hundred year anniversary of the Unification: "All of my relatives are in America and I will go too, once I finish school. My town, in Italy, is only here temporarily: the real Pontelandolfo is across the ocean in New Jersey in the United States. My uncle fought in the war in the Pacific as a Marine. Another one of my uncles landed in Salerno and came to visit us with more gifts than we could imagine. Here, everyone goes to America because it is a tradition. My grandparents once told me that one time Pontelandolfo was destroyed and was set on fire because its citizens were brigands. From that moment onward, everyone became an emigrant. Many made their fortunes as American citizens, but they never forgot where they came from. New York is much closer to us than Milan, and we know English much better than we know Italian. At school they have told us that one hundred years have passed since the Unification of Italy. One hundred years is a long time and we have not even noticed."

"I found this amidst the rubble of a public building," said the host.

He is right: perhaps the inhabitants can reacquire their memory, but Pontelandolfo's identity died in the massacre. In the town (located in the Samnite sub-region where the Romans deported indomitable Ligurians) settled exiles from Siena who had fled from the wars between the Guelfs and the Ghibellines. After the reprisal the town repopulated itself, but of people from different historic backgrounds. They had roots in different places. Pontelandolfo is there, but it has now evolved into something else.

Not everyone is interested in reestablishing the facts: would one insist if their ancestor were Achille Jacobelli (usurper of many state-owned lands and the son of a common delinquent who was condemned to death, but who had been pardoned by the Bourbons) who in order to gain the favor of the Piedmontese soldiers asked them to "raze all of the houses in such unfortunate towns as Pontelandolfo and Casalduni" ("Burn, kill, and remove from the face of the earth each inhabitant of these towns.") Or would one insist if their relative had been the mayor that left his town on the eve of the massacre, perhaps knowing about the massacre but not warning anyone of it, to seek safety in Naples? We still have those names and the resentment that come along with them (Doctor Ferdinando Melchiorre Pulzella, a descendant of the mayor, sought legal action against Antonio Ciano, author of *I Savoia e il massacro del Sud*, and he wrote an essay stating that victims of the reprisal, brought on by the actions of the brigands, were only thirteen).

"Do you remember *Stormy Six*?" asks the host. Sure I do: it is one of those rare but questionable privileges of being my age. They were a band that was active from the end of the 1960s. "Do you remember their 1972 album, *Unità*?" No. "It narrates what happened. One of the songs is called *Pontelandolfo*: 'It was on the town's patron's feast day/The people walked in a procession.... Pontelandolfo, the bell tolls for you/For all of your people/For those who lived and for those who were killed/For the women and the soldiers/for Italy and for the king.'"

One hundred and fifty years have passed, and still no one wants to speak of all of this. "In 2008, at the festival hosted by the Pro Loco Society of Montesilvano in the Pescara province, there were one thousand five hundred people, and our folk group decided to participate by waving a banner with the Bourbon coat of arms. The Piedmontese delegation rebelled and state "Still with this story?" To which I replied, "Why? Would you want us to erase our history? Do you even know our history? If you want, we can meet and talk about it." We made an appointment to meet in Rome.

Every year in Vicenza, the town laid a wreath on the plaque that commemorates a hero of the Italian *Risorgimento*. He won a gold medal for military valor and two silver medals: Colonel Pier Eleonoro Negri. In 2004, a tenacious historical document hunter, Antonio Pagano, discovered that Negri was at the head of the reprisal in Pontelandolfo. It was previously believed to be Gaetano Negri, as he was also a member of the Sixth Regiment. He was another "brigand exterminator" who went on to become the mayor of Milan.

So now what?

Every year, the town of Vicenza continues to lay a wreath on Negri's commemorative plaque in the name of the Italian people, including those from Pontelandolfo, Casalduni, and Campolattaro. The blue soldiers, in order to "build a country," stole the land and lives of many Native Americans. This still angers us. The soldiers from Northern Italy, in order to build a country, destroyed and sacked the South. Doesn't this anger you? Reder and Kappler received a life sentence in prison while Negri received a gold medal for ordering the slaughter of (at least the same amount, if not more) defenseless Italians in reprisal. What would you think if Vicenza were to place a laurel wreath on the tombs of Reder and Kappler?

How many Southerners have you seen, in Vicenza, try to block the ceremony? How many people have you seen casting blood-red paint on the plaque in order to dishonor this noble native of

Vicenza? This is one's acceptance of the status of minority: at most one complains, only to do nothing. A murderer is honored as a hero and nothing is done to stop it. "About twenty years ago," says Nicola Bove, "the mayor of Pontelandolfo asked that the town be given the gold medal, given the blood it shed for the unification. Sandro Pertini was president at the time. The request was declined." The victims receive no medal: only the murderer does. What a strange country this is, where it does not matter how one wins, but whether one loses or not.

When one accepts this inferior status, one is willing to accept anything. I will give an example citing an anecdote from a story by the Milanese philosopher Ferrari regarding the massacre of Pontelandolfo. The survivors received him with dignity. They hosted him in one of the three houses left standing. Amidst the still-smoking ruins and survivors searching for traces of their loved ones and personal effects, they led him to Antonio Rinaldi. He was a landowner (the soldiers had stolen what they could and destroyed his land) who was liberal and in favor of the unification, as were his two sons, Francesco and Tommaso. They had gone to meet the *bersaglieri* and explained that they were fighting for the same side. They were, however, forced to pay a ransom, then executed by bayonet. Pro-Savoy Southerners were useful, but when they had exhausted their purpose they became Southerners just like all they others and were therefore treated in the same fashion. To the honest representative from the North who came to him, the father of those two Pro-Piedmont sons, who had money extorted from them and were subsequently killed, only said, "I ask nothing and I complain about nothing."

Whatever they do to us will be less than what they have already done to us. The betrayed memory of a massacre is worth less than the massacre. The filthy gratitude of the victim for the murderer emerges: after all, the murderer could still choose to hurt someone, but contains himself. The inalienable, subtle need for justice could induce one to invert the blame: Negri is honored because you deserved to be punished. It was written: "The persecuted cried at the funeral of the persecutors."

We are not a country because after the *Risorgimento,* after Fascism, we lacked the common courtesy to examine ourselves and judge accordingly. "You made animal feed out of our hopes/you gave us tears and hunger/it does not matter: long live the king!" was a song that was sung in the South in 1861. Our history is one of crimes that have gone unpunished for the good of the state. This tolerance to impunity and abuse has a geographic connotation. It has generated a notion of inferior citizenship, that is resigned to tolerate, even if it means to their detriment, what for others is deemed to be intolerable. Pontelandolfo is not on Sand Creek. There were no Native Americans in the South, therefore the country's conscience can remain silent.

If Italy were to speak, it would have to condemn its origins. We still do not know how many towns were destroyed by the Savoy troops and of those foreign troops at their command (the most savage of these were the Hungarian Hussars). We have counted eighty-one, so far, though some were forever erased from the maps (this number cannot be found in any history book or official document). It is difficult to predict where this research will take us because in the months following the conquest, nearly one thousand five hundred towns had rebelled against their "liberators." "Against enemies of this caliber (author's note: *he was referring to his "Italian brothers"*) mercy is considered a crime," stated General Ferdinando Pinelli to his troops. "We will purify these regions, infested with their filthy drool, with iron and fire." The atrocities for which he was held responsible were enough to stir the protests by the foreign press and this forced the government to remove him from his post. Before doing so, however, they awarded him with a gold medal.

This campaign of "liberation" continued: from those executed in the town of Bronte to those of Nicosia, Biancavilla, Leonforte, Racalmuto, Niscemi, Trecastagni, San Filippo D'Agira, Castiglione, Noto, Regalbuto, to the two thousand bodies found in the mass grave in Gaeta and the one hundred and fifty to one hundred and sixty from Gioia del Colle, to the dozens of those executed in Vieste (an archpriest, four canons, captain of the national guard, twenty-one soldiers...), to the sixty from Montecillone, the one thousand two hundred and forty-five from Isernia, (more than three times the people that died in the Ardeatine Trenches, but Isernia is not Rome!), the forty-five from Auletta, the forty from Pietrelcina, five from Paduli, two hundred and thirty two from Nola, one hundred and seventeen from Scurcola, five hundred and twenty-six in Teramano in one week's time, fifty in Casamari, from one hundred and thirty-five to one hundred and fifty in Montefalcione; thirteen towns with a total of thirty-nine thousand inhabitants, "part of them butchered, part of them buried under the ruins, or burned by the flames; those who survived the massacre are forced to wander about"; Vena Martello, San Vito (one hundred and fifty three executed and one hundred and twenty deported), Ruvo del Monte was where the Piedmontese soldiers arrived after Carmine Crocco and his men had already left, the soldiers then proceeded to raid the town and slaughter the townsfolk; Pagese, San Martino, San Marco in Lamis, Cotronei, Guardiaregia, Vico, Rignano, Palma, Barile, and Campochiaro were all submitted to the mercy of the flames.... According to *Briganti & Partigiani*, forty-one towns were destroyed. Other lists range from fifty-four to eighty-one.

After taking their lives, the soldiers also took their decency. The bodies of the "brigands," especially the female ones, were displayed nude. Great feelings of resentment rose against the "ferocious dictatorship" that "treated Southern Italy and the islands with iron and fire by crucifying, quartering, and burying the poor farmers alive," wrote Antonio Gramsci, that the "cheering crowds" in Gioia del Colle (according to the historian Lucarelli) applauded Caterina Colacicco, wife of the exiled Nicola Lillo, when she dipped her bread in the blood of her fellow citizen, Vincenzo Pavone, and consumed it. He was responsible for the arrest of her husband and was lynched in the town square. Meanwhile, in Isernia, the women, in a sort of witches' Sabbath, castrated and hung the bodies of the dead Pro-Unification soldiers of the Matese Legion.

The South became a desolate land: bodies were left to rot and fester in the town square. Others were reduced to ashes in the dozens of towns that were razed. There were processions of thousands of refugees wandering the countryside. There were troops everywhere, each fighting their own war: the "brigands," guerrilla soldiers, Savoy troops, private militias of Pro-Piedmontese and Pro-Bourbon landowners (these counted anywhere from one hundred to one thousand armed troops), *carabinieri*, mafia bosses that had been granted policemen and avenger status, national guard, groups of "eager" citizens, and enraged farmers (like those who supported Neapolitan Major Achille de Liguoro and defeated the one thousand soldiers of Garibald's Colonel Francesco Nullo), former Bourbon soldiers, as well as delinquents who were willing to support any of the aforementioned groups, should it prove to be in their interest.

In the towns, families found themselves divided and at war with each other and amongst themselves. That hatred and resentment often remained and became chronic. Still today many communities are fragile and filled with rancor. In this manner, one goes against one's own interest by trying to favor the interest of the "enemy." One of the youngest, most skilled, and best loved Bourbon generals, Matteo Negri, followed his king to Gaeta, along with his brothers Errico and Girolamo. He was killed as he inspected the frontline in Garigliano, despite the fact that he was already injured. His father, who remained in Naples, switched sides to support the Piedmontese.

Several wars were being fought at the same time: a war of invasion, one of armed resistance, a civil war between those who were invaded which was incited by the invaders, and a criminal one of plundering. To anyone who was looking to even out a score, all they had to do was to choose a side ("The patriotic bourgeois went overboard to the point of killing people on the opposite side, particularly the poor farmers, with inhuman ferocity," states Lucarelli, in *Il sergente Romano. Brigantaggio politico in Puglia dopo il 1860*); the possessions of the "enemy" were stolen; women were raped and killed so as to wear the men out (Lauretta D'Onghia, Sergeant Romano's fiancée, was killed in this manner, though he atrociously avenged her death); "people fired their rifles without any warrant, including the troops, national guard, mayors, civilians" (Lucarelli). Convenience, ideals, honor, opportunism, avidity were all roads that led to bloodshed. Much blood did flow. Savagery is a poor means of measuring the depth of the wound that was inflicted upon a country that believed it was meant to greet its brothers and instead found itself gutted. "Francesco or Vittorio?" they asked a young boy, during the siege of Gioia del Colle. What could he know? By chance he said, "Vittorio," the name of the hated Savoy king. He died, as was narrated, asking: "Please ask me the question again." Nearby, a Piedmontese ordered the cutting off of a poor man's lips after he had yelled, "Long live the King!" without specifying which king.

"Terrify these people" was the order given. In only nine months, the official statistics (and therefore false by default, given what the "forgotten" documents reveal) stated that nine thousand were executed, a little less than eleven thousand were injured, over six thousand incarcerated, almost two hundred priests, monks, women, and children were killed. Suppose we accept these statistics to be true: in nine months time. The last "brigand" who expressed his opposition was killed twelve years later, in Calabria. "Entire Southern populations were subjected to a ruthless military repression of which all traces have been lost, because all of the relevant documents were scientifically destroyed. This all brought about the deaths of at least one hundred thousand people, according to reliable calculations," wrote Giordano Bruno Guerri. According to others, the numbers are even higher; Lorenzo Del Boca (*Indietro Savoia!*) reports calculations that are seven times higher, referring to it as a "mass slaughter." It has been estimated that the armed opposition ranged from eighty thousand to one hundred and thirty-five thousand. At least as many as that lent themselves to support them, supply them, and spy for them. They could do this because they had the blatant support of the entire population and the less evident support of the landowners. It was necessary to eliminate all or almost all of them. Antonio Ciano (in is work *Le stragi e gli eccidi dei Savoia* which is a collection of news reports on the massacres as reported by several different authors) adds to the "brigands" those who were executed, the victims of the reprisals, those left to die in the concentration camps, those who fell ill in the prisons or amongst those who no longer had homes. Many went mad and committed suicide. In this manner, the massacre would reach a death toll of a million deaths. This is more or less the same number of victims that was the price paid for the importation of Bush's democracy in Iraq, where four million people fled (from our South, three to five times as many fled). Many cities were destroyed, such as Falluja, in order to drive out terrorists (this does not sound new to us).

The magazine *Civiltà Cattolica* states that the number of bodies left by the liberators exceeded the amount of plebiscite votes (which were imposed upon the voters at dagger point and with muskets), which were over one million. Out of nine million inhabitants. This means that there were more dead than in the recent conflicts in the Balkans, according to Erminio De Biase, in *L'Inghilterra contro il Regno delle Due Sicilie*. In 1860, a brother came to visit us. His name was Cain. "Let us not waste time making prisoners," wrote Cavour to his king. If there were prisoners, they were soon executed out of retaliation, like the lancers from Montebello. They killed sixty-one Southerners to avenge the death of one of their captains.

In the book listing the honors bestowed upon our members of the armed forces, one can count the number of awards that Italy bestowed upon those authors of this "brotherly" massacre; four gold medals, two thousand three hundred and seventy-five silver medals, and five thousand and twelve honorable mentions. What country celebrates murderers in this fashion? Do you believe that nothing remains in our subconscious memory of the fact that the Northern soldiers received awards based upon the number of Southerners they murdered? The medals were only awarded to those Northern murderers: the Southerners who fought in the National Guard, against their own townsfolk, received no medals. Their families did not receive a subsidy if they died in battle, while fourteen silver medals were awarded, according to Molfese, to those Savoy soldiers who heroically massacred those prisoners in Scurcola.

All of this required tactics. Ermenegildo Novelli, from Udine, by orders from Pinelli, wrote a diary that was published after half a century. "In the beginning, they were rounded up, judged, executed, and buried," the soldiers did everything, all one had to say was "brigands." "Everything ended here. When they saw the executed bodies in their churchyards and town squares, exposed to the sun and the rain, things changed." For Novelli, this was a "healthy example."

It was wrong to seek out the "brigands," make them dig a large ditch, line them up on the edge of it, and shoot them inside, burying both the dead and those still alive, and recover the ditch with dirt. This was done in Abruzzo and in Sicily (in 1866) where mass executions were held for three hundred "rebels" at a time. In this manner, one would lose the educational function of the massacre. After all, they were meant to civilize these people, not merely to murder them!

Liberty does not mean doing whatever one wants. It has its limits. Our brothers from the North, along with liberty, brought us several limitations. Commanders, prefects and anyone with power improved upon these limitations according to their own discretion, leaving the penalty unaltered: instant capital punishment. In this manner, anyone who was found in possession of "any type" of weapon was "immediately executed." Included in this list were sickles, knives, hatchets and numerous other implements that farmers would use to work in the fields. Therefore they would have to work their fields with their bare hands and while fasting, since it was "prohibited to bring bread and other foods outside of the town walls" (which angered Napoleon III from France, an accomplice of Italy). It was prohibited to send for food for the farmers from neighboring towns. The farmers were only allowed to have "enough food to feed each of his family members for one day." The concept of "modest quantities exclusively for personal use" had been officially invented. What about tomorrow? What about the provisions set aside for the winter, the dried fava beans, salami, the *friselle*, and flour? If they found you with these things, *kaputt!* Is there any need to state that it was also prohibited to hunt

(How would it be possible with no weapons? With spit? With rocks?). It was prohibited to go into the woods (now, imagine Gargano, which is the town with the most forest in all of Europe, and that the forest was the main source of income for most of the townspeople). Anyone who was caught carrying out any activity in the forest was obliged, within forty-eight hours, to "withdraw their workers, farmers, herders, etc." and to "take down the animal pens and tents that were built there." Or what? Let's see if someone can guess the penalty.

What about the herds? Where do I sleep? What do I eat? In your opinion, if one asks these questions is he a "brigand"? He is definitely a "brigand." Or perhaps not: whether out of doubt or habit, Major Pietro Fumel, from Piedmont, a well-known torturer, first condemned the accused to death, then took note that he ordered the execution of "three hundred brigands and non-brigands" (so what did one have to do to not get executed? Shall I say it and regret it? I will say it: one should not have been from the South). Fumel was the one who ordered legitimate owners to burn their haystacks, to wall up their farmhouses and remove the roofs, to kill their animals. Otherwise? He would give the order to burn everything down. Whoever would like to complain, please raise their hand. Cut off that person's hand. Anyone else? While you are at it, close down all of the bakeries: no more bread.

"Those who spread alarming rumors," for so little, would be "punished according to a brief trial" (there is no time...). Even worse, anyone who provoked the "peasants" to lament or protest would be "executed immediately." Anyone who "insulted the image of the king, the Savoy coat of arms, or the national flag" would be condemned to death. Well, one could refuse to think that there could exist such wicked men that could wound the sensitivity of a portrait or of a coat of arms, but for those who decide to wipe their faces, or at least what most closely resembles their face, is execution still an option?

Death to anyone who sees a "brigand" and does not report him. Death also to anyone who offers any sort of assistance to the "brigand" (as if to say one could choose: if you choose to obey the "brigand," we will kill you. If you do not obey, he will kill you. Free will, in this case, is more arbitrary than free, but this is war). Donata Caretto, however, was only condemned to seven years of prison, because she was eighty-eight years old.... While Antonio Orsolino was executed: he was twelve and dared to defend his sheep from the Piedmontese military's requisition. Therefore, what was the peasant lady complaining about when they sentenced her to a mere ten years of prison when they found an image of the Bourbon king in her home?

Major Du Coll had a system: when he entered a town, he rounded up some suspicious citizens, executed them, and displayed their bodies in the square to rot. He then called for the landowners of the town and ordered them to give his *bersaglieri* whatever they needed (money, provisions, assistance...). Hesitation was viewed as a sign of complicity with the "brigands" and punished accordingly. But during the parade on June 2nd, today, when the *bersaglieri* march with their fanfare, those who are most visibly moved by the scene are the Southerners. Because they do not know (Or perhaps they are happy to have escaped, this time?).

Marsala, was placed under siege because there were some draft-dodgers in the city. Therefore, three thousand people were closed in a catacomb and tortured. A good part of the young men and their families, however, were not even aware that they had dodged the draft (which lasted eight years!). The draft expired on January 31, 1861, but many mayors and local authorities did not display the notification for fear of the reactions (which there were). When the troops came to seek out the draft-dodgers, "boys, young men, mature men approached these soldiers, whom they had never seen before, with curiosity," reports Tommaso Pedio *(Brigantaggio meridionale)*: "all of the young men aged twenty to twenty-five are rounded up" and "in some cases, as in Castelsaraceno, Carbone, and Latronico, are executed on the spot, without being given the possibility to justify their actions." The Duke of Maddaloni, Francesco Proto Carafa, announced in Parliament that "pardons were promised to the rebels, former soldiers, and draft-dodgers. But those who presented themselves were executed without a trial." Luigi Miceli, a deputy, in order to indicate the state of misery that the farmers had been reduced to narrated about a boy who, before being executed, removed his shoes and asked that they be given to his father. He also spoke of a father who removed his jacket and asked that it be given to his son. In other words, he spoke of those possessions that should not go to waste and of the fact that they had nothing more to leave as an inheritance.

Commander Frigerio, from Piedmont, cut off the water supply to the town of Licata (twenty thousand inhabitants), ordered the arrest and torture of mothers, sisters, and relatives of those who dodged the draft: "Youths were killed by lashes of the whip and by bayonet; a pregnant women was killed." A complaint would later be filed against him in the Parliament, but to no avail. The entire population was forced to stay in their own homes, otherwise the usual "instant" execution would be the penalty. This was only where "more severe measures" were not necessary. What does that mean? After you have killed someone once, what else could you do to them? In the Parliament, some honest people made their voices heard by stating that at least those people who were freed by the courts' rulings should be freed. But the soldiers preferred to do things their way and left them in prison. No one knew where to place all of these people who had been arrested. The soldiers began to close them off in caves or, as in Potenza, "bury them in a tomb in an ancient church," where dozens died from asphyxiation.

In only one month, announced Crispi in the Parliament, in the sole province of Agrigento, thirty-two thousand people were incarcerated. This is slightly less than the capacity of all of the Italian penitentiaries put together today. The military issues orders to continue to hold in jail even the accused who had been acquitted. General La Marmora orders that even those who had finished serving their sentences not be released. If they were to be freed, they would risk being shot in the back as soon as they were outside. By the enforcement of the Pica Law alone (the law that allowed the imprisonment of anyone who "seemed" to disagree with the new regime) sixty thousand victims were claimed. Twelve years after the unification, Italy had the largest amount of convicts in all of Europe, despite having a considerably smaller population. In Montemiletto, one of the most tormented towns in the Avellino area, the Southerners sang: "Damn 1860/it left us with these seeds /that grow like mint/ only to bring martyrdom to the poor people."

Eighteen thousand people were forcibly sent home. They were in such poor conditions that the defenders of Gaeta (who had been deported to the islands, despite being guaranteed the right to return home after the surrender) lost at least two hundred of their men. Tens of thousands of Bourbon soldiers were held in the concentration camps in the North. The most infamous of these was in Fenestrelle: it was a fortress located approximately seventy miles from Turin on a rocky ridge that was at an altitude of twelve hundred meters. It was constantly pummeled by freezing wind and the average life expectancy of the inmates was not more than three months. To inflict further torment upon the prisoners, the windows in the dormitories had been removed. Other camps (there never seemed to be enough) were opened in Piedmont, Liguria, Lombardy ... the cattle cars used by the Nazis for the Jews seemed luxurious when compared to the ships and other means of transport used to transfer those prisoners from the South to the North. In 1870, four thousand eight hundred pontifical soldiers were dragged across the peninsula for their derisive acts, amidst insults, spitting, caning, and other punishments: they were only allowed one ration of bread during their three day march.

Many preferred to kill themselves. In Mantua, several fugitives were massacred by the lancers of the local garrison, along with the patriotic participation of some of the civilians. In that lager, during that savage winter, the Neapolitans were left wearing their summer shirts, infested by lice, sick, starving or malnourished. But there is no death toll: they simply were not registered. They were made to disappear and that's it (in Fenestrelle, they were dissolved in quick lime: we still have the tank where this took place, behind the church). We are not even certain of how many tens of thousands of soldiers/prisoners passed through those fields only to disappear (several thousand were able to flee to France, Switzerland and to Austria-Hungary: here many of them fought against Italy.) Like those soldiers that wound up in the German concentration camps after September 8th, 1943, the Neapolitans were asked to recant their oath to their country and to serve Victor Emanuel. Very few chose to do this: the others preferred to suffer the consequences ("all were covered in scabies and vermin," wrote La Marmora, who attempted in vain to convince them, irritated by their "repugnance") and many of them died. Yet they had seen many of their commanders betray their oath and switch over to the invaders' side. They gave up defending their country for the desire to see Italy united, or perhaps because they were inept or, more often, corrupt. Like in the first Persian Gulf War (under Bush Sr.) entire divisions of Iraqi soldiers sought a marine to whom they could offer themselves as prisoners. Here, there were Bourbon generals who surrendered to a few of Garibaldi's troops despite having thousands of men at their service, waiting to fight for them. There were many officials who were attacked (some were even killed) by their troops, who were disgusted by their behavior. General Vial was forced to flee as his own troops shot at him. General Ghio asked for Garibaldi's protection. General Briganti was torn to pieces by his own furious soldiers, because they had been barred from fighting. Other generals were arrested, and for this were condemned and subsequently demoted. A few of them committed suicide. Sometimes soldiers ended up fighting in spite of their commander's orders. Absurd things begin to happen: in the fortress of Capua, Sergeant Bruno, a member of the Thirteenth Division of Hunters who was tired of being restrained from fighting the enemy, pointed a cannon to the enemy, but before he was able to use it, "he was arrested and accused of insubordination by the court-martial and was executed! This is the only example of serious punishment in the entire war," writes Vincenzo Gulì in *Il saccheggio del Sud.*

Perhaps you begin to question whether a monarchy and a country are able to deserve such loyalty from its people. Does it seem normal that in Italy, where everything is published and everything translates, for the young boy that I once was, into traumas in the formation of my morality? I was exposed to the idea of evil with the Sand Creek Massacre, and then saw my principles dashed by reading about the destruction of the Holocaust, only to learn many years later of the criminal act that generated my own country.

Guantanàmo was not Bush Jr.'s idea (It already sounds contradictory in the same sentence: Bush? An idea?!). The system had been tested by the Europeans, with a sort of ethnic "self-pruning." It meant expelling the worst parts of society, or at least those retained to be such, and banishing them to far away, semi-deserted places. How shall I put it: the good with the good in a good place; the bad with the bad in a bad place. The largest penal colony of all time was Australia. Great Britain forcibly populated the continent with convicts and prostitutes (little was needed to accuse someone of something and ship them off to the new continent).

Even the newly formed Italy retained that they could rely on ethnic cleansing to elevate the quality of its population. It is pointless to specify that they intended to deprive themselves of the Southerners. The Minister of Foreign Affairs, Luigi Menabrea, tried to procure a desolate land to which he could deport them: Patagonia, Borneo, Tunisia, Eritrea, the Red Sea (on the island of Socotra), Mozambique, Angola, the eastern coast of Australia, the Nicobare archipelago (Indian Ocean), Timor, Goa, or Macao. This obstinate hunt lasted for ten years. General Cadorna tried to convince the British Minister of Foreign Affairs, Lord Granville (the British expert on colonization) that this was the best course of action, because the mass executions were giving rise to disdain abroad and the locals were rebelling. Granville suggested that he deport them to Northern Italy. Cadorna replied that they were already doing this, but were running out of room. According to the Italian minister's project, the occupation of a foreign land was to merely dispel the doubts of the foreign powers. It was not aimed at the "establishment of a colony"; it was only to be temporary. In other words? "A concentration camp," Del Boca translates in *Male-*

detti Savoia. This issue went on with such insistence and vulgarity that the British diplomats, whom we had asked for help, invited our government, in an undiplomatic fashion, to not insist on the matter; even Cadorna noticed "the repugnance of the entire government (author's note: *the British government*) towards our projects." It was only thanks to the sensibility of foreigners that today we do not have a Neapolitan-dialect-speaking Patagonia or a Borneo filled with turnip tops (someone could have fled, right?).

Who knows if this all would have had a bad outcome, considering that the Southerners, a few years later, would deport themselves to faraway lands out of desperation.

From one day to the next, in the Kingdom of the Two Sicilies, the many companies that worked for the state lost their contracts (which went to the North: from cannons to pencils). The factories involved were closed and shots were fired upon those employees who protested. This happened from the industries of steelworks to the mint, from the building yards to clothing (uniforms) all the way to the railways. A wave of bankruptcies puts tens of thousands of workers into a state of poverty. Many businessmen liquidated their fortunes from their business ventures in order to safeguard them. But "the ruinous, repeated alienation of the Neapolitan market by the two first legateships caused the values to dip from 108-113 down to 75, amidst the alarm and desperation of the thrifty Southerners" (Molfese, *Storia del brigantaggio dopo l'Unità*).

The purging due to the suspected nostalgia for the Bourbon monarchy (real or presumed, there was no need to provide proof or explanations) left thousands and thousands of public employees, judges, teachers, university professors, soldiers, and professionals in the streets. The Duke of Maddaloni presented a frightening list to the Parliament, amidst the protests of his colleagues (he was forced to resign). Even the milk from the wet nurses was deemed unacceptable: wet nurses had to be brought in from the North to feed the newborn orphans of Naples. Luciano Salera reported the words of Angelo Brofferio in *Storia del Piemonte* regarding the morality of civil servants: "Favors were sold. Titles were sold. Positions were sold. Verdicts were sold. Everything was sold" (like Curletto, the patriot from Emilia Romagna, who offered to be a spy for Cavour; when he was placed under General Saint-Frond, the general asked him to kidnap a certain girl for later on that night. This was not the only favor asked of him.) But all of this will go down in history, and passed down in stories as "Bourbonic."

The employees of many ecclesiastical businesses found themselves without jobs. Many of these businesses were quite large and profitable (thousands of people were fed) but they were requisitioned and sold by the city of Turin for profit. This left tens of thousands of people, who were offered assistance by these religious institutions, without any help (five thousand people in Palermo alone). To build the railways, finally, workers were brought in from the North. There were also some Neapolitans: they did the same job but were paid half the salary (tell that *Lega* imbecile this fact the next time he applauds something: he is taking a risk).

Even a country reduced to this state had to maintain its troops: Garibaldi's, the Piedmontese, the "brigands" and guerrilla soldiers (who were just as numerous) as well as the English and French fleets. Just in time for 1860, when the entire continent was suffering a famine.

Those who had assets, in order to preserve them, had to maneuver their way through liberals, "brigands," Piedmontese, and loyalists; sometimes financially supporting all of them, (like in the North during the resistance: people helped both the Black Brigade and the partisans in order to avoid retaliations). There was no guarantee that this would be enough, either. If one was lucky with the "brigands" they could be suspected of Bourbonism and the Piedmontese would execute them. If one was lucky with the Piedmontese, the loyalists would treat them in the same fashion, for the same reasons. One had to hold into account that they would have to bear with some losses; it is credible. The only currency at the time was violence: in the court of Avellino alone, during a period of six months, five hundred trials were held for "brigand" activities (the Piedmontese did equivalent things, or even worse, but they were punished with medals of honor). In one town, Melfi, in the Vulture area, in 1863, there were eight hundred robberies, two hundred fires, three hundred and fifty blackmailings, one hundred and seventy-five murders, one hundred and thirty mutilations, and eighty-one rapes reported. The judges were inclined to "protect and evaluate a defendant based on his professed political principles," admitted one magistrate from the Court of Assizes in Puglia. In this manner, "false patriots" could have four hundred people arrested at one time and then ask the prisoners for money "leading them to believe that they would be freed shortly." A public servant in charge of security was condemned to a life sentence of hard labor because he was not fierce enough; two witnesses for the defense received ten-year sentences instantly.

Let us imagine ourselves to be Southerners in 1860 and in the years following. In this very intense moment, many important notions emerge: the strategic design of Europe's superpowers are delineated, Piedmont's desperate need to make money in order to make history (or is it the other way around?) becomes evident; the ambitions of several capable, open-minded individuals surface; the dream of many to share a common home for all Italians emerges; the general feeling of the time that nationality is determined by a state of mind rather than the delineation of empires (which brought about the dissolution of such multi-national empires as that of the Habsburgs, the Ottomans and encouraged the recomposition of fragmented national identities); the climate diffused by romanticism, that leads noble spirits and hot-heads to seek a nice reason to live and languidly die, not caring where this might take place; the presence of an efficient network (with freemasonry and other associations) of interests and new values, in which the greater part of these drives find a way to express themselves at a "supra-national" level as well as local, uniting a desire for liberty, power, and business with the sensation that one is a part of an elect group of individuals (or perhaps just a group of shrewd individuals) called upon by history to build a future for all (or at least build themselves a fortune.)

In the dissolution of the Kingdom of the Two Sicilies, every action is judged and appropriately sanctioned by those armed, unstable powers that are no longer legitimate, not yet legitimate, legitimist, or neo-legitimist. All of the choices, whether they be a question of loyalty or interest, can be reduced to two: defense of the South that once was, and therefore protecting their attacked homeland with weapons, or the defense of the South that will be, through politics and reason, in the new country that is born. In other words, one either tried to stop the new changes or to try to be a part of them, either because it was the right thing to do or because they had no other choice.

The most audacious Southerners divided themselves between these two possibilities. All of them lost.

There was no alternative when the Unification was accomplished with robbery, bloodshed, and perpetual humiliation of one part of the country (in 1900, "the assassination of Umberto was celebrated with jubilation amongst the Italian emigrants abroad," remembers Ercole Sori in *L'emigrazione italiana dall'Unità alla seconda guerra mondiale*). There is a place where this is best exemplified: Rionero in the Vulture area. Rionero is a town located in the Lucania district, built on the slopes of a dormant volcano (there are lakes in its two craters). It acts as a conjunction between the Basilicata, Puglia, and Campania regions. Lucania is a strange land, filled with many brave and intelligent people that have been defeated or isolated. "Excellent generals, with no army," according to one of my colleagues, "there are very few of them." The history of the Vulture area during the *Risorgimento* has a very meaningful epilogue: the first president of Italy to be born in the newly unified Italy was from this area. He was born in Melfi, just below Rionero: Francesco Saverio Nitti, a great advocate for the South.

Rionero gave rise to the powerful voice of Giustino Fortunato: a jurist and writer who acted as a sort of literary conscience of the South and of united Italy ("This is thanks to a handful of men and a bit of good luck, a miracle, actually"). His ideals brought him to be a member of Parliament, siding with neither the left nor the right. Nitti was indirectly a pupil of his.

However, the greatly feared General of the Bourbon resistance, the "brigand" Carmine Crocco Donatelli was also born here. Of his two thousand men, approximately two hundred survived, despite being injured multiple times. He collaborated on several occasions with Sergeant Romano (and was victorious) and defeated the Piedmontese several times with his guerrilla tactics. He was renown (even by his enemies) for his tactical superiority despite his antiquated weapons.

No one in the South was a more ideal or noble Unitarian than Fortunato, the nephew of landowners who were suspected of collaborating with "brigands." No one was more savagely anti-Unitarian than Crocco (he was a farmer for the Fortunato family, like his most skilled lieutenant, Giuseppe Caruso, nicknamed "Zio Peppe").

The first of the two had delicate features and a dignified air. He was cerebral with a slender profile similar to that of the Chinese: he possessed a deep, meditative, and visionary intelligence. He was the embodiment of an ideal: he was made of passion and erudition. Fortunato was incapable of dealing with conflict and always refused governmental roles out of shyness. ("Wait until I die," was his response when he found out that he would be honored with the erection of a statue in his likeness.) He was a great man, both charismatic and solitary.

The second was hot-tempered and impulsive, with a strong build and the facial features of a true, strong peasant. He was quick witted with the sort of intuitive intelligence that immediately translated into action. He was not rash, and he acted with reason (perhaps even too much, had he led one final attack on a considerably weakened Potenza and established a Bourbon government, history would have undoubtedly taken a different course). Crocco allowed Jorge Borjes's mission (who had been assigned by the Bourbon outlaws to lead the resistance movement) to fail out of jealousy. The Bourbon outlaws had bestowed upon Borjes a higher rank than Crocco. Crocco was a charismatic man, capable of talking to the masses.

These two men were divided by culture, social status, their objectives, and their methods. Yet they were united (for some time under the same roof) by reason and by their life achievements.

All of those who participated in the unification of the South to the rest of Italy passed through the home of the Fortunato family in Rionero. The house is located in the center of the town on the main square, next to the broken fountain, but it is as though it were invisible. All that remains of Giustino the Great, in the house, is the solitude and the silence of his library, which contains twenty thousand books (more than half belonged to him alone). "Students come to use the library, but they are always fewer in number because the Internet is faster," says Doctor Luisa Lovaglio, who looks after this treasure and preserves his memory, managing what is left (though funds would be needed to restore the books and the building). "The Fortunato family was originally from Giffoni, but they loved Rionero and came to live there in the 1700s. They were an enlightened upper class family who did a great deal for the town: they were able to establish the town's autonomous government and on Saturdays they distributed white bread, olives, and some money. But the local residents did not love them very much. They were more in favor of the Crocco family."

The Crocco family were common folk; the others remained the "masters" in the public eye.

"Crocco had ordered that not a hair on any resident of Rionero's head be touched," narrates Donato Di Lucchio, a meticulous reporter and local historian. He says that the Fortunato family, in 1848, was on the side of the people when it invaded the estates of the Doria family in Lagopesole (though some could suspect that they did so in their own interest).

When the Piedmontese arrived, both the common folk and the landowners had an enemy in common. Their interests and their lives became one. The landowners established Bourbon committees and incited, supported, and hid the "brigands." Carmine Crocco, in the influential sphere of the Fortunato family, had established the headquarters of his gang on their farm. As soon as it became clear who would win the war, the landowners and the Piedmontese had an enemy in common: the common folk. The landowners became Unitarians and liberal. The "brigands" and their people were either killed or imprisoned. Italy had been formed.

The Fortunato and Crocco families were actually almost related to each other. One of Giustino's uncles had two illegitimate children from a woman from San Fele. One of those two sons, Giovannnino Coppa, grew up to become head-brigand and lieutenant to Carmine. There are still many heated discussions over this subject in Rionero to this day. Di Lucchio, as a confirmation of the inconsistency regarding several presumed truths, states that many texts refer to the general as Carmine Donatelli, or Donatello, nicknamed Crocco. In actuality, his name was Crocco and he was also known as Donatelli. But in some documents, the brigand with an illegitimate relation to Giustino is actually called Giovanni Coppa Fortunato. The "Brigand Bible" (an enormous file compiled from a mountain of unpublished documents by Franco Molfese when he was vice-director of the Library of the Chamber of Deputies), states in the entry marked "Coppa" to see "Giovanni Fortunato." This should at least offer some grain of truth to the story.

But perhaps the whole affair would be even more meaningful if it were to be proven false. It would then testify to the willingness of the people to unite, in a unified destiny (and perhaps even with a blood relation) the two most important exponents of the South: the fighter and the thinker; the peasant and the gentleman; the defender of the lost homeland and that of the new.... It would be a dualism summarized in one myth and in one house. If it were merely considered gossip or news, it would become too commonplace.

Crocco, an ex-Bourbon soldier, wound up as a brigand because of the abuse of the local bourgeois: a young man repeatedly kicked his pregnant mother (who lost the child, and went mad) and put his father in prison. Another injured his sister when she refused him and Crocco killed him. To be reinstated as a soldier, he fought in Volturno with Garibaldi and became a "patriot" for some and a traitor to others. Garibaldi, however, did not keep his promise and Crocco became a "brigand" for the Piedmontese and a "patriot" for the anti-Unitarians. In the end, he wound up just being a brigand. He stated this himself in his autobiography, *Io, brigante.*

History in those turbulent months is hazy at best. From legal records one comes to understand that in the sole district of Melfi, where Mount Vulture is located, several gentlemen hired eight thousand former Bourbon soldiers for six *carlini* per day, in order to re-establish the overthrown dynasty. This "reactionary movement," as it has been defined in the records, was maneuvered by the important families of the area: the Colabella and Aquilecchia (in this house the provisional Bourbon government was established) families from Melfi, the Rapollas from Venosa, the De Martinis and the Saraceni from Atella, the Corbos from Avigliano, the Zampagliones from Calitri, and the Fortunatos, Catenas, and Gianattasios from Rionero.

Those who did not adhere to the Bourbon cause justified themselves with the other landowners by saying that they wanted to defend themselves from the demands and dangers of the "lower class," who still favored the overthrown king. Those who worked for the reinstatement of the Neapolitan dynasty, when it became apparent that their side was the losing one, would say that they had to comply with the lower class's demands for weapons in order to determine and maneuver their fates. The magistrates who presided over these cases were members of the same bourgeois families that were being tried. The "brigands" were condemned while the gentlemen were restored to their prominent positions. The gentlemen would be the ones who narrated this history. They minimized, notes Pedio (*Brigantaggio meridionale*) the roles played by their families in the resistance against the invaders. Giustino himself (who was twelve years old when the events in question took place) would be obliged by the events taking place to destroy many of his family's papers and correspondence. Still today, it is difficult to find anyone who will admit this. For Giustino, a passionate supporter of the Unification, the shadow of reactionary behavior must have appeared intolerable to his family (his uncles where amongst the few gentlemen to wind up in jail for being "accomplices," and they were released after eighteen months with a questionable sentence). That shadow, unjustly cast or simply not clear, disturbs the town of Rionero. Di Lucchio states that, "Giustino himself wrote in 1916 that 'my Uncle Gennaro, who saved Rionero from the shame of Crocco, a friend of ours in triumph and relative of our slanderer" (in *Ernesto e Giustino Fortunato* by Nino Calice), and that, "Rionero owed so much to the personal deeds of my Uncle Gennaro, a man who was Pro-Bourbon, but still a man of honor as he did not bear the shame of those towns that welcomed and offered Crocco hospitality, like Melfi and Venosa '."

Carmine Crocco wrote in his memoirs, that he penned while he was in prison carrying out his life sentence, that those same gentlemen "who shouted down with Francis II, long live Crocco," then "passed themselves off as liberals." He also wrote that it did not matter what history and politics narrate, the matter is far more simple: it comes down to "us" versus "them"; those who do not have anything and those who do. According to the brigand, the few landowners "who were victims of the counter-reaction should blame their local gentleman enemies" and not "the severity of a law that was allegedly martial." More simply, the landowners fought amongst themselves but they united against the poor peasants in order to use them. Times were dangerous and consistency in one's actions could prove to be lethal.

But when the gentlemen of the Vulture area needed a chief for their gangs that hid in the mountains, they sought out Crocco. The Fortunato family would be the one to break him out of the jail in Cerignola. It is narrated that the brigand established his headquarters in Gaudiano on the land of the Fortunato family.

There were at least eighty thousand armed ex-Bourbon soldiers ready to fight against the invaders. No one was able to unite them under one army: each chief (and there were about four hundred and fifty chiefs) was a god to his men. Only Crocco was able to unite, under his command, a substantial number of soldiers, often of good quality since they had been former Bourbon soldiers. The only other person to obtain a similar result was Sergeant Romano who proposed, out of love for the cause, to submit to Crocco's authority, along with his men: he did not receive an answer.

The tactics of the soldiers were guerrilla style: attack and inflict as much damage as possible and disperse before the enemy (who had superior weapons, better organization, and were more numerous) had a chance to organize themselves and react. Crocco was the only man to respond, at times, by accepting to fight the enemy in hand-to-hand combat. His enemies were obliged to recognize that he was talented and intelligent. This was not only to justify their defeat. Crocco was daring in times of difficulty, prudent in times of victory, but most of all, he knew how to manage his men. The manner in which he maneuvered the cavalry of his most famous lieutenant, Ninco Nanco, revealed itself to be the definitive solution on more than one occasion. General Emilio Pallavicini, who confronted him with three battalions of *bersaglieri* marksmen, four infantries, and various cavalries, was obliged to describe him as being "gifted with true military capabilities."

When it became clear as to how it was all going to end, Crocco saw the landowners switch sides and, "therefore, putting politics and politicians aside, I went back to what I had been before, a common brigand." Then he was imprisoned for life.

In the meantime, from the family that was Crocco's protector, the Fortunatos, rose the voice from the South that declared that it wanted to be a part of Italy: "If Italy must stand for something in this world, it can only be united to do so," wrote Giustino. He dedicated his life's work to this cause: he dedicated his career as a journalist to the "*Unità Nazionale*" and "*Patria*" newspapers. Along with Leopoldo Franchetti from Livorno, he founded the Association for Southern Interests, in order that the fusion might be true and just. Today we must ask how many meanings Giustino's most famous quote has acquired over the course of the last one hundred years: "Italy is formed by its history and nature: to this day it remains a country where two civilizations continue to coexist in the body of one nation." He believed that Italy wanted the South as much as the South wanted Italy. Salvemini chided him for his excessive trust. In the end, with the same disappointment that Carmine Crocco had, he too had to admit his own defeat: "I do not withdraw my concept of 'Unitarianism'," he wrote to Benedetto Croce in 1934. "I only modified my opinion of the businessmen from the North. They are pigs that are far worse than the biggest of our own pigs." "He would go on to say, in his final years," according to Doctor Lovaglio, "that the South was better off with the Bourbon monarchy." He came to share the "same vision of the 'corruption of a people that have been reduced to slaves' that Manzoni and Amari held" states Michele Tondo in *Su Giustino Fortunato scrittore*.

When one exits the Fortunato Palace, one can see the "farewell" that Giustino left to Rionero on a plaque of marble: it narrates that his family came here in the 1700s and restored their residence several times after it had been damaged by earthquakes, as proof of their desire to stay. The family extinguished itself with Giustino (the daughter of one of his brothers married a member of the Alliata family from Sicily who then sold the palace to the town). On the plaque, Giustino writes that he is the "last of his kind." Did he mean of his family or of those like him?

There is one, who has come here, as if on a pilgrimage, for a very long time: first, as a student, then as a member of Parliament, then as Minister of Internal Affairs, and, in 2009, as the President of Italy: Giorgio Napolitano. When one talks to these types of people: you know that they are aware of what happened, and you would like to tell them that what they know is useless because it is not heard. One hears them speak of their children, in London and Milan, attending important universities, working for important newspapers. They become important when they cease to be from the South, from the Vulture area, when they are more and more distant from Giustino, from Carmine, and from themselves.

Upon descending from the mountain, the world spreads before your view and it is a beautiful one: the discovery of the man from Atella, one of our ancient predecessors, demonstrates that our land was amongst the first on the earth to be inhabited. Today, Coca-Cola comes here to buy its mineral water springs. On the right side, towards the horizon, a gigantic barrier closes off the entrance to the valley. "Those are the factories that were supposed to comprise the largest industrial center of the South," Donato di

Lucchio tells us. "It was financed with thousands of billons of lira (after the earthquake that shook Irpinia and Basilicata), to restore hope and jobs to those who had lost everything. *Parmalat* built its largest factory here. Then it moved its production to the North. The Vicenzi company stepped in, and they subsequently closed their doors as well and left one hundred and fifty employees to wander the streets. Other companies did the same. They inaugurated their factories, took the money, then fired all of their employees or let them receive their unemployment checks. Some even went as far as removing their machinery and transferred them to Eastern Europe."

Some of these frauds were punished: a meager consolation. An important Milanese colleague of mine used to send me newspaper clippings, in those years, and highlighted such headings as: "The Potenza police and the *carabinieri* from Melfi arrested in their luxurious villas in Molteno, Brugherio (in the wealthy Milano 3 residential complex), Saronno...." A list of names followed in addition to the amount of billions of lira each had been forced to pay. This was a long time ago, and today, from here, where Fortunato had uselessly "revealed how the eternal promises of public works to address the 'complete and utter re-evaluation of the South and the islands,' in reality ended up accentuating the inequality between the North and the South," comments Tondo, in his book on Giustino, the writer (And what a writer he was! He was reproached for writing too well on technical issues). This happened a long time ago, and yet it is today that those people from Rionero that safeguard their own interests say, "The millions awarded to a great number of factories and building yards are extorted from the poor people of the South."

Going further south, over the hills lies the Ionian Sea. In Patù, on the very last buttress of rock that dominates the border between that sea and the Adriatic, the most hated Italian of the *Risorgimento* lived and died: Liborio Romano. Perhaps he was also the most infamous of the period. Still today, in the South one cannot mention his name without evoking nasty expressions and insults. In the North, few probably know who he is, and the few that do, probably consider him somewhere between a member of the *camorra*, an opportunist, and a useful idiot. For both, however, he is considered a traitor, including from the side that most benefitted from his actions. Without Liborio Romano, Francis II probably would never have left Naples to retreat to Gaeta and Garibaldi would have had the problem of overcoming the third most important capital of Europe. It was wealthy and had abundant weapons and troops, not to mention a population that was very loyal to their king.

All of those other Southerners who lost, for whatever choice they had made (the popular insurrection that ended in a bloodbath, the armed revolt of the "brigands," the convinced, idealist participation in the Unitarian movement), they lost, but saved their reputations. Liborio lost that as well. Yet, he never truly hid what he was or what he wanted: he was a mason and a liberal (a family trait, as he was born from a Romanov who moved to the Salento area) and he wanted a unified Italy. It is for this reason, according to Francesco Accogli, in *Il personaggio Liborio Romano* had suffered through "the persecution, jail, confinement, and exile" and for forty years was "constantly kept under observation " because he was believed to be "a very dangerous man."

The Bourbon monarch knew this while he appointed him as the police prefect, then as Minister of Internal Affairs, and finally as viceroy, all while Piedmont initiated its attack on the Kingdom of the Two Sicilies. Romano did what he perceived his mission to be: to ferry the Kingdom of Naples into the Unification of Italy. He was the linchpin of the entire operation: as Francis II's minister, he prepared Garibaldi's entrance into Naples, while convinced that the city could not save itself, but he had to avert a bloodbath. As a minister with Garibaldi as a dictator, he oversaw the transition, and after only two weeks he resigned. He was offered extremely important government positions, but refused them.

He will forever be remembered by everyone as the man who assigned police duties to the *camorra*. The first to reproach him for doing so were those that came from the North, who had already done the same thing in the South with the mafia. Perhaps there is cause for doubt that this system was not adopted by chance and that continues to remain in effect. He justified himself by explaining that in that particular moment of uncertainty between the two monarchies "no longer Bourbon, but not yet Savoy," it seemed like the only way to remove the *camorra* from a "situation of disorder, or at least to paralyze their sad tendencies, in a moment when I lacked strength, in order to suppress and contain them."

· When Liborio stated his intentions, it is said that the members of the *camorra* cried. "They maintained their promises," assured the man who in those moments held the power of the South in his hands.

He did not like governing style of Luigi Farini (and therefore stayed out of his term in office) whom he "credited with the foreboding idea that the government secretly intended to 'Piedmontize' Italy, and to treat the Southern towns like conquered lands (...) and, in this fashion, to squeeze out as many benefits and money as they could." But Farini was the one who said, "Amongst the seven million inhabitants (author's note: *there were nine million*) here in the South, there are not more than one hundred who believed in the Unification." Had it been true (but it was not) Romano had demonstrated that he was most convinced. Furthermore, if it had been true (and it was not) then with what right, in the name of the Unification, did those one hundred armed men attack the other seven (nine) million?

Liborio returned to the government under the leadership of the Prince of Carignano, but he resigned soon after, again. He was unable to oppose the avidity and pushiness of the Piedmontese. Romano was convinced, out of his presumptuousness, that he would be able to maneuver the events according to his plans. But as soon as the others realized that they could do without him, his power was weakened and his decisions were no longer supported.

So Liborio decided to move his battle to the Parliament, and he went to Turin. Cavour wanted to meet with him, and initially he declined, but then changed his mind and told him that he would come to meet with Cavour. Before Liborio met with Cavour, he sent him a letter listing the issues he wanted to address. The letter is incredible and its subjects are still valid today. He wrote "on the conditions of the Neapolitan provinces" and divided the letter into ten chapters, each of which described "a plague" that troubled the area, and his potential solution. Count Cavour probably understood that he was told a great deal of lies regarding the conditions of the South. So he urgently requested a meeting with Liborio. Finally, they met, after nearly a month, at the end of May in 1861. At this point they were two old men, not elderly, but in poor physical condition. Liborio visibly limped because of his gout. These were probably the greatest minds in politics at the time. They immediately understood one another. Cavour admitted that his information was flawed and that "much of what Liborio says is true," according to Accogli. Cavour took it upon himself to make some changes. However, he died on June 6th, a little over a week later. Liborio never governed again: he saw, understood, but no longer had the power to do anything. The others did, and used it badly. The match was lost.

A century after his death, *Il mio resoconto politico* was published by his descendants. From this text, and from his other documents, the reasons behind his decisions emerge in a new light. "I believed it to be my debt (...) to assist that great "transition" with the least negative outcomes possible. Anyone is free to think otherwise." But he did have one gripe: "I cannot persuade myself that the lone act of serving the monarchy that followed, after having served the one that was overthrown is, in and of itself, something dishonest."

He retained this to be his masterpiece, and that it was absolutely necessary. He wrote in his political testament, "Judge me as harshly and severely as you please, but judge me based on the facts." He entrusted his reputation to "time and history" but he was "always ready, wherever they asked" to shake hands with political enemies "in the name of Italy."

He was extremely popular and was aware of it. He was pleased by his popularity. He was the most voted candidate, with four hundred thousand votes and he was elected in eight districts. This worried the Parliament in Turin: they did not favorably view such power that eluded their control ("Cavour wanted to break my popularity," Liborio wrote in his book. Costantino Nigra, the Count's right-arm-man, was the proudest and most subtle adversary of the minister from the Salento area. He described Liborio as being weak and not very intelligent, and that he was enamored by his own popularity as well as himself. There was some element of truth to this statement, aside from the consideration that he was not very intelligent. This was not very convincing because at age twenty-one, Liborio was a university professor and he had defeated his king (then a Bourbon) in the monarch's court. He was the legal representative of Great Britain in the trial concerning the monopolization of the Sicilian sulfur trade. One could, however, suspect that Nigra was jealous of Liborio, particularly because Cavour defined Liborio as "the best mind in the South."

Accogli reminds us that Denis Mack Smith considers him "bought by foreign enemies." In that orgy of embezzlements, robberies, and raids, there is no evidence that he ever touched a cent: this is the type of honesty that would seem suspicious if not stupid. From his letters, one can read that he asked his friend for more than one loan, which he repaid with seven percent interest. Though he could have done what he pleased while lovers, blackmailers, and basically anyone who walked by, were elevated to important positions, Liborio did not assign a job to any of his numerous family members. He boasted about this. Even though he lived in Portici, he was happy when he received barrels of mussels and oysters from the Salento area (so that this might not sound strange, the mussels from this area are particularly tasty and pure because they are washed and cleared of any parasites, in special sea farms, by freshwater springs that spout their water on the seafloor of that area; concerning the oysters, they were very likely the "imperial" variety that can only be found there).

Liborio finished writing his political testament in Naples in 1866. He then returned to Patù, exiling himself voluntarily. He died shortly after. Some say that he died of heartbreak. A Neapolitan epigraph writer left this comment: "Our don Liborio gave us his final farewell! He died, though it seems incredible, of natural causes!" Amidst the insults Liborio received after his death, a patriot, Carlo Poerio, made this comment, "He did for his country that which no one else would have done: he sacrificed his reputation." He did this without obtaining his final result, as he too was defeated in his attempt to prevent the annexation of the Kingdom of Naples to Piedmont. He wanted to guide the "fusion with the other parts of Italy" so that "they would not be treated as a conquered people, but as equals with the same rights as those fewer, but luckier Italians who dictated the conditions and ways in which the Unification was to be conducted." Other pre-Unitarian states were allowed, if I remember correctly, to preserve a part of their laws during the transition phase. All the South got was the lead from their bullets.

If places could be metaphors, Patù would be one for how the South became a part of Italy. In the year 788, Charlemagne's troops destroyed the Byzantine, Longobard, and Saracen troops that occupied the city of Vereto. Vereto is a city whose origins precede the human documentation of history. It was the first to be founded by the mythical Messapi people. The clash "occurred in the center of the city and may even have happened from door to door," writes Rocco Fino in *Il Capo di Leuca e dintorni*. "The Carolingian troops razed whatever town they passed to the ground."

The superpowers of that era faced each other then and there and the outcome decided the future. The only ones who were not remembered were those who actually lived there; they were absent from the story because they were the paper upon which the others were writing history. What happened to them? "The inhabitants of Vereto, with their town and surrounding lands destroyed, found themselves quite suddenly with nothing," writes Fino. In that place filled with pain (*ager paturius*) at the foot of the ruins of that town, they founded Patù, who in its name carries that inherent suffering. Their past had been destroyed so that the future of many others could be determined. Just like the Kingdom of the Two Sicilies.

After the battle, with the stones of the destroyed town of Vereto, the inhabitants built a unique monument: the *Centopietre*, a sort of temple dedicated to one of Charlemagne's paladins, who tried to prevent the battle from happening, but was killed: Geminiano. Liborio attempted to do something similar, but his remains are in a modest tomb in his family crypt. The Romano family's palace was sold by his descendants to the town despite the fact that they had received higher offers. They would like to erect a library. The minister's collection was divided into three parts. Perhaps they can try to recover some of those books.

I discovered that there is a cultural association dedicated to Liborio Romano in Patù. They have a website, recover documents and books as well as exchange comments and news. They coordinate research efforts with those who are passionate about history and intervene when newspapers call into question the name and actions of that man who guided the passage of his country to another (which he retained even more so as his own). Someone looks after the most forgotten and reviled protagonist of the *Risorgimento*. This means that the need to remember sparks initiatives and emerges: our roots are alive. It is a long trip to reach Patù, which is located at Italy's "heel." But I must go. The association's headquarters is a restaurant. "You will eat very well there," they assure me. The space is large, and half of it is dedicated to books; publications about Liborio Romano and his time. I wonder how many people run this association?

"I am the association," says Giovanni Spano, the restaurateur. There used to be someone who assisted him, but he is longer there. Spano spent twenty years in the Navy as an Italian marine and then he returned to his town. For the past fifteen years, Spano has dedicated himself to good food and the good reputation of don Liborio. He spends the night taking care of the website, searching for documents and maintaining a web of contacts.

All alone? "I try to find the time to be bored."

CHAPTER FOUR

Unequal Opportunities

Piedmont was full of debts. The Kingdom of the Two Sicilies was full of money. How many times have we read that the government bonds of the former, in the Paris Stock Exchange, were quoted at thirty percent less than their nominal value and the latter's were quoted at twenty percent more than their nominal value? How many times have we read that in the South, with only one third of the entire nation's population, there was twice the amount of money in circulation than in the rest of Italy put together?

The impoverishment of the South, in order to increase the wealth of the North, was the reason for the Unification of Italy, not the consequence. This was the practical reason. The idealistic aspect of the Unification was the romantic one. Both the realists and the romantics won.

"We either go to war or face bankruptcy," wrote the Pro-Cavour representative Pier Carlo Boggio in 1859 in his booklet, *Fra un mese*. "Piedmont is lost," he concluded after analyzing the nation's budget. A newspaper of the time, *"Armonia"* (one of the newspaper's founders happened to be Gustavo Benso, Cavour's brother) reported, "their finances will never be restored": Angela Pellicciari reminds us of this episode in her work *L'altro Risorgimento*. Once the Unification had been completed, all of the funds were united as well (although one account was empty, while the other was full). The North repaid its debts in this manner, with the funds from the South. The Kingdom of the Two Sicilies contributed sixty percent of the money, Lombardy contributed a little over one percent, and Piedmont contributed four percent (though it contributed over half of the debt). As more and more states were annexed to the growing Italy, as soon as the Piedmontese arrived, the money disappeared. However, this was nothing compared to the plundering and the massacres that the South was subjected to. The Unitarians saw their dream come true (the survivors ... in seventeen years of rule under Charles Albert, according to Lorenzo Del Boca in *Indietro Savoia!*, there were more patriots executed by Piedmont than from bloody, tyrannical Austria). Someone else paid the price, and the crafty ones cashed in.

"The former Kingdom of the Two Sicilies, therefore," writes Vittorio Gleijeses in *La storia di Napoli*, "paid the deficit of hundreds of millions of lira of debt of the new Italy (author's note: *however, the Kingdom of Sardinia's debts amounted to over one billion lira*). In compensation, the South, which had been oppressed by the extremely severe fiscal system of the Savoy monarchy, was demoted practically to the level of a colony." The Southerners paid more than the other Italians because they were obliged to pay back the expenses incurred during their liberation. The liberation that the South yearned for took years of military operations, massacres, retaliations, incarcerations, concentration camps (which were justified if one effectively preferred not to be free...), large scale and small-scale executions, as well as the destruction of dozens of towns. The Southerners were so obtuse that they fought for twelve years (when the last "brigand" was killed in Calabria) to *not* be liberated and to *not* be better off as a unified nation. When they realized that their armed resistance had failed, millions of them traveled across the ocean rather than be in the company of their greedy liberators. The book *La scoperta dell'America* by Pascarella comes to mind: like the natives of the new continent, the Southerners were savages, so savage that they did not realize how much they would be better off in the newly unified Italy!

Giuseppe Civinini, a follower of Mazzini and Garibaldi along with Francesco Crispi and a writer for the newspaper *"Diritto,"* was not the only one to think this way (as reported by Eva Cecchinato, in her work *Camicie Rosse*): "The North needs to come down upon the South and be violent with these people who need to be dominated. In this manner the Unification will come about, otherwise it will not." Oh come on now!

At least half a dozen times I tried to find excuses to interrupt my writing of this book and to dedicate myself to other projects. The real reason was fear. Everything appeared to be clear (the destroyed documents) and even too easy: honest people had collected irrefutable evidence, both demonstrated and written. Why not leave the nearly completed task to the moral pillars of society?

Fortunato, Salvemini, Saraceno, and other "gods" proclaimed these truths and no one cared; why should they pay attention to me? Then I had the sensation that those truths that had been so arduously recovered and pointlessly proposed, did not reach the masses. An example? The conclusions of a well-documented book *Storia d'Italia dall'Unità a oggi* by Aurelio Lepre and Claudia Petraccone, professors of comtemporary history: "The idea of a nation-community appears to progressively weaken. In the journalistic disputes in the 21st century, we see the return of an issue that was debated at the end of the 19th century: Southern Italy as a dead weight fastened to the ankle of the North or, but with fewer possibilities to prove their case, the North as the conqueror and exploiter of the South." I will translate: Bossi, Calderoli, and associates are the ones who are weakening the idea of a nation-community while the minority (the response is a conditioned reflex by now: when the word South is mentioned, the terminology turns to words such as "lesser" or "minority") is for the studies conducted by Salvemini, Fortunato, Nitti, Rossi Doria, Saraceno, all the way through to Viesti and the National Council of Research of Naples. In the South, even the evidence is guilty of the "inferiority" complex: the Northern troops invaded and, with iron and fire, annexed the South. So who conquered whom? This has not yet been proven? In the same book, it is explained that the invading army "responded with the same violence and fierceness" as the brigands. But the actions of the "brigands," sometimes still in their Bourbon uniforms, were conducted in response against those who had entered with weapons into their homes. This was also, as Machiavelli would have said, "to a more honest end, since they wanted to oppress, while the others did not want to be oppressed" (in other words, that the others started all of this should at least be clear, or does this still remain unclear?).

When you begin to notice certain things, you realize that you are becoming a Southerner, and you discover that they want you to be one, that you remain one, and that you accept it (*terun,* they call you: person from the dirt). Whatever you do, if it is from the South, is minor, exaggerated, too late, too early, or at best, they reply "yes, but...." This is evident even in its apparent reformation, as in the speech given by Giulio Tremonti, the Minister of "Subtraction of Funds for the South," to the young businessmen in Capri in November of 2009, in which he discovers that: "the issue of the South is an issue of national importance" (see what happens when you start spreading the word?); that the Unification was "not accomplished with respect to the territory, but with bayonets" (well now!) hence the "exaggerated reaction (author's note: *here we go with the mistake of "too much"*) by minor literature (author's note: *here we go with the "belittling"*) that brings forth documents of harrowing interest." As we can see, the documents themselves are not discussed, but rather who presents them and how. This diminishes the importance of such documents. This was said by someone who is accustomed to the sobriety and reliability of the likes of Bossi and Berlusconi and who promises to give a "kick in the rear" to his unpleasant colleagues.

The "major" literature, the literature written by the noble forefathers of the Pro-South movement, was not better received. No matter how it presents itself, the South's importance is always diminished: its reasons, what it does, what it knows, its rights and the measure of the facts which support them, even its history and the value of its people are diminished. This is all done with the intent to reduce, by evaluation, the utilities and resources that are destined to the South. Consequently, the ability to produce these things and to market them is also reduced. "The capitalists (and the proletarians) of the North take advantage of the inferiority of the South: we must make this known and continue to make this known," wrote Antonio Salvemini (regarding the proletarians, it deeply bothered him, a socialist, that the workers from the South fought for the rights of those of the North, and then often found themselves alone when it came time to fight for their own).

Nearly all of our Unitarian history is evidence of all of these statements: the laws, the investment of public funds, the infrastructure. It a daily, inexhaustible hunt for opportunities to assert and establish the inferiority of the South. In one week alone, in 2009 (I chose this year because it is recent and relevant, though I could have started from 1861), there was a proposal to regulate salaries on the basis of one's productivity in the lower part of the South. "But everyone knows," explains Vito Peragine, a young economist from the University of Bari and consultant for the Department of Regional Affairs for the law on federalism, "that productivity is conditioned by the efficiency of a place's infrastructures (energy, transportation, location) the likes of which are sorely lacking in the South. The railways have excluded the South for the past ten years from their expansion plans." To bring the South's infrastructures up to par with those of the rest of the country would mean to bring more money to the South and to place it in a position where it could be more productive, while tying salaries to productivity would mean subtracting more money from the South. In this manner, things remain the way they are (if they do not worsen) and the risk of competition disappears.

A billionaire by marriage, Mrs. Veronica Lario Berlusconi, said in an interview that life in the South costs thirty percent less than in the North, but she did not explain where she collected this ridiculous information. And no one questions this piece of information: "It is known to be so," is the common reply. So it happens that this information passes as the truth (does it not occur to this improvised economist that if the costs were so convenient, then why do so many people choose to leave the South?) The Bank of Italy goes on to say that life in the South costs 16.5 percent less; the *Lega* party asks that the salaries be reduced by that much, in respect to the North. He found that the majority of the North, even the non-*Lega* supporters, to be in agreement. It is a shame that this difference disappears when along with the everyday costs one calculates those assets that the Bank of Italy does not take into consideration and, even worse, that of the utilities, which have gone missing in the South, and which are in great abundance in the North (where hundreds of thousands of Southerners are obliged to spend their hard-earned money in order to study and to receive medical care).

It serves no purpose to illustrate that the salaries in the South are lower than the North's by 17 percent, for those lucky few who manage to make them. This means that more people need to live off of one salary than in the North due to the highest rate of un-employment (the youth are particularly affected by this) in Europe: only 17 percent of Southerners between the ages of 15 and 24 are employed. While the difference between the incomes of the "two Italies" continues to grow as well as the poverty level in the South, emigration towards the North, by the hundreds of thousands, has become popular once again, as it was in the 1950s. Let us trust in how the "legs" vote: you will remember a famous response, dur-ing the period of the Iron Curtain, given to those who stated that they were better off in the Soviet Union: "The day I see people fleeing from here to go there, then I will believe it!."

To bolster interest, the *Lega* uses a visceral style (racism: "we are better than they are"), prejudices ("everyone says so, so it must be true"), and ways of doing things that are comparable to the substance of their issues (uncouth). The more ridiculous lies they tell the greater the following seems to be, to the point that it appears that the "North" generated these ideas. This is not true, but it does not matter because only 1-2 percent of Italians (either out of their ideals or interests) wanted the *Risorgimento* and uni-fied the country. Therefore, an equally small amount of people can undo what was done, which is actually easier to accomplish. If for the first undertaking, giants were necessary, for this other under-taking, dwarves should suffice. As the English say, empty barrels make the most noise.

Why is it that South's voice cannot be heard as well as the North's? First of all, it is "inferior," and no one lends an ear to the losing side. Pro-South advocates speak like professors, and hold fast to the provability of data and facts as well as their reasoning (slogans are sufficient for those others). They appeal to people's brains (those others appeal to the "gut") and address these issues in universities (the others profess their beliefs at the local sports bar). They are ashamed if they utter something nonsensical (the others try to do exactly the opposite, but they are protected by the rifles of three hundred thousand residents of the valley near Bergamo, who must be restrained). The "lower" the message is, the easier it is to transmit to the people. If it isn't "low" enough in content, then at least its form should be.

I understood all of this upon reading a heavy text, that from the beginning of the Unification, Milan has been the capital of financial crime (they prefer "moral capital"). The more they evade taxes, the more they complain about them and the "non-Neapolitan" author of the book summarized it best: *"Milano chiagn'e fotte"* ("Milan cries and cheats"). It already "cried and cheated" with the Austrians for the "intolerable" taxes, aspiring to the freedom of the French, who paid taxes that were one third higher than oppressed Lombards and the English, who paid nearly double, while in the Kingdom of Naples the taxes were lower than in all of the pre-Unitarian states.

Well! I thought: when the information is laid out in this manner, anyone can understand. Never mind the statistics put forth by the "criminal" bar associations! I decided to narrate out of my emotional disarray, and to attempt to answer one question: why do the Southerners accept to be treated this way? Why do they speak of the evil that was done to them as though they had to justify themselves rather than ask for justice from those who accuse, insult, and steal from them?

Let us begin at the end, with the invaluable study *Il prodotto delle regioni e il dicario Nord-Sud in Italia (1861-2004),* written by two well-known researchers: Vittorio Daniele, from the Magna Graecia University in Catanzaro, and Paolo Malanima, who heads the Institute of the Study of Mediterranean Societies in the National Council for Research located in Naples. I will spare you the endless pages of tables, charts, and figures, and I will tell you how it ends: "The war ruined us," because, "when Italy was united, there was no real difference between North and South, in terms of production pro capita." Notice that the two researchers begin their study with 1861, while the war in the South had already been under way for several months. It had already been subjected to robberies, massacres, the destruction of towns and factories. One must also take into consideration that the companies that were spared still felt the effects of the ongoing war. Professor Daniele is from Calabria, more precisely from Roccella Ionica, and he intends to remain there. Professor Malanima is from Pisa and set foot in the South for the first time in 1995, when he was 45 years old in order to teach in Catanzaro. His encounter with Daniele brought him to address the North-South affair. "I discovered that there were many opinions on the matter, but little data. The origin of this gap between the North and South was studied from the historical standpoint, beginning from the current situation. This approach carries some risks along with it: for example, if the gap is present now, one tends to think that it was present previously and that it was therefore determined by preceding historical conditions. As a result, many date the existence of such a gap to the Middle Ages or they identify the origins in the structure of the Roman Empire, or even in pre-Roman times.... One is inclined to think that the North is more advanced due to its era of city-states, while the South had been one nation for many centuries, and maintained strong feudal connotations. I suspect that if the situation were reversed, and the South were at an advantage, we would attribute its advantage to the fact that it was not divided into a multitude of fragments, like the North, which harbored many rivalries."

I had never really thought about it before (I realize that I am in good company), but isn't this the reason for which Rome (a unified state) conquered Greece (city-states), and not the opposite, according to what we have been taught in school? (Darwin also mentions this in order to explain the decline of the Greeks.)

"The country that most closely resembled the Kingdom of the Two Sicilies at the time," continues Malanima, "was England, superpower of the time, and only in the 1800s did London overtake

Naples. As far as residual feudalism is concerned, there was certainly less in Southern Italy than in Japan." Japan does not seem to be faring too badly, either.

The professor began his career specializing in modern history. "But I became more and more interested in economics. I ended up teaching just that." This explains the distinction he made at the beginning of our discussion on the differentiation between historical or economic approaches to the gap between the North and the South: he has the ability to evaluate the issue from both perspectives. "Italy was, then, a poor country, and when this occurs, there cannot be great differences between one area and another. I will not go into too much detail, but here is my reasoning: if one establishes poverty to be around 800-900 of an imaginary currency, Italy was close to that figure with 1300. In such conditions, everyone is more or less in the same boat. With the information that I discovered and published in the study I conducted along with Daniele, this appears to be evident."

I have happened to come upon non-Southerners that have been captivated by the Pro-Southern attitude: Professor Edoardo Boncinelli, a Tuscan residing in Milan, who moved there in order to teach, and who speaks Neapolitan after having lived for a certain time on the Gulf. How about Malanima? "I live in Pisa, and I commute." His accent has not been corrupted. I ask if his shedding light on a centuries-long dispute evoked any emotions on his part: "That of being able to give a clear answer to the first question I was asked." I ask him in a more explicit manner: had it not been Italy's South in question, had it been Ghana, would it have made a difference? "No: the trouble, for those who study, lies in the uncertainty of the response. It does not matter what it pertains to. But to insist on the failure of the South, to me, seems misleading. If one does not compare the South to the North, if one considers it a country unto itself, one cannot but define it a huge success. It grew to sixteen times what it was. That is a great deal ... to grow sixteen times more than each individual portion."

This is all in spite of the military occupation, unequal taxation (against the South's interest), the draining of its riches towards the

North.... Professor, could we say "in spite of all these things"? He goes off on a long and serious response. Length is often a defense tactic in certain instances: a way to dilute meaning. So, I ask him again. This time he nods slowly, "You can say so."

"The gap between the two areas of the country," state Daniele and Malanima, "began to manifest itself in the 70s and the 80s (author's note: *of the 1800s, that is*). It was contemporaneous to the birth of the "issue of the South."

But we are used to reading that the gap and the "issue" were already present and that, despite the unification of the country, they were not able to rectify the situation (the problem is that Southerners are Southerners, darn it!) All the while our brothers from the North came to shoot us, "data published in reports on the level of salaries in the North and the South, in both urban and rural contexts, do not reveal substantial differences between the two."

To make the point even clearer, the two researchers use a coefficient that measures the economic differences between different regions of the same country. Then they compare the resulting figure of united Italy, in 1861, to the figure from other wealthier European countries: both Italy and France were both considerably better off than the United Kingdom, while Belgium (to whom we "sold" human meat for slaughter in the mines of Marcinelle in exchange for the coal which they extracted) was, compared to us, in a disastrous state.

"The regional gaps, which were quite modest in the period immediately following the Unification, experienced a net increase for nearly a century, diminishing only in the two decades after World War II" (those were the years of the Fund for the South), summarize Daniele and Malanima. Be aware: in the beginning the difference was not between the North and the South. Because in 1891 (and I apologize, but I must remind you that this is after thirty years of plundering and higher taxes in the South, of which the majority was used in the North), the revenue per capita of the Campania region was still superior to the national rate, "comparable to that of Lombardy, while in Puglia, and in the main islands it was analogous to the national rate." Can I say: could you imagine how things were before? Okay, I said it.

The differences, thirty painful years after the Unification, lay between: a leading group, comprising Piedmont, Liguria, Lombardy, Emilia, Umbria, Lazio and Campania; a middle group, made up of the Three Venices, Tuscany, the Marche, Puglia, Basilicata, and the islands; and one group that brought up the rear, including Calabria, Abruzzo, Molise and lastly, Val d'Aosta.

It is only after another thirty years of administering detrimental "cures" to the South that the *fratelli d'Italia* are finally successful in killing it, and "in 1921 the South can already be considered an area in arrested development." We are speaking of one third of the country that for sixty years has endured an orgy of iron and fire, has been ignored from public spending projects, and is taxed more heavily than the others. Yet the Campania region was still, in 1911, amongst the wealthiest regions (the only one "from the South with a revenue pro capita higher than the Italian average"). But some equality is on the way in the following thirty years, when the Campania region becomes impoverished just like the other regions of the South: "The differences between the regions of the South become blurred and the revenue per capita is clearly inferior to that of the lesser developed regions of the Central regions of Italy. In other words, the regions of the South become like one another" or to put it another way, they all become equally poorer than the rest of Italy.

Cetto Laqualunque[1] would say, "Chiù meno pe' tutti!" ["More of less for everyone!"]

It is during the years of Fascism that the transfer of benefits to the North (money, infrastructure) accelerated, and the worst was shuttled to the South. After its purpose had been served, the dictatorship handed the new democracy a country where "in 1951, the distinction between the Center/North and the South is quite clear: Italy now has a dual economy." It took nearly a century, but they

---

[1] TRANSLATOR'S NOTE: Cetto Laqualunque is the name of the main character in the 2011 Italian film *Qualunquemente*.

finally pulled it off: the wealthiest region of the South, Campania, has a revenue that is barely higher than half of the national revenue; the poorest regions, Calabria and Basilicata, have a little over one third. What would you say now, Mrs. Berlusconi, Mr. Tremonti, or any who may precede or succeed you: isn't this too much? They won't get spoiled and waste their money, will they? Shouldn't we reduce their salaries?

In 1891 (after thirty years of ... need I repeat myself?), the South had 37 percent of the population and still managed to produce around 37 percent of the nation's wealth (can you imagine how much they produced before they were impoverished? Ok, I will stop mentioning it). In 1951, with 37 percent of the population, the wealth produced declined to 22 percent. In the following twenty years, things improve, only to get worse again (anyone who would like can note the contemporaneous rise of the *Lega*'s influence and the greed of Lombardy, not necessarily affiliated with the *Lega,* in the choice of elected officials.) Today, Campania is the region in Europe with the highest rate of poverty and unemployment.

Are you asking yourselves why the South lets itself be treated in this manner and does not react? Me too.

We should try to envision ourselves as Southerners living in 1860: we live in a country (and now we know) that is not inferior to others, in fact, in certain fields it excels, though in others it does not. The capital, Naples, is the third most important city in Europe, and the most important in Italy for its magnificence, modernity, population, and culture (despite the fact that it had more illiterate people than the rest of the peninsula "but this does not constitute a hindrance to development, if not in the long run," states Malanima.) There is poverty at the lowest class levels, but the two capital cities in front of it are Paris, during the period depicted in *Les Misèrables* and London, whose ghettos are depicted in *David Copperfield* and *Oliver Twist.* "I did not see more misery in Naples than in London, Paris, or New York," noted the writer Fredrika Bremer, who was convinced she would find "frightful conditions." Hermann Melville, the author of *Moby Dick*, said that he was not able to "distinguish it from Broadway."

The body of the country had the best components of its "head" in its future (from technology to the social sciences; economically it was certainly more advanced than the rest of Italy, and more on the wavelength with the rest of Europe; Naples and Paris were the most well educated cities on the continent, but even then, and later on as well, "the more refined and robust the culture expressed from the Southern society was, the less it was able to be efficiently represented," according to Francesco Barbagallo, in *La modernità squilibrata del Mezzogiorno d'Italia)*. The laziest part of the "head" of the country, the conservative nobles and those bourgeois living on a private income, adapts itself to the present and the power that governs it. The rest of the body is a pure work force, especially in the internal regions (the coasts have an opportunity to exchange both goods and ideas with the rest of the world). These regions often lived in the past, or at least in a place where time seemed to have come to a halt. In other places in Italy there appear to be fewer examples of excellence, but the body seems, and perhaps it is, more homogeneous.

"Naples had fewer soldiers than France, fewer ships than London, less liberty than America, less art than Rome, and was less polished than Paris, but these things alone do not bring happiness. Yet, Naples had all of these qualities in such a large quantity that, in relation to the territory and its conditions, it was second to none. All things summed, this kingdom was the happiest in the world; foreigners came, enriched themselves, and decided never to leave. The population grew by one quarter in forty years," wrote Giacinto de' Sivo, one of those people who was greatly disappointed by the Unification.

We are one of the most ancient sates of Europe and we are the largest and most economically advanced state in Italy (later, economists of the same caliber as Salvemini will prove this, but by that time we will have been reduced to misery and that affirmation would seem provocative)." For nearly thirteen centuries, the Southerners have been united. They are pacific like all of the most civilized people and their economy focuses on social well-being rather than the well-being of a select few. Their public administration is wise and well pondered. Their religious practices color their character," Vincenzo Gulì writes in *Il saccheggio del Sud*. But life is difficult (though it is difficult everywhere at that time). The shadow of gentlemen weighs heavily upon the necks of the common folk and, despite the fact that legislation focuses on the rights of the common folk rather than the demands of the gentlemen, the common man is still guilty (it does not matter of what) until proven innocent (if even that is enough) and the gentleman is innocent, despite proof of the contrary (just like today, but perhaps a little worse ... maybe). In spite of "what literature, often biased, suggests the condition of the Southern farmers was, in the period prior to the Unification, it was actually better and not worse than it was after," writes Nicola Zitara in *L'unità d'Italia: nascita di una colonia*, nearly forty years before the study conducted by Daniele and Malanima gave us such a well-documented confirmation.

We were ahead in the industrial field and on the cutting edge of many other fields (in the Paris Exposition in 1856, we were recognized as the most industrialized country in Italy, and we placed third in the world). The king's attention toward the wealth of his people manifested itself in many ways: in the contrast of power of the nobility over the common folk, in providing essential utilities (various forms of assistance to the poorest, the first Italian anti-tuberculosis treatment campaign, the first low-income housing assignments, tax breaks for farmers, and pensions for "poor literate people," who were almost always republican). Again in 1883, after the South had been sacked and devastated, (see? I remembered to mention it) in the "Acts of the Council for the Investigation of the Condition of the Agricultural Class," one can read: "In general, the conditions of the farm workers are less wretched than those of several provinces in the North."

"The fact that in 1861, Lombardy was more civilized and wealthy than Calabria cannot justify the widening of the gap that separates them," Zitara observes; in the mid-1800s "even the United States, Germany, and Russia were behind Great Britain (...) but this did not prevent them, over time, from overtaking Great Britain." One could overturn this dishonest comparison: what was the difference between the industrialized Neapolitan area and the extremely poor, alpine, Friuli area? "In the South, before 1860," explains Francesco Saverio Nitti, one could find "more wealth than in nearly all of the regions of the North."

The prized agricultural products from the South were too expensive for the rest of Italy. Only 11.8 percent of exports and 8.5 percent of imports from the Kingdom of the Two Sicilies took place with other pre-Unification states because "the Southern economy belonged to a commercial circuit that tied it closely to the countries in Northern and Central Europe," according to Banti in *La nazione del Risorgimento*.

Let us again trust our "legs" more than we trust our respectable professors: nearly no one emigrates from the South in the years preceding the invasion (only a few thousand), while millions leave the other regions of Italy, from the alpine Northwest to the Northeast from the Padania area (where due to malnourishment, many suffer from pellagra and cretinism) down to large areas of the Center. Only after the occupation, the plundering, and the useless resistance movement do the Southerners begin to emigrate by the millions.

But we shall discover this later. It is 1860 and the taxes are still low and few, and easy to collect. The Bourbon monarchs never increased them in one hundred and twenty-six years. Overall, the tax money is well spent. One continues to hear positive things about our former Minister of Finance, a Tuscan man who held his position for nearly forty years: Bernardo Tanucci. He was a sterling example of rigor and honesty. Political economics, a topic of study in the universities, was invented here; the first university department dedicated to this topic was founded here. As far as infrastructures are concerned, particularly the roads, the South was notably behind (even if we were the first to have a railway in Italy, use an electric telegraph, build iron suspension bridges, have gas lamps to light our cities), because we preferred to focus on the sea. In fact, we have the second most important merchant fleet and the third military fleet in all of Europe. The Bourbon monarchs believed so much in using the sea rather than the land that they personally funded the first transportation fleet that had routes all over the Mediterranean. They supported "the development of a state funded fleet that would promote the convenience of sea travel in a country that was three quarters surrounded by water," as reported in *Storia del Regno delle Due Sicilie*, by Angelantonio Spagnoletti, professor of history of ancient Italian states at the University of Bari. Were the Bourbon monarchs the only ones to think of this? No, another superpower of the time thought this way as well: England. "Paradoxically," says Domenico Cersosimo, an economist from Calabria," my region was better connected in the 1800s by sea than later on, up until the construction of the Salerno-Reggio Calabria stretch of the Italian super-highway." This means that for a century, after the Unification, the region was substantially isolated by sea and by land (aside from the extremely slow, almost untouched railway from the 1800s that borders the cliffs of the coast all the way down to the Strait).

Having to choose between the roads and the sea routes, the Bourbon monarchs chose the latter. Unified Italy chose differently (in the sense that the South lost the sea routes and did not receive the roads until much later, and much fewer than necessary). Today, the European Union has rediscovered its "sea highways" and has seen that they are less costly, faster, and pollute far less.

In 1860, there were many discussions as to how to become Italians under one nation (in the war for independence in '48, the Neapolitan troops fought alongside Piedmont against Austria). This is in spite of the fact that no one really spoke the language: the Piedmontese, Lombards, Venetians, Sicilians.... Aside from the Tuscans, at the moment of the Unification, only 200,000 people spoke what would eventually become the nation's official language out of 22 million. This turmoil was the result of a feeling that pervaded the world at that time which viewed populations and geography as two superimposable entities, as if it were nature that could determine the perimeters of states so as to make them coincide with a nation's soul. Those who held this belief most strongly aimed to diffuse this thought through a vast campaign of proselytism (through poetry, music, theater, and newspapers). The population, however, had more prosaic things to worry about (What will I eat today?). There were various projects for the Unification, and those who found themselves in trouble, because of their ideals, were forced to go abroad: to Piedmont. This wave of notions carried over from one century into the next: multinational empires broke into nations; nations recomposed themselves into states. Not everyone was successful in this endeavor, however.

But in 1860, the Unification was not merely spoken about: everyone knew that we were about to be invaded. It was written in the newspapers of the time. The king's court in Naples sent letters protesting the invasion to half of Europe, but the embarrassment, vacuity, and shamelessness of the responses, and of the lack of responses, led us to believe that the game was already over. The losing side was not even asked to sit at the table with all of the others. What we did not know, and which emerged much later (after a century and a half, we still have a closet that is exploding with skeletons) was that the destiny of the Kingdom had been decided and prepared by Great Britain, France, the masons (who would also collect money in the United States: nearly all of the protagonists of the *Risorgimento* were masons), and Piedmont. Piedmont was the operating branch of the movement and ultimately the area that would derive the most benefits. The spies and agitators of Cavour had already been to Sicily and Naples and had alerted any idealist conspirators and made promises to them, distributed money, made agreements with local criminals and landowners (often, the masons and master masons, would form the embryo that would evolve into the *mafia*). This was an alliance that would never be broken in the way that it became known as the organized crime of the South, an ally of the economy and power of the North. Giovanni Giolitti made this his way of governing to the point of being nicknamed the "Minister of Crime." Still today, large companies based in the North and the Center subcontract jobs to mafia-run companies from the South, and not only in the South. The Milan stock exchange is one of the mafia's favorite places to launder gang money, in perfect harmony with the "elite" of the finance world, whose protagonists can often be found in Masonic lodges. The political party that has governed the country with the greatest majority of votes, *Forza Italia*, in the beginning, was run by a man from Palermo (who was later condemned to nine and a half years of prison for complicity in organized crime) on behalf of a businessman from Milan, who for a time was a Mason. The anti-mafia commission of the parliament was presided by a Calabrian, Francesco Forgione, and certifies the existence of a "long red line" that "unites the *'ndrangheta* (author's note: *which appeared to have been marginal*) to Masonry." In its most modern form, "La Santa," the Calabrian mafia, substitutes its historic "archangels" that are referral points in the "*società di sgarro*"[2] known as *Osso, Mastrosso,* and *Carcagnosso,* with three Northern monuments of Masonry: Garibaldi, La Marmora, and Mazzini. "The mafia-mason system," (we speak of the present day, Forgione's book, *'Ndrangheta,* was published in 2008) became "the formidable instrument by which the mafia was integrated into the systems of dominant power and in the bourgeois of business." Angelo Ravano, from Genoa, landed in Gioia Tauro and proposed to make it the most important port in the Mediterranean for container shipping. The local mafia would receive half of the profits: one and a half euros for each of the millions of containers moved.

What has changed since Gaetano Salvemini wrote: "The moderates of the North need the *camorra* from the South to oppress the democratic parties of the North. The *camorra* needs the moderate parties of the North to oppress the masses in the South"?

In 1860, everything is justified by the end result: "Building a country." Does it not cause you to shudder a little? Do you remember? This was the name of a project implemented by George W. Bush to justify the invasion of Iraq. He had already done the same previously in Afghanistan. Colonialists everywhere did the same thing in order to "bring civilization" to people so backward that they were not able to appreciate the favor being offered to

---

[2] TRANSLATOR'S NOTE: "society of criminal code breaches."

them and consequently would have preferred to continue minding their own business. There is one constant in all of these undertakings: anytime that it is necessary to "build a country," first it is razed to the ground. Then, usually, there is a problem with the second part of the program, and the country is left in ruins, and the survivors are told, "Now that you know how it is done, rebuild yourselves, but well." All this is accomplished while criticizing them if they are unable to rebuild themselves, despite the assistance that has been given to them. The same thing happened to us.

When Garibaldi's ships left Quarto, the kingdom was doomed. A child ruled the empire, Francis II: he was delicate and honest and completely unsuitable to face the brutality of his time and of its protagonists. His father, Ferdinand, was uncouth and more practical. He did many great things for his kingdom, but he also made some serious miscalculations: he spent funds for social politics (reasoning that if the population was happy, it would not rebel) and not on weapons, which rendered his army (the largest in all of Italy) completely useless. He did not feel threatened by the smaller states of the peninsula (his was the largest) and believed that he did not stand a chance against the superpowers of the time. Therefore, he did not address foreign policy. His greatest error, however, was to die shortly before the invasion.

After more than a century, documents chronicling the corruption, robberies, and massacres of the Unification have been published (or republished, because they had been forgotten). These include diaries of Cavour's spies that report the names of those accomplices that had been corrupted in the Kingdom of the Two Sicilies (but also in other annexed pre-Unification states). They also explain the price that "spontaneous revolts" cost to stage, and how deeply involved the other European superpowers were. Those who are scandalized by the revelation of such information shouldn't be. This is the profession in which, to the horror of the idealists, betters, liars, thieves, traitors and assassins thrive. The worst men in times of peace become the most suitable ones in times of war. It is the time of Cain and the best medals are awarded to those who act like Cain. Those first medals (made of gold and other precious metals) were given for military valor: Italy awarded them to those Italians that massacred thousands of other Italians, often out of retaliation. Certain heroes are the victor's criminals.

Now it is easier to understand what Massimo D'Azeglio meant when he wrote, in 1860, about Garibaldi's triumphant undertaking: "When one sees a kingdom of six million (author's note: *there were nine million*) and an army of one hundred thousand men, won with only eight dead and eighteen wounded, those who want to understand, will."

We cannot speak badly of Giuseppe Garibaldi, but Victor Emanuel, who had also just received a kingdom from him as a gift, describes him in a letter he wrote to Cavour while in Naples: "He is neither as docile nor as honest as he is depicted (which is how you view him)," because "he is entirely responsible for the infamous robbery of the treasury and has entirely surrounded himself with scoundrels.... He has caused this unhappy country to plunge into a truly frightening state." Later, the general would go on to be a guarantor for his son Menotti's large loan from the Bank of Naples, which he then refused to pay. Meanwhile, General Wilhelm Rustow, one of the heads of the expedition, confessed that he "desired the San Leucio feud" states Teodoro Salzillo in *1860-61. L'assedio di Gaeta*.

The memoirs of Filippo Curletti, the secret agent provocateur that Piedmont used to create disorder in pre-Unification states to justify military intervention, are a list of stolen items: as soon as Florence was taken, in a few short hours "all of the public funds had been stolen, all without sending a lira to the treasure of Piedmont," he wrote in *La verità sugli uomini e sulle cose del Regno d'Italia*. In that instance, the patriot was Bettino Ricasoli. The same thing happened in Parma, but the patriot was Luigi Farini. He handed his wife the keys to the Ducal Palace. His wife and daughter proceeded to divide the duchess's dresses amongst themselves. Her son-in-law received the Duke's clothes (they wore the same size). The silver was melted.... So many people stole so many things that the spy conceded this point: "I let myself get carried away by my position and am guilty of abuse of power, for which I shared the goods and must also share the shame." This is the only confession we have! As far as Garibaldi is concerned, Curletti believes that "the rapid successes, it must be agreed upon, were due more to Piedmont's gold and less to the weapons of the adventurous general." The spy leaves a few words for the ladies ("the nights were spent in orgies") and the sudden, unlimited profiteering. (But when the Southern army was dissolved, because it was promised a place in the new national army, only the Northern volunteers were selected while the Southern ones, which were double in number, were discarded because it was believed that they were only interested in spoils. Their spoils.) Why does Curletti talk and reveal such details? He does so out of disappointment: "I did not detect any enthusiasm for the Unification of Italy, anywhere," unlike his own enthusiasm.

John Pemble writes in *La passione del Sud* that "while Garibaldi was not mysteriously wise, he was, without a doubt, great in an uncouth way." His undertaking planted a seed, which would develop into a hydra, a monster with many heads, that would come to be known as the "issue of the South." This would dry up the wealth of the Kingdom of the Two Sicilies in order to transfer it to the North and into the pockets of the liberators (the secretary general went from having nothing to amounting a personal fortune that was more than twice the funds of the entire grand duchy of Tuscany). It would demolish a promising economy and would compromise its reconstruction with mechanisms of preclusion that are still in use today after one hundred and fifty years. It destroyed the habit of considering oneself as part of a unified state (they can no longer trust anyone: the old monarch could not defend us and the new one discriminates us). It generates and continues to fuel a condition of accepted inferiority status of the Southerners, with respect to the North. In Northerners, it encourages the idea that their advantage is due to the insufficiency of Southerners, to the point of racism.

(And no one seems to understand why the Southerners continue to put up with this. Have I already asked myself this question before? Let me check and I will let you know.)

Garibaldi lands in Marsala under the protection of the English and Bourbon navies (the entire fleet passes as a unified block) where more British people reside than Sicilians. The *Mille* soldiers quickly become tens of thousands, as members of many nations enlist: Hungary, Poland, Russia, Dalmatia, Switzerland, England, France, Greece, Africa. There are even some rumors that say that there might have been a few Italians in the mix, surely from Piedmont and either deserters or discharged soldiers. What did the *Mille* soldiers do as soon as they landed? They immediately reached for the town funds. Francesco Crispi, Garibaldi's secretary and a Sicilian himself, walked away with five million lira from the Bank of Sicily and one million four hundred thousand lira of "reimbursements," which however were proven to have already been "reimbursed" according to Gulì.

Wherever they stop, the *fratelli d'Italia* take over the best residences and take souvenirs with them: when the owners came back, they did not even find their eating utensils. When Garibaldi sets up his camp at the Bourbon palace, his followers remove anything that could be sold. Twelve chests of documents pertaining to the money plundered on the whims of the Leader and his court would see the floor of the Tyrrhenian Sea from Ippolito Nievo's ships. These whims included Alexandre Dumas' penchant for women, who gave literally everything for the cause and would remain loyal to him. Jessie White and one of her companions used their underwear to make bandages for the wounded during a confrontation with the Austrians in 1866. The deaths of two pro-Garibaldi Sicilians remain premature and suspicious: Rosolino Pilo and Giovanni Corrao, who had initially reached a sort of agreement with the soldiers for their support, were killed. Pilo was shot in the back while he advanced with the Red Shirts in an attack on Palermo. Corrao was shot by people posing as *carabinieri*, three years later, in a citrus orchard (Do you recognize the style?).

They do try to save money on a few things: one can cite the tragic-comical episode of General Francesco Landi. Here Landi's enemy, the Sforza commander at the head of five hundred troops, was winning against the three thousand Garibaldi troops (Landi himself risked his life). Landi refused reinforcements and munitions only to be forced to sound the alarm for a retreat. This would happen nearly every time that Garibaldi was in trouble, and happened so often that Gulì writes: "The trumpeters were the ruin of the Kingdom of Naples." However, when General Landi, tried to cash a check of fourteen thousand ducats, given to him, he assures by Garibaldi himself, he discovers that only on his copy there are three extra zeroes. He died of heartbreak, according to some. It could very well be true: he was old enough, had been swindled for a good amount of money, and the trick was certainly the kind to cause a good amount of distress. His son, Nicola, would obtain a statement of denial from Garibaldi, but....

Naples was like an enormous jewelry box: King Francis left everything behind when he fled to Gaeta. He left the kingdom's gold, works of art, museums filled with treasures, millions of ducats from his own personal estate, and his wife's dowry (when the Savoy family was forced into exile in 1946, eighteen trains left for Switzerland carrying only their "hand luggage"...). Angela Pellicciari reported on the declaration of the Representative Boggio, a Mason, friend, and collaborator of Cavour: "Vast, fabulous, quantities of money disappeared with the same ease and rapidity that they were stolen from the Bourbon funds."

So what happened to that mountain of gold, and how big was it really? Francesco Saverio Nitti, who had access to the documents, counted 443 million gold-lira (of the 664 of all of the rest of Italy, put together). This was nearly half of the Piedmont's frightening debt. To better understand what we are speaking of, I asked Professor Vincenzo Gulì (this is his field of expertise): how much would this correspond to, today? This was his response: "It would come to 200 billion euros, applying currency appreciation and legally established rates of interest. If one then proceeds to add the 33 million ducats from the Bourbon king's personal account, we reach 270 billion euros. In terms of the current economy, however, we are obliged to not stop our estimate with the inclusion of the interest rate. This is because the return on capital for the former kingdom was far superior to this, up until 1861. A plausible doubling of the amount of interest pertinent only to the initial capital could bring us to the more realistic amount of 500 billion euros. Not even the national budget of 2009 (which is "barely" 463 billion euros) would be sufficient to pay for this initial debt to the people of the South."

Could you even imagine that amount of money? What could you purchase? I cannot even imagine. To put this into perspective: the Agnelli family is worth an estimated billion euros. Berlusconi is worth tens of billions of euros. But let us keep in mind that the bill is still incomplete: we have not taken into consideration the wealth that was plundered from public institutions, homes, churches, palaces (that amount, today, is known by God and the thieves themselves). But most of all, the gold in circulation has not been calculated. What is this exactly? The other states emitted paper money, whose value was guaranteed by the accumulated reserves of gold. The system sustained itself on its convertibility: when you desired, you could go to the bank, give them back their paper money and retrieve its equivalent in gold. Theoretically. In the Kingdom of the Two Sicilies, the money in circulation carried its true value in gold. The reserves served to cover the cost of those amounts in circulation that went out of circulation, were used for other purposes, or lost. How much did this other quantity come to? "Some speak of double the amount of the famous one hundred million gold ducats of the reserve. Only half (a proven amount) would then be converted when the currency changed to lira. We are speaking of another trillion euros (author's note: *and the total amount of gold subtracted rises to one trillion five hundred million euros*) that were absorbed by the North in the following years, through the financial drainage of the South. This also happened to the new wealth produced in the South in lira. One must look at the earnings of the state budget and the part that was added by the South, but the amount would still be an estimate. Other damages are certainly more costly, and there we speak of amounts in the trillions of euros."

Professor Gulì is conducting a very complex calculation, and we anxiously await his results. I was given an unverifiable estimate of the possible total from the heir of the last Bourbon Minister of Internal Affairs. However, I can say very little about this: when I asked to see the documents, our correspondence was interrupted. This gentleman lives in Great Britain and still preserves the diary of his ancestor. This diary will likely end up in the estate of a great university, possibly in the United States, after an initial analysis in the University of Cambridge. In those pages, there should be Cavour's commands to transfer the gold to the North. There should also be more exact details relevant to the large-scale robbery. The amount that I was told was of colossal proportions, though I don't believe it makes much sense to state it without explaining the basis upon which such a sum was founded. I maintain, for now, what I know to be certain: the gold in the reserves at the time plus that in circulation, which amounts to 1.5 trillion euros.

How can one understand how much this amount really is? The wealth produced in Italy in 2008 was around 1.2 trillion euros. This does not help us very much. I have a method that helps me rationalize better in these instances: I continue to decrease the scale of importance until I understand. How about if the amount was a "mere" 150 billion euros? This would be the wealth that Italy produces in a month and a half. This also does not seem to help much: how much do you earn in a month and half? We are still far from our objective. I decrease the means of comparison by another step: 15 billion euros. This is the amount of money required to instate a "serious" financial reform or perhaps 2 or 3 "lighter" ones. We would be set for one or more years without new taxes and school budget, health, or utility cuts. Let us continue one step further: 1.5 billion euros. This is one-third of the amount (4.5 billion euros) that Berlusconi and Tremonti wanted to use to launch a "New Marshall Plan" to resolve the "Issue of the South." Let us ignore the fact that they did not follow through with this idea. We never really believed their promises anyway, we merely wanted to use this amount of money to acquire a better understanding of the amount in question.

Now we begin to understand how much 1.5 trillion euros are: they amount to 350 "Southern Issues" resolved (then why was it not resolved even once? What a dumb question: it took them one hundred and fifty years to create Italy, why would they destroy it? What would they live off of?) Naturally, it is not true that with 4.5 billion euros you could carry out a "New Marshall Plan" (renamed, out of modesty, the "Berlusconi Project") that would rebalance the country. Let us say twice that amount. To be absolutely safe, let us say three times that amount and then some. Okay, how about 15 billion euros. Each year. This means that there would be enough money to build a bridge across the Strait of Messina every six months and there would be enough left over to build the streets and railways that they would like, they say, "instead" of the bridge ("instead" of building neither one nor the others). Fifteen billion euros every year for one hundred years. Does this seem like too much to eliminate the gap between the North and the South? Why did it not seem like quite so much when they stole this amount? I think that now I begin to better comprehend how much 1.5 trillion euros really are.

With snobby brutality, Massimo D'Azeglio reported what it was like to convince Charles Albert, upon request of the Masons, to agree to the *Risorgimento*. "It was like authorizing a thief to steal." With the Unification of the country, "there is an enormous transfer of wealth that signifies the fortune of a scant amount of bourgeois, soldiers, and nobles," writes Angela Pellicciari in *I panni sporchi dei Mille*. This is a huge disappointment to those idealists, from the North and South, who spent their lives and personal wealth for the project of a united Italy. In 1899, Giustino Fortunato, a staunch supporter of the Unification to the point of mysticism, wrote a letter to Pasquale Villari, in which he confided, out of discouragement, that the Unification: "was our financial ruin. In 1860, we were in an extremely favorable financial situation, and were at the dawn of a healthy and profitable financial awakening.

The Unification lost us." If even someone such as Fortunato felt prompted to say such things.... In Calabria, the inhabitants took matters up with the Lord: "Those lanky men came down from Piedmont/ they were a race who ate *polenta*/ and on Christmas and Easter they ate two potatoes/ they swore terribly and were not believers/they were brazen and licensed thieves/ arrogant and filled with scorn/ they sit in the shade at large tables/ that we built with our sweat/ and we became colonies/ they became our owners."

But by now, the country was unified. Some portion of the stolen money had to return in some fashion to the South. Put yourselves in the shoes of the Southerners, if you will. In *I vinti del Risorgimento*, (and in other texts as well) you will come upon data similar to this: "From Turin, in one year, over eighty million lira were withdrawn from the funds of the former Kingdom of the Two Sicilies." How much was reinvested in the South: 390,625 lira, "in addition to the 10 million lira that were conceded to the Treasury of Naples. This money was conceded on paper, but was never actually paid out." Apparently, Tremonti's stock has roots that go way back.... With the mere sale of the state and ecclesiastic properties (which were requisitioned) from the former Bourbon kingdom, the New Italy deposited 600 million lira (another 500 billion euros, approximately, in today's terms) that went straight to the North. The country was unified from the North to the South, and not the other way around: the Bank of Naples was prohibited from expanding to the rest of Italy (it should remain in the "Kingdom of the Two Sicilies") while the banks of Turin were allowed to open branches in the South. One could ask the Bank of Naples to convert paper money to gold, while the same operation was prohibited at the National Bank of Turin, who was allowed to keep its gold ingots while taking those of Naples (all that one had to do was print more banknotes and ask for them to be exchanged). When the "Bank of Italy was born," writes Di Fiore, "20,000 shares were conceded to the South, while 280,000 were conceded to the North and Center." This was a curious Unification, in which: what is mine is mine and what is yours is, almost always, all mine.

(Less, always less, little, almost nothing, nothing. Why do the Southerners continue to take this?)

The first extraordinary legislative measures taken in the newly unified Italy for the South were the extra taxes, "assigning the regions of the former Kingdom of the Two Sicilies a war tithe," according to Gulì (it is known that the Southerners want everything for free). At this time, the rerouting of funds from one part of the country to the other resulted in the construction of roads, railways, schools, military expenses, ports, and other large-scale improvements.... These investments were made through to the beginning of the 1900s, as though a large inexhaustible gold mine had been discovered. For a part of the country, this appears to be true: the industrial triangle (Piedmont-Liguria-Lombardy), the Northeast, Rome, a little less In Tuscany and Reggio Emilia. The others paid.

What would Umberto Bossi say if he read that out of 458 million in state funds for improvements that only three were spent in the North? Well, less than three were invested in the South, in the thirty-five years up until 1897. The rest went to the North, which had jobs, and which recovered lands where, what was planted, yielded greater profits, amplified the base of production, and improved overall health. Misery and malaria remained in the South, along with taxes, and still the Northerners shouted insults: "You are incompetent!"

They spoke to us about the residents of Ferrara being the best at reclaiming swamps (sure, but do they know how to accomplish this feat without any money?). They would apply criteria suitable for the plains of Padania, badly, too late, and with disastrous consequences to the torrents of the South. The exception would be when the plans of the great Carlo Afan de Rivera, an engineer from the Kingdom of the Two Sicilies, were found (but only from 1924). The plans first called for the reclamation of rivers and torrents at their mouths (his pre-Unification solutions to drain lakes, marshes, and rivers in Calabria, Puglia, and Campania were widely studied and copied abroad, even at that time).

What would Giulio Tremonti say if he discovered that for a decade, the Fund for deposits and loans released millions to Lombardy, Liguria, Piedmont, and ten thousand lira (over the course of a decade) to Calabria? We already know the answer to this: Tremonti would take advantage of Calabria's distraction in order to take back those ten thousand lira as well. What would Mariastella Gelmini say if laws were passed that allotted government subsidies for schools and that they were conceived in such a manner as to ensure that nearly all of the funds would be sent to the South, while next to nothing reached the North? The opposite was done by the newly unified Italy in order to "distribute government subsidies to the cities based on their wealth, inversely proportional to their illiteracy rate." In this manner, "they continued to be far from eliminating the difference between the expenses of the richest cities in the North and the poorest cities in the South. This made the problem even more serious," reported Giuseppe Donati in 1912. *La questione meridionale*. It is worthwhile to state this again, for clarity's sake: the money from the taxes went to the richest cities in the North, with the lowest illiteracy rates. The school taxes, however, were higher in the South (according to Salvemini's research) where the cities were poorer and had a higher illiteracy rate.

In 1876 and 1886, laws were passed to help small towns, and poor towns (due to the fact that they were small). The South, where the majority of cities and towns were extremely overpopulated (in 1861, there were twice the amount of heavily populated towns than in the North) but also extremely poor, did not qualify to benefit from either law, darn it! Lombardy received 79.44 lira for every ten thousand inhabitants. Piedmont received 68.81, while Calabria received 12.79. In order to finance education, Liguria was given 15,625 lira for every ten thousand inhabitants while Calabria was given 80. "It just so happened," notes Zitara, "that Piedmont, Liguria, Lombardy, and the Veneto regions, for approximately thirteen years, found that they had been given those millions that were destined to towns of poorer regions." What would Tremonti say if he discovered that at the dawn of the 1900s, the state spent 93 lira per inhabitant of the Lazio region (in other words, Rome, for its role as capital), 71.15 lira in Liguria, and barely 8.77 in

Pino Aprile

Basilicata? This one's easy: Tremonti would move Rome's money to Milan, or at most, that of Basilicata to Catania, to pay off the debts of the bankrupt city. Tremonti and Gelmini have invented nothing new. They merely continue a tradition. One cannot choose one's contemporaries. They might not even be the worst of the series. The worst may still be to come.

It is thanks to the passing of numerous laws like the ones previously mentioned that from 1860 to 1998, the state spends two hundred times more in Lombardy, three hundred times more in Reggio Emilia, and four hundred times more in the Veneto region than in Campania. "In the first three decades after the Unification, the vast majority of elected officials hailed from the North," states Mario Meriggi, professor of modern history, in his work *Breve storia dell'Italia settentrionale*. In this manner the government allotted its subsidies. So "for the first twenty years of the Unification, the subsidies were concentrated in the North." D'Azeglio once said, "These chambers represent Italy as much as I represent the Great Sultan of Turkey."

(Sooner or later, I am going to have to ask this question: why do the Southerners let themselves be treated this way?)

In the first decades after the Unification, the disproportion between the North and South in terms of expenses was ... balanced by the fact that the less one invested in the South, the higher the taxes would be. I must continue to give statistics taken from the sacred texts. Anyone who is bored can skip the following paragraphs, which in synthesis state: "Milan is rife with thieves, while the South forgives them" because it forgets and then blames itself for the backwardness obtained for it by those who reproached them.

Italy acquired the Savoy tradition of spending more than it deposited: more than double the amount of all the pre-Unification states put together.

The earnings from the provinces of the former kingdoms of the South tripled by the end of the century (imagine tripling the taxes on your income). But in Liguria, 135 lira were returned for every 100 taken, while Puglia was only given 43.5. In 1904, Ettore

Ciccotti, a representative from the Lucania area, asked that his region be abandoned by the state, so that it might take care of itself with its own resources. The land registry was "calibrated upon the characteristics and needs of the North," so that "the richest provinces" of Lombardy and Veneto were taxed by 8.8% while the poorest, in Calabria and Sicily, were taxed by at least twice that amount, if not more. It was as though one paid a higher property tax the more miserable one's home was.

It has been estimated that out of every 1,212 "unfairly taxed" Italians, one thousand were from the South, 151 from the North, and 61 from the Center. Como, a wealthy industrial town that also thrived on tourism, paid infinitely less than Foggia, a poor farming town that was one third smaller. Even the "cost of the taxes," the expenses incurred to collect them, squashed the South in a disproportionate manner. On Southerners, that tax was five times higher. For Ciccotti, this tax system was "oppressive" and "antisocial" because the more it burdened misery, the deeper this misery became. This would include "additional" taxes imposed upon the South for public projects exclusively in the Po River Valley. These tax laws were passed to keep the "masses of riotous workers" quiet. They were passed without urgency or need and were not even well formulated. Francesco Saverio Nitti calculated that the index of taxation grew in proportion to poverty. Even though the population count was similar, Sicily paid, based on consumption, three and a half times more taxes than Venice.

According to Sidney Sonnino (from Rosario Villari's *Il Sud nella storia d'Italia* these "laws were true acts of spoliation of the poor." In addition to this "financial plundering of the poor," according to the definition of Friedrich Vochting in his work *La Questione Meridionale* was the repossession of the few things of value that were left: linen sets, furniture, work equipment, and houses (for those who owned them). "Plundering" may even be too poor of a word to use because the long arm of the Northern state seemed intent upon destroying the South. That in Lombardy there was one repossession for every 27,416 inhabitants and in Calabria one for every 114, shocks, but it does not explain. I will attempt to explain this better: choose a town of 27,416 inhabitants in Lombardy and one of 27,416 in Calabria. Send an army to occupy the town in Calabria, take the money you find and send it to the inhabitants of its Northern "counterpart" in Lombardy. Close all of the industrial and commercial activities in Calabria and ensure that those left behind are in difficulty and pass laws that oblige the Calabrians to support the businesses of the Lombard town. Also pass laws that oblige the Calabrians to purchase the products from the North at higher prices. Kill all of those who rebel and call them brigands. Impose taxes that are outrageously disproportionate, in disfavor of the Calabrian town, and distribute the subsidies according to the following criterion: "more up, less down, if anything at all." Then, repossess the assets of tax dodgers. You will see one home emptied in the Lombard town and two hundred and forty emptied in the Calabrian town. I repeat: 240 homes, families (which are known to be quite numerous in the South), which means that at least 1,500 people (1 inhabitant out of every 18) will lose everything. Try to envision this: an entire neighborhood, in the streets, exposed to hunger, shame, and at risk to explode in a violent desperate reaction worthy of a "delinquent." Why should I treat this information as though it were outdated: history's collateral damage? This history is not over: it continues with Bossi, Tremonti, Gelmini, and all of the clones of their predecessors and of their successors. It continues in Scampia, one of the poorest and most dangerous neighborhoods of Naples, and wherever there is nothing left but resentment, desperation, or crime to rise above, and some cases to stay inside nonetheless, this decay.

I repeat, 1 versus 240. This is the synthesis in numbers of the aggression and robbery that the South was subjected to. This is the size of the credit, the crime committed.

Now for a little test: after having done this for forty years (in the beginning of the 1900s something favorable happened, but that was short-lived), would you expect that part of the country to be: A) more developed and civilized or B) less developed and civilized?

While all of this was happening, the Savoy monarchy withdrew, from public funds, the equivalent of two points of the gross national product: a dowry "never to be equaled at any time" in the world, according to Lorenzo Del Boca: not by any czar, British monarch, or even the White House. To have a better idea of what this means, it is four times the amount that was spent, then (0.5% of the gross national product) for the Fund for the South. The Bourbon monarchs, with an annuity incomparable to that of their Piedmontese cousins, often withdrew funds from their own personal estates to finance improvements, public works, and technological innovations, so that taxes would not need to be increased).

The agriculture of the South continued to survive, despite everything, and well. It was inserted in foreign markets and thanks to its specialized products (the nickname *"Conca d'Oro,"* the "Golden Valley" after Palermo's orange orchards, was well deserved): "The agronomists and technicians of the time claimed that those orange orchards were the most profitable lands in all of Europe. They were even superior to the fruit orchards outside of Paris, the irrigated lands outside of Milan, and the vegetable farms of Naples," writes Piero Bevilacqua in his work *Breve storia dell'Italia Meridionale.* "The new commercial treaty with France, signed on January 17, 1863, favored the prized produce of the South (citrus fruits, almonds, oil, etc.), as did the constant increase of their prices."

The agricultural entrepreneurs of the South launched a campaign of serious investments in order to recuperate as much land as possible to cultivate their products and to make their current lands even more profitable than the ones already in existence. But when they were ready to gather the fruits of their labor (pardon the pun) the hatchet came down hard. In 1887, the treaty with France was broken, in order to favor the industries of the North, and provoked "reactions that culminated in a customs war with a notable decrease in the exchanges between the two countries. Consequently, misery ran rampant in those regions of Italy that traded primarily with France," writes Luigi del Rosa in *La rivoluzione industriale in Italia.* From one day to the next, Puglia (which was the first to grasp this opportunity and to make the most out of it) went from being in its most florid moment of its history to facing famine. Water became more precious than wine: there was little of the former and much of the latter (which could no longer be sold). There are stories that speak of even exchanges between buckets of water and buckets of wine. The South lost its richest foreign market and was then obliged to pay for more expensive products from the North, which were of even more inferior quality than the foreign products.

The state had deposited great sums of money into its coffers from the South, to whom they had sold state lands that had been repossessed from the centuries-old practice of communal use (where the entire community could use the lands for farming: a buffer against famine and misery) and from the clergy. Those who did not want to take any risks placed their money in the banks. But the commercial war with France entailed the withdrawal of capital from the Italian Discount Bank of Turin, which was already in trouble due to its building ventures. The crisis was kept at bay for a while, but the market eventually collapsed. The collapse of the banks cost a fortune. It was the Parmalat Scandal of its time. It primarily damaged the South because the four hundred thousand creditors of the Italian Discount Bank of Turin were located largely in the South.

"The 'misery' of the South was historically 'inexplicable' by the masses of the North," wrote Antonio Gramsci. "They did not understand that the Unification did not occur on the basis of equality, but on one of hegemony of the North on the South" and that "its economic and industrial growth was directly proportional to the impoverishment of the economy and agriculture of the South."

"The hard-earned savings of the South were extracted by the State through taxes, public revenue, or Treasury bonds, in order to benefit the North," according to Luigi Sturzo. "For many reasons, (the consolidation of debts, sale of public assets, privileges given to businesses) the South's wealth, which could have been the heart of its economic transformation, went immediately to the North," adds Nitti. "When these funds reached the North, an industrial transformation was possible. The protectionist movement took care of the rest. (...) It happened that the origin of the prosperity of certain regions was not perceived to be due to the customs, finance, or politics of the region but rather from an ethnic superiority that never existed. It also happened that those who gave the most appeared to be exploiters."

Already at that time they tried to pass off the gap between the North and the South not as the result of robbery and discrimination, but as a "historical" fact. They also tried to convince everyone that there was no remedy. Gaetano Salvemini once replied to a colleague, the Milanese Socialist Filippo Turati, that "In 1860, we Southerners were ruined in the name of the Unification. In 1887, we were ruined for the sake of industry. The last thing we need is to be ruined in the name of "history"! (We would subsequently be ruined for the sake of war, in the name of Fascism, in the wheat battle, in the name of the postwar reconstruction efforts, and in the name of the industrial revolution. Now they want to ruin us for the sake of Federalism. By now it is not the "ruining" that disturbs us, but rather the monotony.)

The South already had few infrastructures at the dawn of the Unification, especially roads (even if in the last few years dozens of them were built to make up for the delay) and railways (those that the Bourbons began building from Naples to Puglia, in 1855, were stopped with the invaders in 1860, despite the fact that they were already far along). The frugality with which the Italian government (which has long been in the hands of the Northerners) invests in the South is in direct opposition to the generosity that was shown to the North. This only serves to widen the gap. In this manner, the "agglomeration effect" is set into motion: new industries form only where there happen to be others. This is especially true when it is the government that promotes this phenomenon.

(Would you mind imagining yourselves as Southerners, if you are not? I am, and I sincerely hope that Calderoli keeps his distance from me in these moments.)

This discrimination is such that an entirely new branch of economical, historical, and social study has emerged with the name "Southernism." Perhaps it is by chance (do you really believe this to be so?) but its experts are almost always the most highly qualified individuals (in terms of vast knowledge and intellectual honesty) from both the North and the South. This extremely high level of moral and scientific quality of the Southerners is here to stay. Many of the most gifted individuals share the passion against the injustice to which the South was subjected as well as for the research aimed at realigning the South, not only economically, with that Italian social fabric that conquest and robberies had torn. Gunnar Myrdal, a Swedish economist, speaks of "Italy's failure towards its South: a solemn, undeniable, immense failure that should prompt a large scale examination of conscience on the part of all honest Italians."

Piero Bevilacqua states that "there does not exist in Italy (and perhaps not even in Europe) such a movement in favor of certain regions" to *Southernism*, intended as "a form of commitment on a personal, political, or intellectual level that lasts for a lifetime." This fervor on the part of Southerners, in debt to honesty, and those gifted Northerners that chose to know, allowed them to understand the situation. They did not turn away (Franchetti, Sonnino, Zanotti-Bianco, Isnardi, Azimonti, Rossi Doria, Saraceno, Ceriani Sebregondi…). It is only by the example of the first few of those men, and Giustino Fortunato, that, after a generation, an extraordinary "group of men " emerged from the South "who were tied to their country by their hearts and not merely their age, could finally speak as lawyers and address the pain and aspirations of their native lands" (Friedrich Vochting. Oh, if only the Italians loved Italy as much as the Germans do!).

Finally, after half a century, with the special laws passed from 1904-1906, a tax decrease was obtained for the South. This is something that we see still to this day: special laws are passed so that we can be treated "almost" like the others! The first series of special interventions for the South (first in Basilicata, then Naples, then Calabria, and finally for the rest of the South) were launched, with one tiny defect: the field of action was broadened, not only geographically, but also according to sector (from the streets to the aqueducts, all the way through to the decontamination of malaria-stricken lands). This however, did not entail an increase in funds. So to restore the hovels "where hundreds of millions of lira would not have been sufficient, they felt it appropriate to allot a few hundred thousand lira, as if it were an annotation. These would not even be sufficient to cover the costs to survey the lands and sectors" (Vochting).

This may be true, but at least there is now the existence of an intention to repair the situation. This was the reality between the end of the 1800s and the beginning of the 1900s: the South was no longer viewed as a "piggy" bank from which to draw money through the use of weapons and unfair legislation. It was viewed as a part of the country that had been robbed of its wealth and that, for the justice and convenience of all, should be restored. Many great works were accomplished thanks to this new way of thinking, including the great aqueduct of Puglia. It is the largest in the world and for the first time in the history of the region, the water situation is no longer similar to that of the North African desert.

This extra attention was perceived by the South. The state decided to move (and occasionally it still does) "with and for" and no longer "against" the South. The Southern entrepreneurs trusted in this change and continued to do their jobs (with fierceness, even if it was the fierceness of the time). The accumulation of private capital increased and sped up. The end of the "Issue of the South" was never so close to being resolved than it was in the decade prior to the World Wars.

But the War came along and everything stopped: the remaining unclaimed lands were to be freed (They had offered these to us for free, in exchange for our non-belligerence, but peace does not mean business. War does.). We were in the glorious years of 1915-1918. The Piave river would "whisper" and everyone in the country was called to play their parts: the Southerners were destined to die in the trenches while the rest of Italy was destined to cash in on the war profits. When the sums are tallied, it would be discovered that the South contributed the most blood and deposited 7.4 percent of the expenses for supplying the armed forces. The North and the Center would be reimbursed for 92.6 percent of their expenses with the state paying ridiculous "war" prices. The State offered advances and tax money to create new systems (electricity etc.), to modernize businesses, to create new businesses, all tax exempt.... Already prior to the war, two thirds of all of the funds allotted to the military were spent in the Po River Valley and practically all of the supplies for the Navy were assigned to Liguria (numerous larger and more modern shipyards were located in the Campania region, but Unified Italy did not see them. They proceeded to shut their doors, one after the other).

Once all of the fun was over, the social and economic crisis overwhelmed the industries and the banks. What was the solution? The troubles of the businesses were unloaded onto the banks. In 1933, the "*Iri*" was created: the Institute for Industrial Reconstruction. With money from all over the country, the *Iri* acquired all of the businesses shares, and not at their already low value, but at a price that allowed the holding banks to re-establish themselves. Then (always with public funds) businesses were restored and "private businessmen were given back several of their restored businesses" (De Rosa). The state that had abolished any form of assistance to businesses, which were originally stated in the laws of the Kingdom of the Two Sicilies (known as the famously efficient Institute of Encouragement) and condemned an entire economic system to regression and extinction, when dealing with the North, treated them with generosity. It then found itself directly controlling 75% of the nation's cast iron industry, 45% of the unrefined steel industry, and the vast majority of Italy's building sites etc." (*La rivoluzione industriale in Italia*). May I say, that in those circumstances, anyone can be efficient. Yet imagine who objects to all of this. Milan protests "against financial pressures that it deems excessive," states Meriggi in *Breve storia dell'Italia settentrionale*. "The city reaches the point where it begins to refer to itself as the 'State of Milan' to protest against the State's spending towards the military and the taxes." Follow their reasoning: they already received the benefits and in this manner they offered a service to the State, so they couldn't pay taxes too! "The new industrial Milan," continues Meriggi, "looked at the state trustfully, but also with impatience every time they had to turn to it to receive any benefits, privileges, or protection. The cotton, iron and steel manufacturers knew this well." To summarize: Milan only wanted "the protection and profits for private businesses while the expenses should be diffused throughout the state."

"The gestation period of the Padania area's industries lasted for ninety years and meant the complete and utter destruction of the South," wrote Nicola Zitara in *La storia proibita*.

How would Bossi and Tremonti feel if things had happened in the opposite manner? Naturally, at the head of most of those businesses, institutes, and banks were Northerners (Giovanni Floris in his work *Separati in patria* tallied the results: all that was state-run and full of money or that depended on political decisions, from the railways to the highways, to energy through to the banks, rested in the hands of the Northerners, with the exception of three Romans and a Neapolitan). In the Parliament, at present, the North holds the relative majority while in the government (of "triumph" for the *Lega* party) they have absolute control. (twelve ministers from the North, of which nine are from Lombardy; four are from the Center; seven are from the South).

Don't be surprised when the state intervenes in the South's affairs, they do so to benefit the North, with few exceptions.

One of the best examples of this remains the drainage of the swamps in the province of Latina. The Fascist regime assigned the new and extremely fertile lands almost exclusively to the North. Expertise (both the North and the South were experts, judging by what was accomplished in both areas) and money were required in order to salvage the marshes and swamps. Money was what was mainly required to drain these swamps and the regime decided to invest in this mission, and the task was accomplished. Those who lived there and had contracted malaria for centuries, soon saw their potential employment taken from them by people from the North. In 1906, Minister Pantano launched a project to subcontract the improvements to be made in the South, to the North (with public funds, you understand). Decades later, Vochting would write that the North, "after having conquered the South as a colony for the sale of its industrial products, was preparing to colonize it demographically by populating the area themselves at the expense of the locals. They would take over the South's wealth in the strictest of senses and would utilize the entire community's subsidies," including the South, which would be called to co-finance its own dispossession and colonization.

To drain the swamps from 1922 to 1932, 47 million lira were spent in Basilicata (75 lira per malaria-infested hectare), 936 million lira in Reggio Emilia (781 lira per hectare), and 576 million lira in the Veneto region.

I am not sure it is worth it to ask again why the Southerners allow themselves to be treated in such a fashion. After so long, we might have an answer: out of habit.

Let us forget that the Kingdom of the Two Sicilies was the first Mediterranean country to practice specialized farming, which is incredibly profitable. While the South conducted a transfusion of biblical proportion of its public funds for the benefit of businesses in the North, the Fascist regime condemned the South to the production of wheat. This is in favor of the few landowners, who were supporters of the party. In the beginning of the 1930s, Italy was unthinkably reduced to having to import olive oil due to a scarcity of its production in the country! In this manner, "a drastic reduction" was applied not only "to the farming network in the Mediterranean, which was primarily geared for exportation, that in those years following World War I had come to be quite diffuse in the South," but also their animal husbandry, according to *La questione meridionale prima dell'intervento straordinario*.

This decision would crush the best agricultural businesses of the South. To better illustrate what abilities the South had to adapt to the market's demands, take as an example the terrible crisis that occurred in the first half of the 1800s. Puglia had become an enormous olive grove to produce lubricant for Northern Europe's machinery during the industrial revolution (especially for the British and the Flemish). In Gallipoli there was the Oil Stock Exchange with the consulates of the most important and most advanced countries in the world. Every year, when the price of the oil was determined (just like we do today for crude oil) there were already fleets of tankers ready to take the oil away while on the roads there were numerous carts with barrels ready to do the same. From one year to the next, all of this came to an abrupt end. The industries discovered that vegetable oils derived from seeds were cheaper and that mineral oils proved to be the cheapest. What would become of Puglia's olive oil, which had now been rendered useless? In 1830, "the French agronomist Pietro Ravanas applied the theory behind Pascal's vases to the press, and the hydraulic press was born," write Umberto Mairota and Cosimo Lacirignola in their work *Olivi, oli, olive*. "It was all over for the regular press." The olive-growers from Puglia "let Ravanas convince them that they should adopt farming techniques (by perfecting their pruning) that would create an ideal environment to extract oil that would be fit for human consumption. The hydraulic press did the rest. The area north of Bari became the most technologically advanced olive grove in the world." (And then they were asked to abandon everything to grow wheat?)

After the Unification, farming in the South was exposed to constant changes: first, the treaty with France; then the treaty was broken; then the sale of the Church's lands to private owners; then those who illegally occupied state-owned lands were considered usurpers; and finally the destruction of their vineyards due to parasites...: "Within a few decades, faced with threats from both the inside and the outside, the fields of the South were in a state of disarray, the woods were leveled, old crops were uprooted and then replaced, though the new crops were launched on the market only to be uprooted again with the same fury with which they had initially been planted," summarizes Andreina De Clementi, professsor of modern history at the Oriental University of Naples, in her work *Di qua e di là dall'oceano*. We are talking about vineyards, orchards, citrus orchards, and even olive groves, that require years of investments and work before they yield any profit. "*Ci voli fidi pi' chiantari nu pedi d'auliva*," recalls Leonardo Sciascia in *Occhio di Capra*: one needs faith when planting an olive tree, on the part of the fathers to give to their sons and grandsons. While the state continued to save poorly led industries in the North, the South, amidst a slalom of punitive laws and disappearing markets, burned their efforts and their savings. They lived hard lives as farm laborers: many Southerners would die begging for jobs and this would last through the years of the "economic miracle." The Fascists used their weapons of mass oppression in the South: from hostile takeovers of "red" lands, to the first assassination of a member of Parliament, not the well-known Socialist Giacomo Matteotti, but Peppino di Vagno from Conversano, South of Bari. It is the cavalry of Caradonna, from Cerignola, that would break the skulls of those who did not bend to their will (the *mazzieri* were an invention of the Pugliese, which they loaned to the Fascists): "For those who do not know us/ Oh! For Mary's sake/ we are the fascists/ of Peppino Caradonna."

The Fascist regime's order to produce wheat would deliver a very hard blow to the South, and would only serve to widen the gap, which was no longer merely an economic one. In the "two Italies," this law was most profitable to the wealthy in the North (where the income pro capita grew) and took from the poor in the South (where in those same years, from 1928-1938, the income pro capita decreased). In the meantime, projects to bring electricity to the South were also blocked, "In order to avoid affecting large businesses in the North," who were notable sponsors of Fascism. In these years, all of the regions of the South became poorer than those in the North, and for the first time, the internal inequality acquired a distinct geographical configuration, as Daniele and Malanima demonstrate.

If that wasn't enough, the tax reform raised the taxes "of those poorer rural classes," the same that were already paying the extra city taxes. The resignation of properties soon followed. "The numerous bankruptcies, that ultimately buried the remaining savings of those farmers, did the rest," according to Vochting. Now that the North had the South's nest egg, they did not want the South to lose its former landowners. So a law was passed, that affected only the Southerners, which prohibited the unauthorized transfer to other areas of the country, so that there would not be any "clandestine immigrants": of Italians in Italy! (There, now I have done something stupid: now someone from the *Lega* will want to reinstate this law and those members of the Parliament from the South will minimize the whole affair because "it would only be a way to regulate one's inalienable right of mobility.")

The Committee for Migration and Internal Colonization was established. Its task was to prevent the millions of Southerners who intended to go to the North (an exception was made for "young maidens") and to facilitate the emigration of the Northerners to the South to those lands that had been redeemed with state funds. The agricultural policies of the Fascist regime, which determined the abrupt drop in the employment rate; the halt of emigration for work (even for family reunification of Italians who were already abroad); the rigid restrictions to new immigration imposed by the United States since 1921 grew worse in 1929; France who, from 1930-31 organized special trains to send emigrants home (it is said that "after they used the power of their arms, they refused to take care of their mouths") and even paid for their tickets home (just like we are doing today with the Romanians): all of these factors left the Southerners with one direction to flee to avoid going hungry: the North. The Fascist regime tried in every way they could to discourage emigration to the North, but with poor outcomes. In 1923, the regime thought it would be a good idea to involve the excessive number of males in the population to embark upon imperialistic initiatives, where they could release their animosity usefully without endangering the established order at home. In this fashion, in Sardinia, the First Legion for Colonization was born. It guaranteed room, board, clothes, and a sixteen-lira salary. The only mission worthy of note was the one in Libya. "When the order was given to attack a rebel tribe, the Sardinian legions mutinied," according to Giacomo de Antonellis in *Il Sud durante il fascismo*. It just so happened that the announced salary of sixteen lira actually turned out to be seven. The food was also terrible. When the state refused to improve the food and the pay, the Legion disbanded. They figured if they had a choice between going hungry abroad or going hungry at home, they chose to go home.

Everything that happens today with the clandestine immigrants happened to the Italians from the South. According to Anna Treves in *Le migrazioni interne nell'Italia Fascista*: "There are too many of them" (shantytowns appeared on the outskirts of the major cities that Mussolini wanted to "ruthlessly disperse" as he stated in *"Popolo d'Italia"*: the majority of its inhabitants were from Puglia.) "They steal our jobs," an unemployed man wrote to Mussolini. He also stated that employers "favor hiring Southern Italians, first one from one town, then his friend from the same town, and all we receive is hunger and misery." Another accused the Fascist regime "After you have eaten, you believe everyone has eaten and it is easy to give assistance to those with large families, so that their children can live. We have had enough. Regards and Fascist greetings."

It was an exodus that was not recounted often, yet it was larger than the one that nearly emptied the South in the 1950s-1960s. Milan has never grown so much in so little time. While in the general indifference (and even hostility) of the country towards the South, entire areas remained deserted for the first time after many centuries. Only in 1960 did the number of "emigrants" reach the million and a half mark that was previously reached in 1937. This was embarrassing for the Fascist regime that chose to register the internal migrations as "address changes," despite the fact that many studies were published on the "Southernization" under way in the country. Since they were not able to stop this migration, they hid it: in the census of 1936, only the arrivals were registered, not their place of origin. The Southerners disappeared! This was pure genius. It was rogue genius, but genius nonetheless. Regards and Fascist greetings!

Actually, I take back the "genius" and leave the "rogue": while all of this was happening, the ad hoc Commission was busy selecting "human material to transfer" according to political and health criteria as well as whether they were prolific and competent. The selection was done on a national level and the chosen ones were only from the North. The area selected for colonization, with public funding, was in the South. What a hoax. The state-supported colonists "went in the opposite direction to that followed by the spontaneous migrations," writes Treves. "At most, the situation concerned a hundred thousand people" migrating "versus the many millions" that traveled North on the peninsula. "It was a small wave against the tide" (Dudley Kirk in *Europe's population*). The idea of helping the Southerners in their own homes instead of forcing them to flee and then offer incentives to the Northerners to take their places, funded by the state, must have appeared to be a subversive idea. Regards and Fascist greetings.

When World War II ended, Italy's industrial capacity returned to its 1884 levels. The industrial capacity of the South was subjected to serious devastation because the South had been used as the battlefield for the confrontations between the Allied Forces and the Nazis since 1943. The North managed to get by without too much damage. Furthermore, for a year, from July 1943 to May 1944 from the landing of the Allied Forces in Sicily to the penetration of the Nazi "Gustav line," two distinct monetary areas were created. "While in the South an intense inflation was under way, in the rest of Italy, that was occupied by the Germans, the prices remained relatively contained" (*La questione meridionale prima dell' intervento straordinario*). With the military advancement and the victory, prices realigned themselves, but for approximately a year, they were four to five times higher in the South, thus generating a monetary crisis only in the South. This "further weakened the economic structure and its ability to recover."

Peace brings about indemnities, and two ugly things happened (only to the South, you understand):

1.   The money from the Marshall Plan arrived in Italy in order to restore the systems of productivity that had been destroyed during the conflict. But the South's system (35% of its industrial factories had been destroyed, while over 50% of its power plants were lost as opposed to 12% in the North) was too badly damaged: the money would be better used by the North. For this same reason the billions that were destined to rebuild the devastated Southern territory ended up in the Center and the North. We

reach the paradox that while the most damage was done in the South, the funds go to the North. This was also valid for the two hundred million dollars that the Anglo-Americans deposited in Italy for war damages (indemnities "were split in an inversely proportionate manner" according to Vochting) and for the ten billion per month that the Institute for Industrial Reconstruction (IRI) took from public funds.

2. Is that enough? It is not. "While industries in the Center and the North opened themselves to international competition after having been protected for such a long time, during which they had a chance to consolidate their positions, the South was taken by the new economic foreign policy. It was no longer protectionist, but more of a free enterprise system, in its initial phase or at least in the way it was set up. The collision could not have been more dramatic and discouraging," writes De Rosa. Let me summarize: in the Kingdom of the Two Sicilies, there was a sort of Ministry for Participation of the State (the Institute of Encouragement) in order to support economic and industrial growth. With the Unification of Italy, this protection was abolished in the name of free enterprise, only to be reinstated a few years later. This time, it only benefitted the industries of the North in similar ways but with incomparable proportions. Then it was reconverted to liberalism again when the Northern system of productivity was capable of standing on its own and that of the South was out of the race (even still, in 1950, Germany requested that the customs tax be reduced on several of its imported goods, especially machinery and cars, by threatening to drastically reduce the importation of Italy's agricultural products. At the expense of the work of the South, the industries of the North continued to be favored).

The result of these decisions can be translated into two numbers: in 1860, the year of the invasion, the economy was worth 100, in 1947, it was worth 60. Thanks, Italy! Twenty years of Northern dictatorship had accelerated the marginalization of the South. The pro capita income of the Campania region, once one of the richest lands in all of Italy, was now slightly more than half of the national level. In other areas of the South the situation was even worse: the pro capita income was equal to one third of the national level.

The creation of the South's inferiority status was built with the use of massacres, plundering, and unfair laws. It was the biggest business affair for the North, who did not stop at merely devouring the South, but nibbled on everything, even the crumbs. Few examples depict this notion better than the Parliamentary debate in 1912 regarding the "criminal" law on emigration, which made a distinction between those who emigrated "out of misery" and those who emigrated "in search of better luck." When the South's armed resistance proved to be useless, and the Southerners abandoned their lands en masse, newly United Italy referred to them as delinquents and traitors. It placed an atrociously high per capita tax on those who "emigrated out of misery" (emigration from the South overseas). With the money received from that tax, the state paid for the expenses of those Northern emigrants (especially ice cream makers) that went to work for part of the year in Switzerland. After a few years, the Parliament determined that there was an "error" in the law passed that allowed for the poor to finance the wealthy. Girardini, a representative from the Udine region, recognized this mistake, but to "fix" it would be another "mistake." So, thanks to the good fortune of the electors, the law remained, with their sincere regrets, untouched. His colleague, Basilini from Como, agreed with him: it was an injustice but for the sake of "brotherhood and national solidarity" (of the less towards the more) it was no longer the time to make "distinctions." Hurrah for Italy, we are all brothers! (Cain and Abel were also brothers). Salvemini wickedly remarked that the only distinction that remained was that where "one group paid and the other profited" (*Movimento socialista e questione meridionale*). Finally, the words of the Sicilian, Pantano, were heard. But to the great misfortune of the electors he said that there was no need to "diffuse egotistical feelings amongst the proletariat": in other words the aspiration of the desperate to not continue to finance those who were financially better off than they were. For the Minister San Giuliano, the debate was "tiresome." For the representative Morando the discus-

Pino Aprile

sion "must end." So it ended. The abuse, however, did not. The miserable people in the South continued to finance the Northerners "in search of better luck" (now try to imagine the debate if the situation were reversed).

The real gold mine was the money that was supplied by the emigrants, who actually saved the state budget. In 1938, a Parliamentary investigation revealed that, of those that were traceable, four hundred and fifty million lira had entered Italy per year. Over 70% of that amount was from the Southerners. According to another subsequent investigation, after the war, that sum was confirmed, but it was in dollars (four hundred and nine million dollars). While the amounts that were not traceable (sent by mail or carried by hand) were twice the "officially" declared amounts. A stream of money that, was born from the South's affliction, was drained from the banks and sent to the North.

The Italy that emerged from the destruction of the Second World War believed that it would be useful not to change their methods due to their profitability. I do not remember where I read that Giuseppe Di Vittorio, a man of enormous strength who was a hardcore defender of the labor unions, left a meeting on the reconstruction of the country in tears. The president of the *Confindustria* (the Italian Manufacturer's Association) Costa, opposed every idea that involved moving industries to the South: ("It is absurd (…) it is more convenient to transfer labor towards the North." The economic importance of the North was enough to allow it to express itself politically, govern the state's money and work orders. If there were any tears cried, they were cried by those millions of Southerners who were obliged to uproot themselves because no one wanted to bring the factories where the laborers were. Di Vittorio, a former laborer from Cerignola, knew what tragedy was about to start again. First Torino took the lands of the South, then it took the Southerners.

Another five million people left. More or less the same amount as during the Fascist regime; more or less the same as before the other World War, when only the "countable" were accounted for (just as many were probably clandestine). Numbers, numbers,

numbers.... Try to imagine faces, stories, and loves lost. Try to imagine their fear, humiliation, rage, and hope. Have you read about the tragedy between the Bulgarians and the Macedonians, who had to leave their lands because of the war? They were two hundred thousand. How about the tragedy of the Germans who had to abandon their lands because they had become Polish territory? They were seven hundred thousand. And the tragedy of the Greeks that had to flee Asia Minor? There were a million of them. For them, the war meant the delineation of a new geography that rendered them incompatible with their land. For the Southerners it determined peace. The enemy had the same flag and boundaries and spoke the same language as they did. To better understand the numbers, I give you these examples: it was as though, in one century, Sicily, Puglia, Basilicata, and Molise had been emptied 3 or 4 times. Three or four times in one hundred years!

The Italian Manufacturer's Association "did not want to create competition with private industries in the recruitment of laborers." Therefore, public employees were paid less in the South. (Less, less: the South is the land of "less." It seems as though the North does not have its own identity if it is not compared with that of a "lesser" South. One can sense the anxiety of those who need to put someone else down in order to feel superior themselves. Those who are superior, simply are. They do not seek to penalize others through unjust laws and privileges in order to artificially create an imbalance, without which they would fear confrontation.)

"The ruthless resistance of the Northern industrialists to the industrialization of the South," states Manlio Rossi Doria in *Scritti sul Mezzogiorno*, "lasted until 1962" (and after the period of the State's investments in the South, things became much worse than they were before). The North's fear of an industrialized South prompted it to block any initiative that would improve the infrastructures appropriate to sustain a lasting development in the South. Subsidies are better than roads and airports. In this fashion, however, those same capitals of the North, when they needed to expand to new locations, were obliged to migrate out of Italy, thus depriving themselves of the advantages they could have by operating on their own soil and depriving the country of a portion of their economic "strength."

The North's refusal to allow a South that was "equal" to it allowed for a paradox: we are "the country that contemporaneously exports labor (in recent years these were mostly composed of young people, many with college degrees) and capital that could be better invested "in those regions from which the emigrants left," according to *L'emigrazione italiana negli anni '70.*

I cannot be cold and calculating when I narrate these things. This is not just Italy's history. It is the history of my family. I counted the many faces that disappeared around me when I was a child. The first time I interrupted my writing of this book, typewriters were still in use. I broke mine with my fist.

People have a value, in economic terms, and they produce. Areas subject to immigration become wealthier because they receive workers that have already been trained and are capable of producing. The cost of their training is paid for by the regions they abandoned, but they benefit the regions where they decide to settle. Professor Antonio Mastrodonato, from the University of Bari, in his book *I capitali umani*, (emigrants are often referred to as this, "Human Capital"), calculated the amount of wealth acquired in the Center and the North due to the 5.1 million Southerners who moved there from 1952 to 1981. With the official statistics of the cost of living and by applying (as Manlio Rossi Doria did as well) "the methods of calculation normally used for work animals, to the emigrants" he obtained the "human capital" that the South ceded to the North. In those thirty years, it came to 547,000 billion lira, according to prices in 1986. We can compare this amount to the amount that was given to the Fund for the South in the same thirty year period (102,800 billion lira) and "notice that it is less than one fifth of the loss" to which the South had been subjected to through emigration.

While many emigrated, others chose to work the fields in spite of their owners (who became such, at times, by usurping the lands). This was the season of massacres. The laborers were shot at by the landowners, the *carabinieri*, the riot police (armed tanks were actually used), and the bandits hired by all the aforementioned groups. The Southerners fell by the dozens in Melissa, Montescaglioso, Andria, Corato, Eboli, Portella della Ginestra.... In two years more than ten thousand Southerners had been arrested (Giuseppe Gramegna, *Braccianti e popolo in Puglia*). The landowners were so arrogant that Paolo Cinanni in his work *Lotte per la terra nel Mezzogiorno: 1943-1953*, quotes the words of Tommaso Campanella, spoken a few centuries ago: "They stole honor, wealth, and blood or became 'impromptu' husbands, and mocked all the wretched people." When agricultural reform laws were passed, those assets were dispossessed and indemnified. Baron Berlingieri was dispossessed of lands that were not even his, which were delineated by markers stating that the land was pro-perty of the state!

The South was a place from which to flee. "Learn a language and leave," were the words of the honest President Alcide de Gasperi, who had nothing else to give and nothing else to say. Those millions of brothers (that is how the national anthem refers to them?) that made the country rich through their own misery were left to fend for themselves, in their moment of need and suffering. They were not given a special train, a discount on their ticket. A system of reception was put in place to accommodate ten percent of the nation's population that emptied part of the country only to clog another part. They were alone, mistreated, and mocked. "Italy has been one of the few countries in Western Europe to carry out the most important phase of its industrialization in the 1950s and 1960s without having to resort to external labor forces" observed Gerardo Chiaromonte and Giuseppe Galasso in their work *L'Italia dimezzata*. France had the Algerians and the Moroccans. Germany had the Turks and the Italians. The Southern Italians were treated as foreigners in their own home. Count Rossi of Montelera gave an "extremely fun" speech at the Rotary Club to support the notion that the Southerners should take courses in their native towns before leaving, with the use of the Funds for the South, to learn how to wash themselves, learn how to behave with young ladies, and to learn how to speak the dialect of Turin. (Why aren't you laughing?) What an insult to the cities of Piero Gobetti, Primo Levi, and Norberto Bobbio!

Impartiality would oblige them to register the evident improvement with respect to the migrations prior to the First World War. Perhaps it was because they no longer emigrated that this time no tax was imposed upon them. The law that prevented internal migration was even abolished in 1961 (to mark the end of the Fascist regime). The South would offer its eternal gratitude towards the state, but up until that point, the law that forced them to work in secret in their own country "was exploited in the large factories in the North" according to *L'emigrazione italiana dall'Unità alla seconda guerra mondiale*, "as a threat in response to insubordination of the new working class of immigrants." Would you please put yourselves in the shoes of the Southerners for a moment?

While in the South, the Fund for the South was being used to pay for all of the things that had already been accomplished in the Center and the North, and that they continued to accomplish with their funds (build schools, improve infrastructures, build power plants, roads and aqueducts) many people continued to leave the South. They landed in Germany and Switzerland along with their "clandestine" children, whom they hid in their homes. They were educated in silence, so that their cries would not betray their illegal presence to the Swiss authorities (or even just their neighbors). If they happened to rejoice, they had to do so silently.

People left even the sub-Apennine area of the Daunian mountain chain, where the Puglian plains become populated with hills. They settled in the bitter climate near Irpinia. I will speak of an anecdote that is not well known (at least not in Italy: the national television channels and newspapers have ignored it, while Reuters and the BBC sent news crews to speak of this to the world). I speak of this event because it is one of the anecdotes that best explains the rapport between the North's economy and the lack of initiative on the part of the South's politics, to oppress the Southerners and to deprive them of their resources.

The sub-Apennine area of the Daunian mountain chain is a beautiful place. The area is full of rounded, sensual hills in the

East. In the northeast, on clear days, the Gargano Promontory stands tall and is the same color blue as the sky. The plains seem to return to what they were originally: an enormous lagoon with low-lying fog. Southwest, one can see the massive Mount Vulture. Many great wines and great minds hailed from this area. The remains of the great forest that once covered the entire area explain why Frederic II came to hunt here and they explain his studies on falcons (many birds of prey fly overhead). There are dialects here that are quite unexpected: the musical Franco-Provençal dialect was the language of the troubadours, who sang the *chanson des gentes*.

Here, in the 1960s, the people believed the illusion that an economic miracle would be possible without having to emigrate: the largest natural gas deposit in Italy, and possibly in all of Europe, was discovered here. It came to about forty billion cubic meters of methane gas. For that area, which was beautiful, but in a state of depression, it could have meant jobs, refineries, professional institutions, a culture of industrialization, and industrialization of agriculture with low-cost energy. God had smiled upon the poor people of the area. The local people greeted the representative of the SNIA-Viscosa, the engineer Casini, with more flowers than they do in Hawaii. But they came to understand that something was not right, perhaps the State did not think like God. The people of Candela, Ascoli Satriano, Deliceto, Accadia, Castelluccio dei Sauri, Rocchetta Sant'Antonio began a battle that would last for years, would involve everyone, with such methods of self-organization that would raise interest of foreign observers, disorientation on the part of political parties, and the reaction of the state. Thirty thousand people, including senior citizens, men, women, and children, marched on the capital of the province. They feared that their methane would end up like the bauxite from Gargano, which litters the area with nothing but waste and unemployment. It only offers the benefits of jobs and wealth to the Port of Marghera in the North. Mario Giorgio, in his book *La sconfitta del Subappennino Dauno*, recounts this historical episode almost day by day as it unfolded. I will tell you how it ended: ENI

(Italy's multinational oil and gas company) did whatever it pleased. It used the State's and locally "assembled" political parties in Rome, as well as on location, to get its way. One of its executives actually launched his political career from this affair. The Daunians were bent by false promises, the cooperation of some of their local leaders, the request for hundreds of millions of lira in "lost wages," threats, and brutal police interventions. This resulted in hundreds of people being sued, many people being arrested, and many expatriations being denied to emigrants. Many diplomats were placed under investigation and risked to be excluded from the possibility to advance their careers.

ENI said that the industries of the North needed the natural gas. So that is where it went. That is also where the Daunians were forced to go. A pardon law was passed to erase the "crimes" committed by the nonviolent protests. Order returned to the Sub-Apennine area: the resources were stolen and redirected elsewhere, the people were oppressed and emigration became the only solution for survival. Then, there was a telegram: "Due to the intervention on the part of the Honorable Romita, the Undersecretary of the Ministry for Internal Affairs, twenty million lira are issued as of today to the prefect of Foggia as aid for the unemployed in the towns affected by the methane gas affair": they are not compensated with jobs, but with unemployment and with charity, this way, in the future, the methane gas thieves have the right to shout, "We don't want to work to support those people in the South!"

The Italian economic system was built upon the status of inferiority of one part of the country with respect to the other: the South was deprived of its wealth and its most qualified people but was assisted as long as it did not produce anything. The North could not allow for internal competition: a war of annexation was fought to prevent this from happening. In an *a posteriori* analysis, the Fund for the South and the agricultural reform laws passed in the South "expressed a project that aimed not to resolve, but to establish a dual economy in the country," according to Domenico Novacco in his work *La questione meridionale ieri e oggi*, "and to define the roles of the North and the South: an industrialized North with a propulsive function and a South that exports low-cost laborers, but endowed with an *in loco* agricultural economy that is more efficient and with a more consistent income to consent the North to expand their markets here and increase the sale of their products."

The South was essentially a geographical area that was created to place the North's goods and to supply them with a sufficient workforce as well as clients. It is the "disabled" liberty that is granted to a colony: they are called to consume according to the will of others while they are disabled from doing anything for themselves and, heaven forbid, from competing. In a unified state, however, money needs to be spent in the South. At the very least so that these funds can return to the North. For example, one can analyze where the funds for the improvement of the South's infrastructures went: economists discovered that one third of the amount went to the North for the acquisition of materials and salaries, while two thirds were spent for goods produced in the Center and the North. The South supplied the swamps only because those could not be transported. The other elements needed to be sent from the North. The system would be perfected: to create industries in the South, the State gives money to the North, who deposits the funds before disappearing. The South complains and the state "becomes filled with indignation, and throws in the towel, with great dignity" (I stole this quote from Fabrizio De Andrè).

Not even the law passed in 1957 is respected. It was passed to encourage the industrialization of the South and obliges public businesses to invest 40% of their total investments and 60% of their new ones. This continues until the "oil crisis of 1973 marked a division in the politics behind the assistance given to the South," writes Barbagallo in *La modernità squilibrata del Mezzogiorno d'Italia.* "The public funds would no longer be given to bolster industries, which are generally more productive, but will become more charitable in nature, and would be aimed at supporting the incomes of the population" because the State (Who would offer these funds otherwise? Those directly interested?) needed to support "the renovation of the industries in the North."

This actually works: taxes are low, evasion is tolerated and actually encouraged. The North gets to keep its money. The State transfers funds to the South by increasing public debt, where the Center and the North gain 90% of the interests. On the surface, everyone wins: the South lives better than it would be able to otherwise (as long as it agrees to remain "behind"); the more the deficit grows, the more the North profits, because it was the creditor of the State and producer of the goods that the South would otherwise be unable to afford.

Even politics manages to profit from this situation. Politicians "buy" votes in the South by showing that they intended to give (subsidies, disability pensions etc.) and in the North by actually giving things, even through the South, and by supporting the businesses there.

In the scheme of the Italian economy, the South confirms its position as a cushion: money bounces from here. For the reconstruction after the earthquake in 1980 in Irpinia and Basilicata, the state offered an advancement "of public funds of up to 50% of the expense (in other words, thousands of billions of lira)," writes Giovanni Russo in his work *Baroni e contadini*, "to those same businesses that would be accused of corruption by Antonio Di Pietro in the Milan bribery scandal: *Grandi Lavori*, Pizzarotti, Cogefar, Lodigiani, Recchi, Maltauro, Golani, Vianini, and Zanussi."

But while the economy continued to grow, this mechanism appeared to be sustainable. We only needed to pretend that we did not know that we were spending the money of our children and grandchildren (that's what a deficit actually is).

Towards the end of the Eighties, the system began to collapse. In the South, for every 100 lira produced, the state spent 73 (46 in the North), preferably in salaries and disability pensions (those senior pensions, the best ones, go for ninety percent in the Center and the North). "This rapport has no equivalent in any other country or area, aside from the Lander areas in the former communist Germany in the years immediately following the reunification," write Giorgio Bodo and Gianfranco Viesti in *La grande svolta*.

A vicious cycle begins that brings the increase of taxes, debt control in order to adhere to the unified European currency, shrinking incomes, and finally the world crisis. This game is no longer convenient. And, after having prevented it from being and from doing, the South is reproached for not having been and not having done anything. In the midst of the worst part of the crisis after the war, the North (as usual) aimed to save itself at the expense of the poorest part of the country. The first thing that a politician needs is an enemy, and the North finds one in its home: the South. They indulge their animal instincts through the *Lega* party, which has been condemned more times by the European Committee against Racism and Intolerance, ("The racist activities and the propaganda that certain members of the *Lega* party promote [...] are indicative of the lack of control on the part of the Italian State.") Umberto Bossi, the head of the *Lega* party, is the quintessential example of the North's protest against the do-nothing South: he has never worked a day in his life, he has been supported by his parents and then by his first wife (who later discovered, after a year and a half of marriage, that her husband did not go to work every day at the hospital, as he said, and that he was not a doctor. In fact, he did not even possess a degree, despite holding three parties to celebrate this event over the course of the years). He was then supported by his second wife (a Southerner, just in case any of you appreciate metaphors) and then by the Italian people. This is the man who proposes to give a lesson to millions of Southerners (and the clandestine immigrants) that give their lives and blood for bread and "*chi vrazza svacantanu a panza da terra*," who with their arms empty the belly of the land, according to the poet Ignazio Buttitta from Bagheria.

Why do the Southerners tolerate all of this? Maybe they no longer know who they were. They believe that this has always been their situation, that "historically" our land has always been a land of emigration (this is not true), and that we were always poorer and less active than the North (this is also not true).... But who believes that this is not true?

"The conflict is not a political one, it is a geographical one," according to one of the technicians who worked to define the criteria and the laws for financial federalism by participating to the meetings between the government and the regions. "The *Lega* party, in those meetings between all of the delegations in question, was often overlooked in lieu of the proposals of Mercedes Bresso, President of the Piedmont region, who represented the center-left. The basis of the proposals was the federalist project presented by Lombardy, by the Catholic, Formigoni. It was a true act of secession and a monument to egotism. However, the majority of the representatives from the South had approved it, without actually reading it, I fear." That project would move a monstrous amount of resources towards those regions and, in particular, to the wealthiest of those regions.

In order to have a better idea of what would be left of the state and of the equality amongst the citizens, one must take into consideration that "in the beginning of the Nineties," according to Robert D. Putnam, professor at Harvard University, in his work *La tradizione civica nelle regioni italiane*, "the regional governments were spending a tenth of Italy's gross national product, an amount that is just slightly inferior to that allotted to all fifty American states." For the worst parts of the North (who was unfortunately victorious) Italy is only of value if there is something to be gained from it. Otherwise, they could do without it and make off with the funds. From recession to secession.

Egotism, however, hides some insidious traps. Those who believe that they would be able to swindle the South with the federalist laws (the *Lega* and Formigoni deny this because they are liars) don't ask themselves "what would the weight of Lombardy or the Veneto regions be when placed before the likes of united Germany and united France," asks Agazio Loiero in his work *Se il Nord*. While the idea that federalism would put an end to the "scandal" of an assisted South and the North as a forced donator, it does not take into consideration that "the North includes the four Italian regions (Piedmont, Lombardy, Veneto, Emilia-Romagna) that in the rapport between the taxes paid and the respective public utilities, these regions give more than they receive. However, it also includes," according to Meriggi in *Breve storia dell'Italia settentrionale*, "another four regions (Liguria, Valle d'Aosta, Trentino, and Friuli-Venezia-Giulia) that interpret the opposite role: they are the ones who receive assistance."

There are even more sophisticated traps than those mentioned. Professor Federico Pirro of the University of Bari, in a large volume entitled *Grane industria e Mezzogiorno 1996-2007*, which he wrote with Angelo Guarini, director of Brindisi's branch of the *Confindustria* (the local Manufacturers Association) and with the preface written by Luca Cordero di Montezemolo, counted 904 industries with 500 employees or above, largely part of multinational companies with factories all over the South. In many instances, the legal headquarters of these companies is in the North or even abroad. The largest iron metallurgy plant in Europe (which also happens to be the largest Italian factory based on the number of its employees) is located in Taranto. This is also where one of the largest cement factories is located, which uses blast-furnace slag. The military's Arsenal is located here, along with one of the seven plants that refine, in the South, half of the crude oil that is refined in Italy. Nearby, Basilicata happens to have the richest non-marine oil wells in Europe and the number one factory in Italy (by number of employees) for the production of blades for windmills used in the production of wind power. Two of the world's most important pharmaceutical companies have their factories located between Bari and Brindisi. Two imposing factories that belong to the Alenia company (Italy's cutting-edge aerospace company) are located in Foggia and Grottaglie. In Brindisi, there is an important aeronautic coalition that comprises three large factories; while in Atessa, Melfi, Pomigliano d'Arco, and Termini Imerese (which is currently being dismantled), Fiat produces more than half of the cars that it builds in Italy, including a good part of its lightweight commercial vehicles. Fiat also has other factories that produce parts as well as contribute to the design and engineering aspects of the company including the assemblage of buses and heavier machinery. These are located in Sulmona, Naples, Termolu, Foggia, Avellino (two factories are located here), Bari, and Lecce. One of the vastest areas in the country dedicated to the assemblage of auto parts (both national and foreign) is located in Bari. Brindisi is home to the most powerful thermo-electric power plant that runs on "clean coal" in all of Italy, plus two other minor plants as well. The large shop that the railways of the Center and the North (erroneously considered property of the State) used to carry out routine maintenance on their rolling stock is located in Foggia.... I will stop here.

Can you imagine the turnover, in billions of euros, that this productive force has?

With federalism, the state would give back to the regions on the basis of the wealth produced and the taxes paid. In the North and the South many believe that the turnover obtained in the South by Northern companies, or with their legal headquarters based in the North, the regional funds would be replenished by the State-granted subsidies. This was another devious transaction, however, on the North's part, and the umpteenth injustice for the South. The South is burdened with pollution, dioxin poisons, and smoke while the money from the taxes, that could be used to combat those things and to repair the territory from the damage incurred, ends up in the North. These funds further help the North by increasing the regions' level of production, thereby entitling them to even more of the State's money.

It is important to remember, explains Professor Pirro, that businesses pay the Ici, Tarsu, Iva, Irap, and Ires taxes in addition to contributing to the pension fund. The first two taxes are paid to the towns and cities, in proportion to the size of the factories and the waste produced. The third tax is paid to the State, which allows for the deductibility of the Iva tax for purchases. The fourth tax is paid to the regions where the factories are located and is based on the number of employees. The fifth tax is also paid to the State and is calculated according to profit. None of the taxes are paid directly to the region where the business, that has its factories in the South, has its legal headquarters. Only the Ires tax could have this potential, but only in the instance where the business declares gains and not losses. Professor Pirro has told me that there are already discussions being held at the Parliamentary level addressing the possibility that part of the Ires tax could remain in the region where the factories that generate the profit are located. By this same reasoning, one could imagine the birth of businesses that use the South as the location of their legal headquarters, though still controlled by the larger businesses in the North or elsewhere in the world. According to Professor Pirro, this could "hold many positive surprises in store for the South": that part of the Ires tax could be given back to the regions that produce electricity, refine crude oil, forge steel, and build cars.

Imagine the disappointed and embarrassed faces of the Northerners when this notion is explained to them. The trouble is that while things appear to be simple, they rarely are. The mere utterance of this issue opens the door to endless complications. One evening, I embarked upon a similar discussion with Mario Cervi. To my umpteenth objection, he rebutted, "You (us, Southerners) are too good at complicating things." To which I replied, "Do you intend to say that it is our fault if they are not as easy as you (Northerners) would like them to be?" "There, you see?" Cervi replied. So we both agreed: it was better to focus on our dish of spaghetti with Tropea onions at the *Sorrisi e baci* restaurant. They are the best in Milan, maybe even better than you could find in Tropea.

"The South has been abandoned by the development policies in the moment it needs them the most," write Bodo and Viesti in *La grande svolta*. The Fund for the South was done away with in 1992. It was easily accused of wastefulness, gifts as well as assigning jobs that inexplicably cost double or triple what they were actually worth. This is similar to the kilometers of subways in Milan just prior to the *Tangentopoli* Bribery Scandal, or that of the High Speed Train (TAV) after the same scandal. The Bologna-Florence portion of the highway cost 68 million euros per kilometer due to the mountains. The Rome-Naples portion, though it cost less, still cost 24 million euros per kilometer. Even though the stretch of land that accommodates the Turin-Novara portion of the highway lies entirely on flat plains, it cost 54 million euros per kilometer: God and perhaps someone else knows why (This means that over one hundred billion lira was spent for a kilometer of railway on flat land. I repeat, over one hundred billion lira were spent for a kilometer of railway with NO tunnels). The French manage with 10 million euros per kilometer, while the Spanish manage with 9. Can you even imagine what the cost would be to build a stretch of highway between Matera and Foggia, should they decide to establish a train to reach Matera one day?

Still today there is an uproar when one mentions the "thousands of billions" (one hundred and forty billion euro) that went to the Fund for the South over the course of forty years. That amount constituted 0.5% of the gross national product. Some calculations place the amount at 0.7% Wow! Is that a great deal? It is almost nothing: it is between one hundred and fiftieth and one two hundredth of the annual wealth of Italy. That comes to 3.5 billion euros per year, which is more or less the amount "the yield of the local property tax on the first home that was abolished by Berlusconi's administration" (*La Stampa*, 23 August 2009). It was abolished in all of Italy, only for first homes purchased that happened to be luxury homes (for the other types of homes it had already been removed). These funds were subtracted from the improvement of the roads and ports of Calabria and Sicily. The Fund for the South was a scandal, but for the opposite reasons.

After the Fund was suppressed, 0.8% of the gross national product was spent to improve the South: more, not less. Does this mean something? Yes: only in the last years of the Fund's activity was an investigation conducted to determine if the funds were effectively used in addition to the State's normal subsidies. The answer was no. Other things were financed, in the rest of Italy, by ordinary means, with those funds. Listen to what they built in the South with the thousands upon thousands upon thousands of billions in the Funds for the South from 1950 to 1992: eighteen thousand kilometers worth of roads, twenty-three thousand kilometers of aqueducts (it was sufficient to guarantee that water reached the plains of the Metaponto area: the farmers were then responsible for cultivating the lands and making them worth three times the amount invested in the iron and steel factory in Taranto. They gave life to the most advanced agricultural enterprise in Italy. To better understand the importance of this undertaking, around a century ago, a farmer from that area, who had emigrated several times, participated in one of the investigations performed in the South and said in an interview, "I have walked the world over, but I have never seen land this poor for farming.") forty thousand kilometers of electrical cables were laid, one thousand six hundred schools were built, along with one hundred and sixty hospitals. The construction of these basic elements required a special government committee and the creation of special fund? How is it that the South has an endowment of infrastructures, specifically those infrastructures, that is 30% inferior to that of the North? With what money did the North accomplish so much more without a "Fund for the North" or special committees? A consequence of this gap is that the medium-sized enterprises of the South, when they grow, decide to move to the North. In this fashion, they can enjoy the ease of transportation available, better infrastructures, discounts from the banks, and less crime. They also enjoy the added benefit of not being branded as "Southern," and therefore considered to be "inferior."

I am pretty good with numbers, so stick with me here: 100-0.7=99.3. I am using the "special" percentage, 0.7% of the gross national product (the highest estimate is that given by Pasquale Saraceno, a Pro-South advocate from Sondrio, and he says it is 0.5%). We plan on hiring Lieutenant Colombo to discover where the other 99.3% of the funds, that did not cause any scandal, were spent. Then, we will ask ourselves the reason for the unequal distribution of bread and fishes (loaves and filets for the North and crumbs and fish bones for the South).

We always seem to reach the same conclusion: "The growth of an economy that depends on the regions of the South is one of the most important components of the entire model of development of post-war Italy" (Bodi and Viesti). There exists a phenomenon of subjection and inferiority of one part of the country, with respect to the other part, but that oppressed part of the country also represents the motor behind an opportunity for development.

One of the main reasons for the North's resentment towards the Fund for the South is the scant result obtained as compared to the rest of the country's best efforts (perhaps they are getting carried away here). According to Domenico Ferrara in *Le ragioni del Sud*, "Taking into consideration the depressed conditions of the South, under all aspects, the Italian government tries to solicit internal productivity through unsecured subsidies, loans, tax exemptions and rewards for production and exportation. This is in addition to the limits placed on imports from foreign countries in order to protect the country from foreign competition. (...) The Italian government invites foreigners, experts, technicians, and workers to take up residency in the South, but despite the assistance offered, the results obtained in that area are quite modest, and are certainly not proportionate to the financial commitment offered by the State's revenue." Now you must forgive me, because I have lied to you: I am still referring, here, to a "Fund," but for Lombardy. In order to read the above quote correctly, you must substitute "South" with "Lombardy," and "Italian" with "Austrian." Don't be surprised if in Vienna, after having invested in Lombardy's soil, up to nine times the amount of what was spent in other regions of the empire, they reached the conclusion that those Lombards were ethnically inferior.

All things considered, things went much worse in the South. Pasquale Saraceno (*Studi sulla questione meridionale*) states that "the economic value of the protection from which the North's industry benefitted from its inception, and for decades after, (...) was much greater" (with respect to what was given to the South). The State was forced to "cover the losses that the banks were subjected to from 1930 to 1932 due to industry. Despite this intervention, an important part of the businesses became public domain" through the Institute for Industrial Reconstruction (Iri) and other such institutions. Furthermore, "many forms of tax relief, similar to those implemented in the South, were also implemented in the Center and the North. These both have about one third of the population in the South" (and I am certain they did not have near as many financial problems as the South). Saraceno places emphasis on the inherent contradiction behind providing incentives for areas of Italy that were considered "depressed" only because Southerners migrated there. A distinction needs to be made between areas "defined as being depressed" and areas that are "truly depressed."

The residents of the Padania area have a different concept of equality: equality means giving the same financial assistance to all. A few years after the Fund for the South became defunct, the new project for financial support was launched. Thanks to the alliance between Tremonti and the *Lega* party, some of the richest areas in all of Europe are included in the "depressed areas" of the country: Turin, Milan, Genoa, Trieste, and Reggio Emilia. Thirty-two percent, 11.5 million people, of the Center and the North's population discovers that they are living in "depressed" areas! Businesses receive incentives to invest in Busto Arsizio, so that they might save the desolate residents from poverty. The true masterpiece on the part of Tremonti and the *Lega* party (for considering the South amongst the "depressed" regions) was to give rise to numerous protests, because this new project would allow for the umpteenth financial "present" to be given to the Southerners. In fact, this law would only further contribute to widening the gap between the North and the South. Yet again, the industries in the North would benefit from this law (summarized: insults for you and more money for me). Goffredo Fofi, in *L'immigrazione meridionale a Torino*, states that the Italian Manufacturer's Association (*Confindustria*) in 1960 had already asked for funds for the North for schools where Southerners sent their children. The money would have been managed by local industrialists. The reasoning behind this was that if the Southerners came here, then the Fund for the South should spend its money here. This of course implies that he might have missed the entire point (or did he?) of the Fund in the first place: it existed to provide decent conditions in the South so that the Southerners could stay in their native land.

This all reminded me of something that I had read about Gaetano Salvemini, more than a half century earlier. Piero Gobetti was right when he called Salvemini "a genius." One could also consider him a prophet. Here is the sentence he wrote well before any of the authors of that wicked *Lega*-Tremonti law were born: "'Special' laws are sterile deceptions. For a privilege that only a tiny corner of the South will ever see, there is someone elsewhere that has longer arms to reach and ask for favors that are much bigger."

This is the South's advantage in being able to do everything but that which is truly essential. What is it missing to make its businesses and territories more competitive? Roads, railways, and energy at an acceptable cost and with the same efficiency as the rest of the country. The South is also missing fast connections with its ports (even I noticed that!). In other words, their infrastructures are sorely lacking: there are somewhere between 30% and 60% fewer in the South, according to the only former president of the Italian Manufacturer's Association to come from the South, Antonio D'Amato. But "instead" of doing what is necessary, the South is "compensated" for what is missing and each time the occasion presents itself, territorial pacts are made, special loans are granted, tax breaks are granted, business incentives are offered, laws for young entrepreneurs are passed.

Roads, ports and railways are not transferable. They were built in the South, and must stay there, so it would be best if the South were rendered accessible to foreign markets (though the North would deem this dangerous). Perhaps it would be better if any assistance offered to the South to "catch up" were conceived in such a fashion that eventually it could be extended to the North as well, "for justice's sake." In this manner, we could continue to favor those who are already ahead. For example, the law for young entrepreneurs had proven itself to be quite useful. However, when it came to include the rest of the country (which was already favored by better infrastructures and economic status) it removes the very region it was trying to assist from the competition. There is a very comical anecdote surrounding when Tremonti announced that he wanted to create a Southern Bank. Immediately afterwards, the head of a movement called *Impresecheresistono*[3] requested on the behalf of all of the industries of the North that a Northern Bank be created as well. He was ignoring the fact that all of the Italians banks originate in the North; or from the Center, at best. There isn't even one bank from the South. It is the only macro-region of Europe, from Iceland to the Ural Mountains that does not have a bank. Would you even dignify this request with a response? Would you tell him that in 2003 there were complaints that 98% of allotments from banks ended up in the 12 regions of the Center and the North and only 2% was distributed among the 8 regions in the South?

One can say that "any subsidies determined by politicians will largely be spent to support the North," writes Floris in *Separati in patria*. "Do you want to help businesses? You will find them in the North. Want to bolster consumption and increase the income available to families? The businesses will benefit from this and therefore, the North. If one takes into consideration that many of the funds that support this assistance come from the funds that are allotted for the poorest areas and that the South somehow is unable to use, we once again see money swimming away from the South, upstream."

It has always been this way (in 1996, it was discovered that the bank that was created to help the South's development, the Isveimer Bank, actually financed Berlusconi's financial holding company, Fininvest, with four hundred and fifty billion lira). The difference is that with the passage of the millennium, the money went directly to the wealthiest part of the country, without necessarily using the poorest part as a cushion (to exclude the South, it was sufficient to accuse it). From that time onward, and always more explicitly, the nation's, and Europe's, political and economic decisions, tend to forget the South and penalize it whenever the occasion arises, either under the direct influence of the *Lega* or the influence it has on its other allies in the government. This culmi-

---

[3] TRANSLATOR'S NOTE: "Businesses that fight to resist."

nates in an absurd pact that an Italian minister (ok, fine. He is a member of the *Lega*) made with the European Union to damage the Southern part of his own country. "This was the disastrous Paglierini-Van Miert Pact of 1994," according to Antonio D'Amato, it includes "an abnormal rise in the cost of labor" in the South (*Mezzogiorno risorsa nascosta*). The mere elimination of those cumbersome taxes on the businesses of the South would be worth one hundred thousand jobs. When one traces the priority routes across the continent (using highways, railways, and air space) the swift route between Bari and Otranto, which is the continuation of the Patrasso-Salonicco route, is sacrificed for the sake of Malpensa, the airport located in Varese. It will bring about the failure of Alitalia, in its attempt to steal the Roman Fiumicino airport's primary role as Italy's hub. This is in spite of the fact in the North there is an airport every fifty kilometers and only two out of every Milanese, one Lombard out of every ten, and zero Venetians out of every million that actually use Malpensa. Then Italy is elected as the European Authority on Nutrition, whose headquarters is located in Parma, while the rest of the world identifies Italian food with Neapolitan pizza and spaghetti. It is the Mediterranean diet. (Alternatively, a member of the *Lega* who disastrously ended up being the undersecretary for the Ministry of Health, proposed the federalist "Padania Diet." This shows that the ridiculousness of an idea doesn't necessarily serve as a brake to its promotion. Angel Keys, a professor from California, analyzed the methods of nutrition of millions of people from Lapland to Japan. He discovered that the diets of farmers and fishermen in the Cilento area of the Campania region and Puglia are the most suitable for the human body. He himself offered the ultimate proof of this: he moved to the Cilento area, just south of Salerno and proceeded to live there until he was over one hundred years old. Fortunately, he passed away before our friend from Padania noticed the absence of *cassoeula*[4] from his diet.

---

[4] TRANSLATOR'S NOTE: "a boiled cabbage-based dish typical of Northern Italy."

Investments for public works in the South are slashed in half over the course of five years (1991-1996). During this same time period the gross domestic product plunges below the level it reached in 1991 and 600,000 jobs are lost. This means that one out of every ten people lost their job. It was a disaster that has no historical precedents and we are the only country in Europe that has such a vastly different employment rate amongst its regions. The *Lega* party is the only racist movement in power in Europe. When similar situations occur elsewhere in Europe, such as Haider's Carinthia movement in Austria, the country in question becomes the "infected" member of Europe. Even in France and Germany there are movements of this type, but they are not in power even when the right is in power. In Italy, the *Lega* members have also wielded their influence when the center-left was in power. In fact, to gratify the *Lega*, the center-left launched the first federalist laws, which were then followed by a belated bout of remorse.

The money that goes to the North does so in silence, or it is destined "to the country." Is there a world crisis? Are we on the verge of collapse? The State pumps billions into the national banks to support businesses, which means that only the North benefits from this because there is not even one great Southern bank and the network of businesses (aside from slightly more than 7% of the small and medium sized businesses) is located from the South upwards. There is much unemployment, which again favors the North, while there are those that die in silence in the South, with their illegal factories, where workers are paid poorly and taxes are evaded just to survive and to compete with the Chinese.

In the opposite manner, money for the South is always well advertised. However, it must be seen whether that money actually makes it to its destination: the Fas Funds (which were to be used for under-utilized areas) were to be spent largely in the South. Instead, these funds were stolen and distributed between Milan's Expo Convention Center and other Northern destinations such as the acquisition/salvation mission for 100,000 wheels of *parmigiano* and *grana* cheeses that remained unsold; interventions that favored navigation on the Como, Maggiore, and Garda lakes; to establish the European Authority on Nutrition in Parma... In 2009, Sicily rebelled and threatened to form the Political Party for the South. Four billion euros of the South's funds were blocked. These funds theoretically already belonged to the South, but Tremonti and his cronies keep them blocked in the Cipe (Committee for Economic Planning). A national television news program immediately broadcast a poll: is it right that "other" "special" subsidies should go to the South? There was a heap of "no's" from honest and offended people. Of course no one tells them that the money the news program is referring to is only hypothetical. The real money has already been stolen and sent to the North.

Even when the money arrives, it is not necessarily true that it is usable. Giovanni Floris remembers one of the methods of virtual multiplication of funds: first the money is allotted for a specific task, then it is allotted for another, then another, then.... This results in funds that "have been around for years, but that will very likely never find a destination." None of the projects for which the funds were allotted were ever started or finished. If you ask, "What about the money?", then the answer is "They took it back." However, the publicity is only reserved for when the money is allotted, not for when it is subtracted.

Do you remember the funds allotted for the bridge over the Strait of Messina, that the Prodi administration redirects to other infrastructures, always in Sicily and Calabria? Tremonti, the new Minister of Economy and Finance uses these funds to offer a property tax abatement for all of Italy. "The resources that were supposed to be used to assist the South ended up in the Center and the North. Furthermore, the Ici[5] had already been abolished for the lower classes by the Prodi administration. Therefore, the resources that were set aside to help the poorest areas ended up assisting the wealthiest families" (*Separati in casa*).

The South is Italy's ATM. The country that was born by C-section and that bled the South and revived the North does not know how to exist any other way. Every birth has some blood-

---

[5] TRANSLATOR'S NOTE: property tax.

shed. Then the scar blocks the flow of blood and the child grows. If we are the only country in Europe where this fracture remains unable to heal for the past century and half it is because the Italian economy is supported by this. Banks, the Fund for Deposits and Loans (over forty of its one hundred billion euros are comprised of the South's savings) have always drained the money from the South and sent it towards the North.

Even statistics seem to focus on serving this purpose. Take, for instance, how the statistics determine unemployment: "Starting from 2004, Istat[6] begins to consider all those that carried out 'at least one hour of compensated activity (even payment in kind) in any field, or even if it is not compensated (such as in a family-run company)" explains Luca Montrone, founder of a major private television network (though it does not receive national coverage: it reaches nearly all of the Southern part of the peninsula from its location in Conversano, near Bari), in his *"Lectio Magistralis"* speech given for his *honoris causa* degree. So basically if once a month you bring groceries to a client of your cousin, who owns a delicatessen, you are not considered unemployed if she gives you a sandwich or she allows you to touch her bosom (that's payment in kind, isn't it?).

"Also, since 2004, Istat considers all those who have conducted an active job hunt in those thirty days to be unemployed." The others are not. So, in the South, where the lack of jobs is such that those who are unemployed, after numerous unsuccessful attempts, abandon their search, the unemployed disappear from Istat's statistics. In this fashion, the official figures are cut in half. Paradoxically, "in those regions where jobs are available, many seek them. This, however, increases the level of unemployment in that area." It is as if to say anyone who eats a sandwich a month either is debilitated to the point of not seeking food anymore or he is not considered malnourished by our Central Statistics Institute. We have finally discovered how to erase world hunger!!!

---

[6] TRANSLATOR'S NOTE: the Central Statistics Institute.

This system is used by all of Europe. However, in other countries, that data is based on an efficient network of social aids. A welfare check is guaranteed for those unemployed people that are registered in records that are constantly updated. They also do not lose this right if they refuse to accept a job. Our country is the European country that spends the least amount of money for the poorest members of its population. It also does not provide a welfare system for those without jobs. However, it has excellent support systems for those who lose their jobs. What is the difference?

In the first instance, the majority of those who would benefit from such a system are located in the South, where the difficulty of finding a first-time job is enormous and the jobs are much more unstable. In the second instance, the majority of those who would benefit are from the North, because the Fund for Unemployment and other forms of assistance act as a flywheel and lighten the load of costs for businesses. They also act as a support for workers that are temporarily in excess. If the world crisis destroys millions of jobs, in Italy, the first to be assisted are banks and businesses (primarily in the North), while in other countries the unemployed and families in difficulty are helped first (which in Italy are prevalently in the South). This is because our system offers assistance in an inversely proportionate manner with respect to need. This is incomprehensible from a social viewpoint, but not if there is a distinction between the Northerners and the Southerners. When viewed in this light, the criterion applied is coherent with both history and geography (according to Formigoni, a Christian from the "Milanese" rite, this would also be done in accordance with religion).

Italy is very generous, compared to other countries, with its pensions granted for seniority, which are granted from their jobs. Italy is, however, quite stingy when it comes to those pensions allotted for invalidity (one cannot live off of the amount that is allotted). 90% of the people in the first category live in the North, while the majority of the second category lives in the South. Here, the invalidity pensions are largely used as a point of focus in electoral campaigns to gain votes rather than to actually assist the handicapped. Again, there has been no attempt to render things equal in this country. The North was offered guarantees while the South was bribed for its silence (it was easily bribed as well, due to its many needs). "Solidarity in the defense of pensions has united a large part of the population in the North," including the unions, the *Lega* party, and even the left, according to Isaia Sales in *Riformisti senza anima*, while nothing comparable has been done for those "who have been left out: the youth, the unemployed, in other words all those who fully represent those affected by the hardships of the South."

Why do the Southerners put up with all of this? I think that they have been convinced that they receive more than what they actually deserve.

What do you think of the distinction between "relative poverty" and "absolute poverty"? There is a statistic that is derived from the averages of all of a country's incomes. If you earn below this number, you are considered to be poor. This could, however, favor the South because there, with the same amount of money, you could purchase more things than in the North. For this reason, the term "relative poverty" was coined. It takes into consideration a good amount of assets that are considered to be indispensable, as well as the prices in a given area. If you cannot purchase these goods with your salary then you are considered to be poor. In this manner, the number is higher in the North than in the South. Seems right, doesn't it? This of course does not take into consideration the notion that if one lives in a high-income area, the opportunities to emerge from one's situation of poverty are much more numerous. There are more instruments and means of assistance available. The State spends nine times more money in the Emilia-Romagna region than in the Calabria region for families in financial difficulty. Calabria's handicapped can count on assistance that is eight times inferior to what is offered in Lombardy. Calabria is the only region in Europe without a project for a welfare system. This discrimination is still geographical, territorial.

So the Minister for Education, Universities and Research establishes that only worthy Universities will receive funds. The allotment of funds would be based on a series of impartial criteria. This merely served as another way to remove funds from the South and to give them to the North, Lida Viganoni observes. She is the president of the prestigious, but punished, *Università Orientale di Napoli*. Among those "impartial criteria," notes Raffaele Lombardo, governor of Sicily, is the ability to attract donations and funds from businesses (that are located in the North) and to guarantee jobs immediately after graduation (this really sounds like a joke in the South). The minister claims to want to renew the scholastic system (or at least what is left of it), but she is actually in a traditional rut that is rooted in the *Risorgimento*: she tries to pass off what is old as something new. One hundred and fifty years ago, as soon as the Northerners reached Naples, they destroyed the scholastic system. When they arrived, the Northerners found fourteen middle/high schools, two specifically for noble young women, and thirty-two conservatories. These structures had a total of nearly 4,000 students. Alianello, in his book *La conquista del Sud*, reveals what the Northerners left behind them: "For secondary education, in a city of five hundred thousand inhabitants, we only have a high school that has sixty or seventy students. This is with the guidance of an intelligent minister, full of good will." Can you imagine if we had a minister that was not as capable? We could even say that courses could be offered to teachers from the South so that they could catch up. This wouldn't be because they are bad teachers, but rather only because they are from the South.

There has been much debate about the modest score given to average Italian students according to an internationally given test. Immediately, it is highlighted that the higher scores are in the North and the South's students have lower scores. In this manner, Italy is below average and it is "the South's fault." Professor Vito Peragine analyzed those statistics in detail and published, amidst general disinterest, the results of his findings. There are several things that influence the results of South, including the conditions of the school buildings, which are in considerably poorer conditions than those in the North. The buildings are often crumbling and the equipment needed is often absent entirely or of poor quality. Furthermore, the situation of the students in their homes is considerably more difficult than in the North. Often, in the South, the students have to contribute to their family's income. "When one calculates the influence that these situations have," says Peragine, "the geographical distinction disappears and the real source of the problem emerges. The students that have better equipped schools, fewer financial troubles at home, and more guarantees that they will be able to put their studies into operations in the job world are more productive." No way! Who would have ever thought that to be true?

Now, we should either give Peragine the Nobel Prize or the Ignoble Prize (yes, it exists) to those others. Luckily, no one speaks of meeting "impartial international criteria" as a means of certifying Ministers of Education. At least we have been spared that humiliation.

They would also like to reduce the salaries of teachers in the South, to further emphasize the level of hardship present. In this manner the schools are worse, the results of the exams also worsen and the quality of the teachers would also decline. This is because they would head to the North in order to earn higher salaries, all with a simple address change (yet again we would have the same influx of the best talent moving to the strongest area at the expense of the weakest).

It is never the case that we conform to the European standards—internationally established criteria—that require equality in the distribution of funds so that we might improve these school buildings in the South and make them decent. Perhaps we could elevate the South's network of highways to "European standards," or at least elevate the railways to "Italian standards." We could introduce a welfare system and improve the efficiency of employment agencies.

"Do you want me to summarize all of this?" asks Professor Peragine. You bet! This way I can stop listing anecdotes where, although the times and locations may change, the result is always the same. "To better understand the issue at hand, we must consult the accounting for the public territories. This means that we must find out where Italy's public funds actually go (and not where it is said that they go). The Dps (the Department for Projects of Development) finally engaged in such an investigation. This department was created by Italy's former president, Carlo Azeglio Ciampi, in 1998, in order to focus some attention on the South. The first piece of information that emerges from this investigation is that public funds are not used towards development but largely towards running expenses. The second piece of information is actually the exposure of a myth: that the State spent more funds pro capita in the South than in the North. The opposite is actually true. The third piece of information is that the South has actually been erased from programs that include investments in infrastructures. The most scandalous example of this is that of the railway companies, that for years have only invested in the Center and the North (there are only about one hundred kilometers worth of high-speed tracks in the South while there are more than a thousand from Rome upwards). It is this way for the schools, roads...."

There was actually an instrument to ensure that the State would honor the commitments it made to the South: the Dpef (Document for Economic and Financial Planning). It was launched by the D'Alema administration in 1999. It was approved upon receiving some changes to its later versions. What did it say? It stated that the "special" expenses should be considered "additional" expenses (this is trivial, otherwise the expenses would be considered "ordinary," but in Italy it is important to make this distinction), and therefore in conformity with European law, they should benefit those who are disadvantaged (see previous parenthesis). In this manner, it was decided that 85% of the Fas (Funds for Underutilized Areas) should go to the South, while the "ordinary" funds allotted by the State should be distributed according to population density. In this manner, 30% would be allotted to the South and 70% for the Center and the North. The total comes to this: the Fas plus the "ordinarily" allotted funds comes to 45% of the total expenses for the South and 55% to the North.

The commitments were not respected by the center-left administration and even less by the center-right (even though the government may alternate sides, geographical discrimination is always respected). In the best instances, such as in 2004, the South was able to remain only 4.6 percentage points below that amount (if this does not seem like much I would remind you that half a point was what the Fund for the South spent. Therefore 4.6% is the regular amount spent plus the Fas, which equals four times the amount.) In the worst case, as in 2007, the South received 9.7 percentage points below (that is 8 or 9 times the amount spent by the Funds for the South!). In the years between 2002 and 2006, one million eighty thousand jobs were created in Italy (according to *Le sfide del cambiamento* by Gianfranco Viesti). All of those went to the North, while barely forty thousand were created in the South. Are you surprised?

The most Lombard head of state ever, Silvio Berlusconi, tried to decrease the enormous gap between what was said and what was actually done. By increasing the funds spent? No, by decreasing the percentage allotted for the South from 45% to 42.3% and then to 41.4%. Then they canceled it altogether. This way no one knows how the amount allotted is spent and the Southerners can stop complaining. So what happened to the department that Ciampi created, that made the passage of funds visible, and that was headed by a qualified and honest individual? Well, they got rid of that person....

While, in spite of the commitments made, the "ordinary" funds allotted grew in the North and collapsed by 10 percentage points in the South, the "special" funds allotted were used to partially compensate for this robbery.

"Not only does the State systematically spend less for the residents of the South, but today, with the laws of financial federalism, the South runs the risk that even the funds it uses to satisfy basic needs could be cut off," according to Professor Peragine, a consultant for the Department of Regional Affairs regarding federalism and territorial equalization (this is why I wanted to speak with him).

A member of that group says that the conflict is not "political, but geographical." In other words it has nothing to do with the *Lega* or the right or left. It is about the North versus the South. Would Peragine confirm this?

Here is his answer, and it is subject to interpretation: "Our country has always been supported by the principle that all citizens need to be treated in the same manner by the State, in regards to, for example, healthcare, schools, transportation...This principle, today, is not always respected. This idea is, and must be, at the base of a well-ordered federal system. The State and regions are assigned specific tasks (you take care of the schools, and I'll take care of healthcare etc.) based on the principles of subsidiarity: funds are assigned according to the tasks assigned. What does this mean? That there are no "sovereign priorities" amongst the various entities involved. Each one is like the other according to the tasks it carries out. Therefore, federalism does not mean that resources are withheld by the territories that produce them, but rather are used to perform the tasks assigned and to have adequate funds to perform them. This principle is present in the bill that has already been approved by the Parliament. Nonetheless, there are strong pressures to pass another interpretation of the bill, which is inspired by territorial egotism rather than the desire of a well-organized state. At the same time, the bill upholds the principle by which not all of the tasks are compensated by the State with the same treatment for all of its citizens. For the essential tasks (like healthcare) a basic minimum is established that is the same for everyone and those who can afford to pay more, do so. For other, non-essential tasks (like tourism and road maintenance) only partial coverage is offered." (A century ago, something similar was proposed and it was called "decentralization": "this would be like" according to Ettore Ciccotti "acting as an intermediary between two people fighting by tying the arms of one of them behind their back and giving the other a better chance of winning the fight.")

Excuse me, but wouldn't this be like legalizing the schism between category A citizens and category B citizens? Why should the South accept this? Why shouldn't the South go about its own business?

Professor Peragine is young and athletic (he is a mountain climber) and is passionate about his job and in particular about, if I am allowed to invent a field of study, the "construction and concealment of poverty in advanced countries." I think he suffers from the frustration of those who see, understand, and can explain, but cannot modify a given situation. They are not listened to. Up until this point, we were both leaning towards each other over opposite sides of the same desk almost to the point of touching heads. He then sat back in his chair with his arms splayed on either side of the armrests. What he tells me hits me like a slap in the face. He knows it. It is one of the worst things that he uselessly knows: "It is better to be poor in a rich country. Either way, I cannot imagine a South without an Italy or a Europe."

With federalism, everyone would receive funds based on what one gives. Perhaps it would be better to say everyone receives funds based on what they have. The wealthy keep their money and the poor keep their troubles, plus a few "compensations" through "equalizing funds," whose governing body remains a shameful and inconstant mystery. This would amount to about 1.5% of the gross domestic product with the current version.

The undertaking launched a century and half ago with armed force, massacres, plundering, humiliation, and furthered by the false belief that we were a country that shared common principles is now looking to be legalized into a sort of "regional apartheid." Article 1 of the Constitution would read: "Italy is a Republic founded on the prevalence of the rights of the Northerners and on the inferiority of the Southerners." Do we want to use garbage as a means of comparison? "The expenses in the urban refuse sector: between 2000 and 2006, 138 million euros were spent in the South and 574 million euros in the Center and the North," reports Viesti in *Mezzogiorno a tradimento*, "in other words 6.7 and 15.5 euros respectively per capita."

Pino Aprile

The Southerners are dirty and it is useless to try and clean up after them. For this result, we have spent two and a half times less for their dirtiness (this may be ... but when the Piedmontese sacked the Palace of Caserta and they took an inventory of all the loot, they mentioned an unidentifiable object that was shaped like a guitar: they had never seen a bidet in their lives.) While Naples drowns in garbage, until Berlusconi and Bertolaso arrive and re-move it from where everyone can see to someplace where no one would look, there is Genoa. Genoa was the lowest ranked city for recycling amongst the cities of Italy, though today it is the first (ahead of Milan, Turin, and Rome). It is the city that costs the least for its citizens with a budget of one hundred and twenty million euros (five years prior, it did not have a single euro). Traffic used to strangle it, while roads now are more free thanks to the numer-ous parking lots on the outskirts that are well connected to the city by a network of public transportation. The beaches have been cleaned and the asbestos that polluted them has been removed. The most decrepit neighborhood was completely restored. The city looks forward to the completion of its new subway and its new business center, which was built in only 11 months. It is large and quite impressive and was built with European funds as well as private ones as well. Its Agency for the non-repressive fight against crime is now being studied by the United Nations as well as cities like Madrid, Goteborg, and Bogotà. This was all accom-plished in four to five years. Even Moody's, an international com-pany, has taken notice (it measures the reliability of institutions and countries throughout the world) and has attributed to Genoa, and only very few other cities, the "AA3" qualification.

Oops. I made a mistake. This virtuous city is actually not Genoa. It is Bari. It is in the South too, just like Naples. All of these wonderful things were accomplished with fewer funds than Genoa, Milan, Turin, and Rome. "We know how to manage the few funds we receive," says the mayor Michele Emiliano, who boasts of such results. He is the same mayor who is responsible for the demolition of the "monsters of Point Perotti," those horri-ble buildings that hid the sea view. But the only thing that is

174

known to be from Bari are the prostitutes who visited Berlusconi's homes. You probably have not heard about these other things. "My colleagues from the North," narrates Emiliano, "tell me that Bari does not seem like a Southern city. Why, because if it works, it can't be from the South?"

I consoled him by telling him that the same thing happened to Salvemini: "It seems impossible that you are from the South!" They wanted to pay him a compliment, for his acumen and his legendary honesty. A friend from the Emilia Romagna region said this to him. He was an honest, well-educated man who was hardly affected by racist intentions (aside from this unwitting exclamation): in other words, it seemed impossible that he could be from the North.

CHAPTER 5

Southerners Have No Industrial Culture

"**D**id you know that we had the biggest and most modern steel mills in all of Italy? They were the only ones capable of competing, for both quality and productivity, with the best in all of Europe," Sharo Gambino told me. He is a prolific writer from the area near the Angitola River and the Ancinale Woods. He was the one who showed them to me, in the mid Eighties, shortly after the program to renovate this industrial complex was launched.

Mongiana is in the middle of the Serre mountain chain in Calabria. It is filled with wild natural beauty. The roads that ascend the mountains are narrow and they hang from the edges of these unstable mountains. Time increases the long distances even further because the roads are difficult to travel. One gets a sense of resentful pride from the people there because they know that yesterday they were great. This area was the richest mining and metal works district in the Kingdom of the Two Sicilies and of all of Italy. It was shut down by the new government because it had a serious structural defect: it was located in the South.

Why do I always come back to this? I do this so that you all might notice that when you speak of history and economics, data, ideas, and events appear while people disappear. If you narrate the life of a man, you can measure the joy and glory in it by comparing it to your own, but how could you do this for an entire population? Your life becomes an insufficient means of comparison. They destroyed the industries in the South, but how can you see the way this changes the course of existence of an entire population? I chose Mongiana as an example because this town was born because of a steel factory. This factory received so many recognitions: for its size and its technical efficiency. Then it was forgotten. All of those industries that were reasons for the Kingdom of the Two Sicilies' pride were canceled and removed with violence. Perhaps nothing is a better example of what was done to us than the damage this incurred on our abilities and our desire to accomplish.

At the dawn of the Unification, the South had approached industrialization with vigor. The North did as well, and was advanced in a few sectors while the South excelled in others. On the whole "the percentage of the population that worked in the industrial sector was higher in the South with respect to the North," according to Amedeo Lepore in *La questione meridionale prima dell'intervento straordinario*). This advantage seemed ridiculous, however, when the size of Italy's industrial sector as a whole was compared to the rest of Europe. Piero Bevilacqua, a historian, illustrates this using a few examples in his work *Breve storia dell'Italia meridionale*. In the textile industry, Italy had tens or hundreds of thousands of spindles. England had thirty million and France five million. In the metal works industry, we produced thousands of tons of cast iron. Germany produced six hundred thousand tons, France one million tons, and England produced nearly four million tons of cast iron. While the rest of Europe had many enormous factories and mills, we only had a few, plus many small workshops (some of the largest factories like the paper or cotton mills, were located in the South. These were seeds from which giants were generated (in France and Germany, up until World War I, somewhere between 94% and 97% of their businesses did not have more than ten employees). But the North, (after the Unification, the heads of state were primarily from Piedmont) was given every possible opportunity to grow, while the South was blocked in so many ways that most of the industries that were already there were suppressed. Which is saying a great deal because in 1903, despite the pro-North politics adopted by the newly unified Italy, the area surrounding Naples was second only to Milan for the number of factories and was home to 5% of the nation's factories. The largest cotton factory was still located in the South in 1925. In the decades prior to the Piedmontese invasion, the Kingdom of the Two Sicilies, which traditionally exported raw materials, actually became an importer (wool and cotton) in order to supply its industries of transformation.

The South's economy had been integrated within the European economy for centuries, as well as other economies. Its landscape changed according to its own industrial needs as well as those of others. The land of mulberry bushes (and silk) became a sugar plantation (still today one can see that the sugar mills are much like the ones you can see in the Antilles), or an olive grove (the oil used to grease Europe's industrial machinery came from Puglia and Calabria) or orchards of almonds, hazelnuts, citrus fruits or vineyards, when Northern Europe and the United States became, in the first quarter of the 1900s, great consumers of fresh fruit.

Ships from the Kingdom of the Two Sicilies, as well as foreign ones, loaded themselves with cargo and the South was introduced to the world market. The South was the weakest part of the system (although this was not always the case), but it was still nonetheless a part of the system.

The Bourbons, the supporters of Napoleon (with their Institute of Encouragement) and then again the Bourbons (who did not cast away all the good things that those who dethroned them did, unlike the Savoy monarchs) launched on-site initiatives for the transformation of their basic products. These worked and foreign businesspeople came to invest the money in the South (the British, French, Germans, and Belgians). They set up factories that employed hundreds of thousands of people. The powerful Schloepfer textile company, owned by Alberto Wenner, was born this way. The paper mills of Courier and Lefebvre became the largest in Italy. Then our "brothers" came to free us of these most unwelcome guests (In this manner, the enormous wool industry in Arpino met with a dire end. To think that it had been active since the time of Cicero, whose father had a wool business there.)

"If you are from Mongiana, every day you see what you once were and what you were reduced to," said Gambino. They don't even have a locksmith there today, where once there were anywhere from 1200 to 1500 expert blacksmiths and specialized metal technicians. These were responsible for rendering the industrial sector of the Kingdom of the Two Sicilies entirely self-sufficient.

The Phoenicians had already mined iron from these mountains. In the nine hundred years that preceded the Unification of Italy, the production of iron and steel were the main industries of the Serre Mountain area. Even the monks of Saint Bruno were involved in metallurgy, with the permission of King Ruggero II, the Count of Puglia and Calabria. This industry was assisted by the iron-rich minerals in the rocks of the area, which were then processed by technicians and workers from nearby towns with the energy that they derived from the waterfalls in the woods and the fossil fuels derived from the surrounding lands. Only Cesare Fieramosca, Ettore's dumber brother (the one from the Barletta duel), who was given a feud comprising the entire metal works district, did not have a clue as to how to manage this business.

Mongiana steel, and that from the surrounding areas, rendered the entire kingdom completely independent when it came to the production of weapons and beams for the construction of the first iron suspension bridges in Italy. It was independent when it came to supplying the shipyards of the second largest merchant fleet in the world, after England: the arsenal and shipyard of Castellammare (in 1931 they built the *Amerigo Vespucci*, the "most beautiful training ship in the world" where still today, it is used to train Italian officials). In 1860 it was the largest shipyard in the Mediterranean with 1800 workers and 3400 (half of the amount that worked in all of Italy) worked in those of Naples. Calabrian steel supplied the stupefying Neapolitan railway industry located in Pietrarsa (the Royal Mechanical and Polytechnic Factory), which was the largest industrial complex on the entire peninsula. This was of course over half a century before Fiat, and it had twice as many workers (1000) as the Ansaldo energy company from Genoa. It was the only Italian company that could build everything from the rails to the locomotive entirely by itself (this disturbed the French and the English, who had a monopoly of the railway industry, and disappointed the Austrians who saw themselves surpassed. It also caused the czar to copy and identically reproduce the Neapolitan factory in Russia: and so the celebrated Kronstadt Workshops were born. As far as the Savoy monarchs were concerned, they were the only ones who sent a general, La Marmora, to study the Neapolitan factories that had given rise to such admiration in Europe, with the intention of recreating similar versions in Piedmont. After the country was unified, the Neapolitan factory was reduced to a condition of decay and was impoverished. The workers protested against this destruction and soldiers fired shots: fifteen or so were killed or wounded). It was the only company in Italy to build both ship engines and railway tracks. The government post-Unification, however, preferred to subcontract the latter to the French.

The supporters of Garibaldi arrived, and this spelled the end for Mongiana. They told the residents that what they knew, what they were, and the pride that they had for their much desired and achieved skills were now worth nothing. They took their world away: the world that they knew so well and that recognized their worth. I remembered the words of Enzo Biagi, after RAI pushed him aside upon harsh orders from the head of the government at the time, Silvio Berlusconi: "In order to kill a man, you need not take his life. It is sufficient to take away his job." We slowly saw him fade away.

They acted with such "savagery" wrote Gaetano Cingari, author of *Nordisti, acciaio, e mafia*. "A fortune's worth of technical experience was instantaneously erased, even if it has remained the specialty of the local population of the Serre area. What happened to the Calabrian metal works industry happened to the rest of the South as well. "Within a few years after the Unification, the industrial legacy of the Kingdom of the Two Sicilies, which was wrongfully diminished, was completely destroyed. This brought about irreversible damage." The South was not the only one who lost that wealth and opportunity for growth: all of Italy did. Egotism, while it seems to offer something in the short run, takes away your future, tenfold.

Calabria did not only produce steel. It was also extremely important in the South's silk industry. It "exported highly valuable damask fabrics abroad, as well as satin, furniture upholstery and velvet. The glassworks of the Bourbon capital were also widely appreciated outside of the country, as well as ceramic tiles, perfumes, soaps, paper from the Liri Valley, Neapolitan gloves and other leather goods. These goods were all world famous. (...) The construction of a national merchant fleet, which was eventually built, was encouraged with such rewards that they provided for the larger part of the traffic of importation and exportation. Its cargo rose over the course of fifteen years (1824-1838) from 8000 tons to 166,500 tons, in other words it increased twenty-fold," writes Vochting.

The Calabrian metal works industry was too big and located too far South. This constituted a serious imbalance in the North's prejudices and plans. Italian industry needed to be "Northern".

The blast furnaces of Mongiana, which were the largest and most technologically advanced in all of Italy, were renamed "Cavour" and "Garibaldi" (rather than keep their original names, "San Francesco" and "San Fernando" after the two namesakes of the Neapolitan kings who funded their construction). Soon after they were turned off forever. The rails that were used to transport the minerals that were extracted from the local mines were torn up and sold by weight, just like old scrap metal. The entire factory was put up for auction and was sold to a former tailor, a Garibaldi supporter, who then became a member of Parliament. He later was involved in a colossal fraud case against the State. In the sale price, the element that held the highest value (four fifths of the cost) was the forest that surrounded the factory, and not the facility's equipment. This was the ultimate insult.

When it closed, Mongiana had 1,200 workers, but in its moments of peak production, this number increased to 1,500 (In 1845, in all of the factories of Liguria, Piedmont, and Val d'Aosta, about fifteen factories put together, the total amount of workers equaled that of the factories of Mongiana and Pietrarsa. However, the quality and quantity of cast iron produced was much higher than in the factories from the North. This has always been the case with factories in the metal works industry of the North, with the exception of the Rubini factory located in Dongo del Lario, which passed into the hands of Falck.).

Officially, Mongiana was condemned because the new industrial theories sustained that metal works factories located in mountain areas were inferior to those by the sea, which could run on hydroelectric power and could use organically derived coal. However, when Mongiana was closed, a steel factory was built in Terni, which was also located in the mountains, and was actually even farther away from the sea. Furthermore, "much more money was spent to build this factory than would have been necessary to renovate the factory in Calabria," according to Brunello De Stefano Manno and Gennaro Matacena in their work dedicated exclusively to this subject: *Le Reali Ferriere ed Officine di Mongiana*. Financial support for industries were only considered a detriment if they were allotted to industries in the South. The courtesy extended by economic theories depended largely on latitude. From 1887 "the industrial sectors that were most favored by the protectionist policies were the cotton industry (…) and the metal works industry, *that was literally invented from nothing by the State*" according to Marco Meriggi in *Breve storia dell'Italia settentrionale*, "with the construction of the Terni factory, continuing through to the development of the industry in Tuscany and Liguria." How would you feel if you were from Mongiana today, or worse, from that time period?

The technicians and experts from Calabria, who were obliged to emigrate to Umbria, were immediately hired for their competence in the new factory. Others wound up near Brescia where they contributed to building the fortunes of the Lombard foundries. Today, Mongiana's proud and well-documented appeal to the Italian government sounds pathetic. It made note of its large production of goods and its advanced technology and its extremely high quality (which received many national and international recognition). The appeal assured the government that the factory's workers were willing to cut their already small salaries in order to pay the salaries of their chief technicians. They volunteered even for modest jobs as long as it meant that they could continue to work. They were even willing to adapt themselves to produce weights that cost half of what the State was willing to pay, or even to assemble meters for mills at 75 lira a piece. But their appeal was ignored and they assigned the contract to an iron mill in Turin who delivered the meters for a starting price of 100 lira per piece, but whose quality was so poor that they were eventually just thrown out.

Again, in 1861, when Mongiana's fate had already been decided, their steel received an award at the Industrial Exposition of Florence. The year after that, they received numerous awards at the International Exposition in London for their iron, cast iron, damask blades, precision rifles, sabres, and many other weapons. But for Turin, "the best factory with the largest production of quality products that Italy possesses today" (as the local administrators proudly wrote) needed to be shut down.

It was at this time, when the soldiers arrived from the North to Mongiana, that the "Issue of the South" was born throughout the entire South.

To those who speak of lack of ability and industrial culture on the part of the Southerners, Calabria's centuries old history of metallurgy narrates a different story. "First, the iron mill came into existence around two hundred years ago, then the town," Marisa Tripodi states. She is originally from Mongiana, but is now the administrator of a foundry in the town of Lumezzane near Brescia. "When the factory closed, the town began to die as well. The people began to leave."

However, the demand for iron and their ability to manufacture it allowed them to resist for a time. Despite this, nearly a century later, a new wave of emigration emptied Mongiana once again.

"I was nineteen years old," remembers Mrs. Tripodi "it was the 1960s. One hundred years earlier, when the factory was first shut down, only the men left for the Americas, because they believed that they would return. We no longer believed this. Entire families left. We closed the door to our home behind us, and our home became one of the many that remained empty and mute.

My grandmother, Jacopetta Maria Rosaria, and my great-grand-mother as well, both worked in the steel factory. Their weekly payday was announced by the peals of local church's bells. Those who showed up late did not receive their salary. I am not certain if our metallurgic tradition actually determined our path (my father, however, was a forest ranger) but those of us from Mongiana who emigrated found ourselves working in the foundries in the Brescia area. There are one hundred and fifty families from Mongiana (around five hundred people) in Lumezzane alone. By now, Lumez-zane is the real Mongiana, while the original, as we have now come to call it, has been nicknamed "Mongianella."[1] We have spent the better part of our energy and intelligence far from our home. If today these places are as important as they are, they owe it also to our presence. I am disappointed that I did not do this for my town. This is a deep regret I have, you know? A regret that bor-ders a feeling of guilt. But what could we have done? In the sum-mer I go back to Mongiana, beautiful and dying."

Dying?

Sharo had asked me, "Haven't you ever gone to see the iron factories?" The question mark he added was out of politeness: he already knew the answer. His tone reminded me of that of an old Greek man I encountered when I was in Cephalonia who asked me, "You are Italian? Have you gone to visit the memorial com-memorating the five thousand Italian soldiers from the Acqui di-vision that were *kaput* by the Germans?" I couldn't find anything better to say other than "I am on vacation."

Mongiana reveals its origins: the iron factories and foundries are located on the edge of the Alaro gap. The Alaro River spouts across a marked slope into a deep and narrow gorge. The houses line the only road that crosses the town and that ultimately leads to the ruins of the factory.

To further tie the workers to the factory, the administrators of the iron mill imposed duties on the workers and offered numer-ous advantages thus convincing the workers to live in shacks

---

[1] TRANSLATOR'S NOTE: little Mongiana.

nearby. That shanty town soon acquired stone walls for its homes, then a priest, then a church.... With the arrival of the Napoleonic administrators, when the French Revolution reached the shores of the Kingdom of the Two Sicilies, came a pay raise, as a cost-of-living adjustment. "The workers obtained a doctor, a pharmacy, a justice of the peace, and exemption from the military draft." Also, according to De Stefano Manno and Matacena, the workers were granted a healthcare fund in case they were injured on the job or suffered an illness (this was an innovation that came to light for the first time in the history of the Industrial Revolution, in the Kingdom of the Two Sicilies. There was an analogous fund only in the silk factories of San Leucio in Caserta).

The element that most captured the imagination of Mongiana's inhabitants, and not only theirs, was the particular attention paid by the Bourbon monarchs to even the least of the workers' needs. For the workers they built "filthy places": restrooms fit for gentlemen, not shrubs. The population grew to approximately two thousand people. Today that number is less than half.

Three members of the local government came to greet a visitor. They were young and quite prepared on the subject, without being invasive. They know that your presence means nothing, but they are also aware that if a visitor comes, that he knows the true value of what they can show him and that he has come to pay homage. Merely getting to the place is a sign of determination: the road that ascends to the Serre Mountains bisects the town and ends in an open space on a ridge that has been carved by the river next to what is left of the iron factories. The road served no other purpose but to connect those factories to the port city of Vibo Valentia. To give the iron factories an outlet on the Ionian Sea, a stretch of road was built that crosses Calabria and connects the two seas. It is the first in the history of the region, from the time of the Greek colonies, and remained such for one hundred and thirty years after the Unification of Italy. Why would the Savoy monarchs need to do better when they had destroyed the original reason the road was built for in the first place? Today, the new road is under construction with rhythms dictated by the trickling of the necessary funds. It will connect Soverato to Tropea, the two gems of Calabrian tourism.

In 1974, the Neapolitan architect Gennaro Matacena happened to visit Mongiana. He was specialized in the restoration of monuments and he restored the Medici Foundries in Follonica. "What impressed me the most were the cast iron columns, " he narrates upon finishing his work. "I asked for information about them in the town, but no one remembered anything out of reticence, embarrassment, or modesty.... I then went to the mayor of the town at the time, Vincenzo Rullo, a real gentleman, and said, 'Do you know that you have a treasure here?' He immediately understood what I meant and was able to procure funding from the Fund for the South. He purchased the part of the factory that had become privately owned, by acquisitive prescription. He then asked me to take care of everything. The first difficulty I encountered was to find the documented proof that the factories even existed! Not even the monumental *Storia di Napoli* alluded to the existence of Mongiana. The metallurgical settlement had simply been canceled by the annals of history."

Today, its value in the history of metallurgy is celebrated the world over by Italian, American, and Russian scholars. "In the residence of the colonel that governed the town, (the factory was militarily strategic for the Kingdom)" continues Matacena, "they pointed us to a chest: 'There are some papers in there...': we discovered a map of the town and of the factories! Then it was restored by the specialists from the Abbey of Cava dei Tirreni."

At that point, the re-discoverers came to know what it was and how it used to be. "The element that elicited the most excitement was discovering in the state archives letters, documents, reports, as well as questions and answers regarding the factories' activities. Everything was perfectly catalogued and was perfectly comprehensible. The inefficiency of the Bourbon bureaucracy instantly became a false myth! Finally, the lives and the work of all of those men came to light."

"The kings of Naples, " Gambino explained to me "cared very much about the efficiency of their iron factories as well as the speediness and assurance of the transportation of their products. Ferdinand II, despite the difficulties in reaching the location, wanted to visit Mongiana in order to emphasize with his presence as sovereign, the strategic importance of those factories for the military and civil aspects of the Kingdom.

On a previous trip, he had ordered the construction of a bridge over a sunken torrent. When he reached Mongiana, he remembered this request and asked the official to whom he had given this order, in Neapolitan dialect: "'Guagliò e 'o ponte addò sta?' 'L'avimm passato, maestà.' ('Hey boy! Where's the bridge?' 'We passed over it, your majesty.') The king, quite certain of the contrary, burst out: "Aggio capito: m'avite futtuto!"[2]

When the supporters of Garibaldi arrived, the inhabitants of Mongiana understood that a larger nation was to be built, but even in the regret for the one that would be lost, they believed that one certainty guaranteed their future: steel. Italy could not do without it and everyone in Europe knew of their excellent metallurgical skills. Only a few months were sufficient for them to realize that the government in Turin intended to ruin the efficient and highly productive factories in Calabria to favor the development of others (and to build new ones) in the North. This discovery prompted incredulity, then vexation and protest, and finally, violence. The factories were the object of robberies, pillaging, and vandalism. The brigands appeared in the nearby woods. The commander's house was attacked and the crowds trampled the tricolor flag.

This explosion of disorder and protests transmits the sense of disappointment on behalf of the citizens of Mongiana because "in a century since the establishment of Mongiana," according to the local government in their letter to the State, "the civil authorities can attest to the fact that there was not one single murder, nor robbery, nor any crime of any sort here." Who knows if any of the inhabitants of Turin ever read that the poor inhabitants of Mongiana, despite their oppression and hardships, "they continued to

---

[2] TRANSLATOR'S NOTE: "I get it: you've screwed me."

respect the law as something sacred as well as their fellow citizens and their property. They preferred to die of hunger out of honesty." This European aristocracy of technicians and workers was forced to die of hunger. Even alcoholism was absent, which is quite unusual considering the conditions of the workers at the time. Are these all exaggerations of the Southerners?

"Let's go," Sharo Gambino invited me, "I will take you to someone who will tell you the story of the man who was declared the 'most honest Italian in America': Francesco Roti, a former shepherd from Mongiana." "Yes, he was a former shepherd, " began Father Giuseppe Scopacasa, the parish priest of Mongiana, "but he knew how to rise above certain situations and remain honest."

"When our factories were reduced to ruins, our town began to empty itself. There are more people from Mongiana in America now than here. Francesco Roti left during this time and he was able to improve his life and grow. He became aware that banks took advantage of the hard earned salaries of the immigrants with heavy taxes. So, in Chicago, he created a bank where many of the immigrants entrusted their earnings. Francesco Roti's reputation was well known to everyone. Unfortunately, there was a robbery and the bank could not withstand such a blow: it was forced to close.

Roti was put on trial but was acquitted because it was immediately clear that he had no responsibility in the disaster and was actually its primary victim. However, he did not share the opinion of the judge. He thought of the situation in this fashion: "People put their trust in me and suffered a wrongdoing." He began to work for years like a beast and was able to repay all of his clients all of the money they had lost, even at the expense of his own family. He paid them back with interest. In that moment, he was declared "the most honest Italian in America" and the newspapers of the time told the story of this former shepherd from Mongiana with admiration. My uncle (yes, he was actually my uncle) then retired and with his family's permission, he became a monk" (before he died, Father Giuseppe Scopacasa narrated this story in a book: *Lo zio d'America*).

When the referendum for the annexation to the Kingdom of Sardinia came to a vote, Mongiana's bitterness turned into an outright rejection. The polls revealed that the area of Mongiana registered one of the highest percentages of votes in disfavor. More than one third of all the votes in disfavor in the province of Catanzaro came from the district of Mongiana-Fabrizia. To make this statistic even more important is the fact that the vote was not secret. One's vote was expressed in front of a panel of soldiers that wrote down the names of those in disfavor. One either needed to be very brave to vote "no" or despondent.

"With the Bourbon monarchy," Vincenzo Caracciolo, an engineer who is the director of the forest rangers, narrates, "there were jobs, growth, and prestige. The inhabitants of Mongiana were protagonists and competitors of the best iron manufacturers of Europe. Only through memories can one relive the pride in this excellence that has been lost. This makes the events after the Unification even more bitter. There are still some families who are still proud of their ancient abilities. From these abilities and from the factory derived a sort of hierarchy that trickled into the town. One still gets a sense of their belonging to an industrialized world upon speaking to them. I overheard someone say, '...my grandfather counted the bearings at the factory....' In the Serre Mountains, still today, many still know how an iron mill works."

Umberto Galimberti wrote in his work *Psiche and techne*: "It is said that animals live in an 'environment,' while mankind lives in a 'world'": that which is built by actions and the consequences of those actions. The world of the inhabitants of Mongiana was founded on the industries of mining and metallurgy, while they lasted. It was synchronized with the rhythm of the machines and of the furnaces. It was organized according to the hierarchies of the factories, with a language that left their workplaces and trickled into their homes.

"The work was hard and the salaries were low. The people were almost obliged to work," according to Mrs. Tripodi's mother. Yet, it was all a privilege and this was Mongiana's way of 'dominating nature'."

"And since we usually call this domination 'culture'," explains Galimberti, "'culture' becomes for mankind what the 'environment' is to animals. It is the circumstance that is essential to our survival."

This is what was taken from Mongiana: the circumstances necessary for their survival.

The inhabitants of Mongiana began seeking these circumstances elsewhere, rather than completely give up on their world: in the United States, Canada, Argentina, and even Terni. Over a century later they continue to reach places like Lumezzane and other places near Brescia. The Serre Mountains were the "environment" of the inhabitants of Mongiana. Metallurgy was their "world". They gave up the former so that they would not have to give up the second, which made them members of the human race (the only culture that they had lived by, nurtured, and built for two hundred years was metallurgy.

This, however, could still be considered an amputation.

"Today the dream of the youth who does not want to emigrate from his land is a job that is socially useful: becoming a forest ranger," according to Caracciolo, with realist-laced bitterness. "With the little money they made and the mushrooms they picked in the forest they somehow managed to survive. Who would ever believe that this area was once as productive as the Ruhr area in Germany?" As always, at the end of a civilization that came to an abrupt end, its temples and government buildings were left standing. These were the bare bones (without flesh, blood, or skin) that represent an economic ability that was sucked dry as if by a vampire. They are the muted cathedrals of gods who no longer have priests. It is this way in the Serre Mountains, in the Rossano Valley below, in all of Calabria and in the entire South. There are skeletons of textile mills, sugar mills, tuna canneries, licorice factories, shipyards, workshops, paper mills and pasta factories. This makes the site a paradise for industrial archaeology.

The Calabrians, on the other hand, have forgotten. It is as though the memory of the region removed the insult it had been subjected to because it was too unbearable. "Still today, however, in Mongiana about one third to one half of the male population is named Ferdinand after their grandfather. In this tradition, the respect for the king that gave them a reason for existing continues to live on, up until another king took everything away," noted Father Scopacasa.

"But now, we can finally narrate this story,": I returned to Mongiana after nearly twenty years and I was greeted by Doctor Vito Scopacasa, a cardiologist and a nephew to Father Scopacasa, who is now deceased. "Once I have finished this, I can stop being mayor (he was not re-elected)." "This" consists of the transformation of the factories into a museum, so that they might be used for holding events that would bring some life to Mongiana and awaken some memories. The last portion of the funds allotted for the security of the buildings and the acquisition of the furnishings has arrived: six hundred thousand euros from the Regional government (they had never received anything from the Ministry of Culture). "Then we will begin to have tourists here at the museum. A private foundation will run the museum and the town council will have a part as well. This took thirty-four years to accomplish."

How can one even begin to recount the pride one feels upon crossing the threshold of the building, which is marked by those two historical cast iron columns at the entrance of the resurrected factory? He showed me the area of the blast furnaces, where concerts are held today. "People that are seventy years old, that have never left Mongiana, have come up to me and said, 'Mayor, I did not know this was even here. I never came this far'."

"Here" is not that far. It is in the town, that small town. The factory is located between the houses on the outskirts and the blast furnaces were right nearby. "These memories were completely repressed," explains the mayor. "They wanted to forget." It is a self-defense mechanism for dealing with a pain that is too strong to bear. Not everyone was successful in achieving this.

Expert technicians from Germany, Switzerland, France, and England all came to Mongiana to discuss and compare techniques of production in their countries. Often they would partake in an international competition, in the name of industrialization and progress. We even won, though perhaps there was some trickery involved. The King of Naples commissioned the best metallurgical scientists to conduct a spectacular mission of industrial espionage. These austere scholars (researchers and university professors, not James Bond) with the support of the embassies and foreign colleagues inspected factories and analyzed the techniques of fusion and materials used and obtained data.

This trip lasted eight years and brought the most daring Southern scientists all over continental Europe as well as Scotland, Ireland, Iceland, and the Orkney Islands. Out of all of them, the eclectic Puglian Doctor Matteo Tondi distinguished himself. He studied chemistry, but also became one of Europe's foremost experts in mineralogy (he obtained recognition in Germany and France). As far as spirit of adventure and spy skills, he could easily be compared to any invented movie character. He was able to gather and take with him from the British Isles, who were extremely jealous of their trade, dozens of chests of minerals and samples of craftsmanship. He was offered six thousand pounds at the time (a fortune at the time) for his collection, but he refused out of honesty.

He was able to reach Naples by crossing through a Europe that was at war with Napoleon. His ship was captured by the French shortly after departing England. He pretended to be Venetian (who were not hostile to Napoleon) and was set free. He was arrested later on by the Austrians who became suspicious of his behavior. He was accused of espionage and was sentenced to death. At the last minute documents that pardoned him surfaced and he avoided the executioner. He would then wind up being captured by Bavarian soldiers. He understood, at this point, that he would never make it unless he escaped. He devised a plan that worked perfectly and he was able to escape through Switzerland and Austria and he reached Trieste, where he was finally able to board a ship for Naples.

The information he collected was of enormous importance. The Mongiana experts now knew all there was to know about metallurgy in the rest of Europe.

The only ones to truly comprehend the threat of the Mongiana factories were the English. They tried their best to block Mongiana's production. This was without any success because the engineers from the Calabrian iron mills were able to deceive the British defense and bring back tons of samples from the factories in Liverpool (as well as others) back to Naples.

The English, with a production that was much larger than that of Mongiana, were always proud adversaries of the Calabrian iron mills. Either they sensed Calabria's dangerous opportunities for development or they believed that "there are no small enemies, only enemies." This hostility reached the point of sabotage when the Bourbon king commissioned one of the greatest mining engineers of the time, who happened to be British, to operate the new fossil coal vein that had been discovered in the Serre Mountains. The engineer, who was given the utmost trust, conducted this operation in such a way to render the mine completely useless. Before he was finally removed from his post, he was able to waste substantial sums of money, to the point where the mining activities would be forever damaged.

Yet it was from Great Britain that businessmen like Pattison and Guppy arrived and created the most active metallurgy factories in the South, often with the collaboration of Neapolitan engineers. In the Serre Mountains, (that, like the rest of the South, came to know emigration only after the Unification) two waves of Brescian and German workers and technicians arrived. They did not last long. The inhabitants of Mongiana were very jealous of their abilities and in both instances they demonstrated that they could manage without the extra assistance.

"Mongiana had scientists," states Gambino. "It had managers, visits from the King, and many families from neighboring towns moved there. Finally a garrison was erected there so that the artillery's engineers could manage the weapons factory. Schools were built. Local craftsmen had their shops where they further processed the iron to produce valuable objects that still today adorn the most beautiful homes in Naples. When one referred to 'Mongiana iron', everyone understood that it was of the best quality."

The workers were overworked, just like in the rest of Europe during the Industrial Revolution. However, Mongiana's workers worked eight-hour shifts, or twelve at the most, as opposed to their colleagues in Liverpool, who worked sixteen-hour shifts. Mongiana's workers were the first to have health insurance and a pension fund, upon the initiative of the company itself and with the financial contribution of the workers themselves.

"What is Mongiana today?" asks Caracciolo. "Their primary concern is work. The town council, forest rangers, and other 'socially useful' jobs make up the bulk of available work here." The rest comes from the forest: the sawmill, the gathering and drying of wild mushrooms and the sale of products made with them, and the gathering of strawberries. These are all accomplished by a handful of small local businesses. They have a very poor economy. In fact, it may even be insulting to consider it an economy. But they live off of this out of need, not out of the evaluation and development of their potential."

Mongiana was once a capital of the metallurgical industry, and today it contends with the neighboring town of Nardodipace for the title of the poorest town in all of Europe.

The little money that the Forest rangers make ties them to the town. "By now the balance between man and forest is such that if mankind moves away, the forest will disappear. If the forest disappears, then Calabria disappears with it. To cut a tree, one must ask the Forest Rangers for their permission. These rules, I assure you, are respected, " explained Caracciolo.

"Those who come here cross wooded areas that are filled with streams and springs. However, they do not realize that they are in one of the most destabilized territories in all of Italy. At the end of the 1800s, the vast Calabrian forest (approximately eight hundred thousand hectares) was cut in half due to irrational exploitation. This is extremely dangerous in a region like Calabria. But twenty years passed before the Forest Rangers were established. The first law dates back to 1914 and was completed in 1923. This law actually copied, almost to the letter, the law with which the Kingdom of Naples established the Institute for Water and Forest Management and commissioned its own Forest Rangers." The Savoy monarchs had abolished the Forest Rangers and discovered the need for them only much later.

Calabria's mountains are fragile. Its slopes are marked with signs of the many earthquakes there have been (historically, this region is famous for its violent earthquakes). Two centuries ago, a violent earthquake caused serious landslides that affected hundreds of mountains. These landslides came down from the mountains on both sides of the many streams and rivers and obstructed the valleys. Two hundred lakes were formed in this manner, by highly unstable rock mounds. These mounds could have given way at any time and could have provoked serious floods due to the sudden emptying of the lakes.

The Bourbon engineers of the time studied a system of "controlled overflowing" in which the water spilled over the rocks slowly and in so doing, eroded the rock mounds progressively, thereby freeing the valleys of danger. This technique was later applied in 1987, in Valtellina, in the North.

Calabria is composed of one long string of mountains that rise from the sea. If one were to empty a bucket of water at the top of one of these mountains it would arrive at the bottom with the force of a bomb if nothing were to slow it down. Removing Calabria's forest means the region's certain destruction. The major flood in 1951 not only killed many people, but it provoked the abandonment of entire towns. These towns are empty to this day and are ghost towns. The health and management of the forests in this region are, for those areas that are considered at risk for earthquakes and landslides, a matter of life or death.

Mongiana, whose metallurgy industry was ruined, was chosen to be the headquarters of the Forest Rangers. "But still today, one hundred years later, one cannot consider this adequate compensation for the damage inflicted. In forty years," narrates Caracciolo, "the forests that had been destroyed were replanted and new wooded areas were created. The mountain is no longer subject to landslides. Ask yourselves why in this region there are no longer disasters of the same caliber that have tormented the regions of Tuscany, Campania, and Liguria in the last few decades. The old landslides have been stopped. Once in a while, when work is done on the mountains, old braces built to reinforce the sides of the mountains are uncovered. They still hold up after all these years. This is quite exciting for us. There is danger only on the extreme part of the mountain chains that border the sea, where the jurisdiction of the Forest Rangers ends. Here, the areas near the last stretch of the river are still subject to floods."

The engineer has a dignified but resentful tone of voice. It is a tone that I know well and I hear it quite often: if a person does something good, in the South, they are suspicious, and you can see that the person spoken to is asking themselves "What is the real story here? Where is the catch? What is this person hiding?" One is only credible if they do something bad. The Forest Rangers (they are considered to be workers, because, proportionately, there are fewer of them in Calabria than in the Veneto region) are quite numerous here because they are a sort of safeguard from misery. This was similar to the "official rectilinear swamps" from a century ago in the North. These only existed as a means for giving money to unemployed Northerners courtesy of the "voluntary" payment of taxes imposed on the South (who actually had its own fair share of unemployed workers). In other words, these are "socially useful" jobs (though the ones in the North were not exactly useful).

The Calabrian Forest Rangers saved the region's territory (but no one has really taken notice of this). They are summoned to do their job in other regions as well because their competence is widely known. The Spanish Forest rangers have based their training methods on those established by the Calabrians, to adapt their methods for use in Andalusia. The Calabrian Forest Rangers do not dedicate themselves exclusively to the forests, like they do in other regions. They also take care of roads that border the coast and even build new coast roads. They build town squares, public pools, manage the plants and greenery in local cemeteries as well as those plants at the airport of Lamezia. There are so many rangers that it is scandalous. Someone must resolve this situation. The orthodontist who was called to rewrite the Constitution, what was his name again? Roberto Calderoli proclaimed himself a "commissioner" and asked Berlusconi to grant him God-knows-what decisional powers. He then proceeded to announce, "I am not familiar with the problem, but I am the right person to solve it." Can you imagine what would have happened in a serious country? Well, here, they were not able to imagine it. Calderoli is a member of that party who was able to procure for one of Bossi's sons a job (which was later denied) with a ten-thousand-euro paycheck. Per month. A Forest Ranger could hope to see that same sum of money in a year, if all goes well. But it is the Forest Ranger who is the thief. As for Calderoli, the "constitutional orthodontist of the forest," he was able to solve one problem immediately: he disappeared. This act alone did wonders for the view.

The *'ndrangheta* managed to infiltrate the Calabrian Forest Rangers (as with the jobs in the Expo, the fruit and vegetable markets, the Stock Exchange, construction and other entities of Milan). It was advantageous for them to control the forests so that they might oversee the places where they could hide their henchmen and bosses (for a time they used to hide the people they kidnapped here as well). This piece of information is widely known. "Forest Rangers" have become synonymous with "*Mafioso.*"

"I don't like to speak with journalists," Caracciolo told me. "I will be frank in telling you that I would not have accepted to speak with you had you not come here with Doctor Gambino. I have nothing against you, but then again, I have no reason to trust you either. A few years ago reporters were sent here from an important weekly magazine based in Milan. They asked to visit our construction sites and we helped provide them with all of the things they desired to see. We showed them documents and everything. When the article they wrote was published, they only spoke of *mafia*-affiliated Forest Rangers and photos of the officials that had accompanied them throughout their stay here, as though they were the delinquents being written about. Sometime later, another important weekly magazine put out by the same publisher published the same photo again, attaching it this time to an article about the *mafia*. There was no mention of the landslides that had been halted, the forests that had been saved, those that had been created where there once was nothing. Not one word was written about these things. They simply were not interesting enough."

Now the greatest former metallurgical district in Italy wants to recover its memory and render it productive. "A museum, plus all of the businesses that will flourish because of it, and the Forest Ranger's Center for Biodiversity: all of these things will not merely resurrect Mongiana, but give rise to its proper birth. In this day and age, that is something." (Scopacasa would go on to lose the election by eighteen votes. He would be replaced by the daughter of the mayor with whom he began the project to renovate the iron mills.)

Why is it so difficult to recuperate a past inclination towards business and industry? Why is it that the Southerners are incapable of once again being who they once were? Pippo Callipo (who is specialized in preserved goods especially fish and tuna of extremely high quality) held a public discussion with representatives from regional and national institutions present. In his speech, he listed the many obstacles that a businessman must face should he decide to operate his business in the South, taking into consideration that one not only has geography and the mafia (who stipulates work contracts, the payment of "protection" money, and personnel) against them but also the state, for its policies that are the allies of "bad" businesses and the government that subtracts incentives from the trenches of the South, only to invest them in the comfortable "living rooms" of the North. While he was delivering his speech, this large, indomitable man was overwhelmed by his sense of powerlessness and the general disinterest of the government. He cried. He had already been subjected to numerous attacks on the part of the *mafia* and had to consider the possibility of closing his business and transferring his company elsewhere. However, he did not give in. Rather than continue to wait for the government to mend its ways, he took matters into his own hands and ran for President of the Region, as a complete out-sider candidate.

I asked him to remember back to the moment where he sur-rendered to his feelings. "When they killed the vice president of the Region, Fortugno, the Minister of Internal Affairs, Pisanu, came to Calabria. A meeting was held at the Regional Council in Reggio Calabria. I spoke, as President of the region's branch of the Manu-facturer's Association (*Confindustria*). Only the officials that ac-companied the minister were present at the discussion because the minister was attending another meeting in the same building. 'What a pity,' I said, 'I would have liked to ask him what I should reply to my son when I accompany him to the airport to leave for his studies at the university when he asks me, 'Dad, do I have to come back?'" It was at that time that he could not stop his tears from flowing.

Callipo has managed to build an exemplary company. He has two hundred employees, the majority of which happen to be women. To read his name on a label is a guarantee of excellence. What other element of pride must a father transmit to his son? But his factory has been the target of shootings and a Regional Coun-selor has sent his officials to try to find any irregularities in his company. In the recordings of the phone taps, which ended up as evidence in a court of law, the inspectors reported to this coun-selor that at the Callipo Company, everything was frighteningly perfect. Everything was in order, even beyond the regulations. There was nothing to question. They, however, received a direct order to return (and they would do so, uselessly) with the promise to be promoted to director, should they find something wrong with the Pippo Callipo's tuna cannery. If this is the situation, what would you tell you your son? "Come back here, so that you can spend your life fighting the *mafia* and politics!"

So what answer did he finally give his son?

"Nothing." His voice cracked. Again. I thought, but didn't say, "Who is obliging you to continue to do this? Why?" Then he told me the rest of the story and I had my answer. His son is twenty-five years old and graduated from the Bocconi University in Milan with honors. He then pursued a master's degree in business management in Barcelona. He then returned and asked to be hired by his father's company. His first job consisted of canning tuna filets.

I spoke with Callipo only once in my life, while writing this book. Anyone from the North who believes himself to be a business entrepreneur should see if they can manage to be so when facing the same conditions that Callipo and his colleagues face every day. One must pay for electrical energy, which is more expensive than in the North, despite its production in the South. One must put up with the possibility that the machinery could stop working at any given moment, without warning, due to the electrical network's inadequacy. One must accept that bank credit is 30% more expensive and that the time it takes to process it is much longer. One must also accept that loans have an extra 3% worth of taxes. One can also add to their list of expenses, should they decide to pay it, the "protection" money that must be paid to the local *mafia* (if the *mafia* agrees that it is sufficient). Transportation expenses are greatly influenced by the inadequacies of the roadways, railways, and ports: the largest container port of the Mediterranean, Gioia Tauro, does not sort goods that are imported or exported from the regions or the rest of the nation. It has only had a functional connection with the railway, despite its existence for decades, since 2007, and even then, the railway was only equipped with one track! Cersosimo, an economist, defined this as "a port that is close to the entire world, but very far away from Calabria." One must also take into consideration that the Minister of Economy and Finance, Tremonti, will remove the tax breaks for businesses in the South, the tax credit, and would invent others in favor of the North. One must understand that the government cannot be counted upon, not even when your regional vice president is killed did the Prime Minister consider it appropriate to show his support for the State against the *mafia*. Berlusconi did not attend the funeral. He sent no telegram to the widow and the orphaned children. He did not even offer his condolences over the phone! Do you believe that the *mafia* and the people don't know what this means? "This is their business. We will not interfere."

This is exactly what organized crime wants: everyone rules their own household. The government rules in Rome, and we rule here.

One cannot count on the Manufacturers' Association either: "It has been in existence for over a century and has only catered to the interests of the North. In one hundred years, it has not taken one legislative measure to support the businesses in the South. Even Emma Marcegaglia, the current President of the Manufacturer's Association, has taken notice of this," according to Luca Montrone of the Telenorba television channel. He is a Southern business entrepreneur who has taken the initiative to design a Manufacturers' Association exclusively for the South. I ask if it is not risky, in the establishment of this contrasting association, to break the country into pieces? He answers, "The country is already split into pieces. It is time to sew these pieces back together." Montrone always weighs his words with care, but when he speaks them, he does not soften their meaning. When I ask him on a scale of one to ten, what the chances are that it can be sown back together, he replies, "Three or four. But it will take a very long time. I will not live to see it."

From October 2008 to spring of 2009 from his television network and the radio (and then TeleCapri, Channel 21, and Channel 8) a massive advertising campaign was launched: "Telenorba would like to invite the businesses of the South to abandon the Italian Manufacturer's Association. It does not represent the South's entrepreneurs" and it is controlled "by the large businesses of the North to the enormous disadvantage of the businesses from the South" the South's entrepreneurs should "rally to render the regional and provincial business associations of the South independent from the Manufacturer's Association" and form a Manufacturer's Association for the South.

What response did this campaign receive? Hundreds of businessmen, economists, and politicians proposed to support this theory with analyses, studies, and personal experience. Montrone was expelled from the Italian Manufacturer's Association (well, almost: he was expelled from the association's branch in Bari, but he was also a member of the Lecce branch, which did not expel him.) "In the businessmen's union, the importance of a company is determined by its number of employees, " explains Montrone, "There are two things to note: small and medium sized businesses, which make up over 70.8% of Italy's wealth, have little power. The South, which does not have large companies, counts for 7.5%. On the Manufacturer's Association's Board of Directors, only one of the 17 representatives is from the South. When it comes to dealing with the government, only the large companies are taken into consideration, and they are located in the North. The South is penalized twice. I have written to President Emma Marcegaglia five or six times and have received no response. " After they threatened with secession, a dialogue was opened. "I ask that the Italian Manufacturer's Association have three presidents," Montrone explains to me, "one for the large companies, one for the medium and small ones, and one for the South. They should be elected by whom they represent and not be appointed from "above". At a time they establish, they should meet with the government together. If not, they should each go their own separate ways." In case this request were to be denied, the South would proceed with its plans for establishing its own association, out of necessity.

Even the information-advertising monopoly RAI-Mediaset works to damage the South. It "kills local television stations as well as small and medium sized businesses, to favor larger businesses, especially foreign ones" states Montrone. What do you mean, I ask. "RAI and Mediaset sell television commercials at prices that are too low, damaging paper advertisements and local television stations. In France, the same spaces cost twice as much. In this manner the large Italian companies, who want to advertise outside of the country, are obliged to invest twice as much money for advertising. In Italy, their French competitors spend half as much, and they are favored. This system is profitable in either case for RAI and Mediaset. To further prevent that local television stations become an obstacle, they are penalized. A law passed in 1993 imposes that 15% of the public television fee paid to the RAI should go to local television stations. That would be equivalent to two hundred million euros. That money would be ours by law. But in 2008, that amount was reduced to one hundred and fifty million euros. In 2001 that amount was further reduced to sixty million euros. We have to stop our investments, reduce our production teams, and not renew our renewable contracts. They want to make us disappear."

But what does this have to do with the South? Montrone shows us a map and a chart. The trends of local advertising, industrial growth, and increase in jobs appear to be linked. "The market increases with advertising. The South is the land of small and medium sized businesses. If your market is Lecce, you need to let the people of Lecce know what products you manufacture. Local television stations serve this purpose. Otherwise, small businesses could only advertise on a national scale, where they would be left out." Remember the advantages of that law, that for three years allotted fifty million euros, not to the businesses of the South, but to the advertising of their products? "It was a small sum of money that yielded great results. Curiously, this law was not renewed." Perhaps because it worked too well, like the tax credit.

Montrone suspects that there might also be another reason: "Many small voices equal freedom. If they are silenced, only the strongest voice will be heard. Before the electoral reform that abolished the indication of one's preference, members of Parliament had to answer to their electors, now they only have to answer to the secretary of their political party. They cannot allow themselves to represent anyone else. The South has never had the Italian Manufacturer's Association on its side. Now it no longer has its members of Parliament either. It also risks losing its local informational and advertising advantage with respect to its local businesses. What do we have left?"

What would the editors of the North's daily newspapers say at this point? "The South should quit complaining and do something to improve its situation." Then it would cite the industrial data of the North-East portion of Italy. It pains me to not have a powerful voice like that of De Andrè so that I might follow his advice. But someone has.

Pino Aprile

In Mongiana, Father Giuseppe Scopacasa did not accept the idea that his town and parish emptied itself a little more as each day passed. To keep the inhabitants tied to their town and homes he tried to invent jobs for them, and when he was unable to do so, he tried to help them as best as he could to emigrate. He let no one too far out of his sight, however: his project was to bring everyone back home. He was a clever shepherd of souls: one that you could say is one of the true leaders of the town. He knew everything there was to know about everyone. He knew what to ask of whom and to whom he should give something. In this manner, he protected the destinies of many people.

Father Scopacasa organized conventions to recover the town's history and to recuperate the ruins of the iron mills. He compiled and published reports for this purpose. He formed an association to favor the return of emigrants, if not permanently, at least temporarily, so that they would not forget their roots. Father Scopacasa also organized a sort of party during which the local, provincial, regional, and parliamentary representatives, who were concerned about the emigration problem, were present when these emigrants returned home to recount their experiences. It was an homage to nostalgia, to those things that the emigrants had lost and to the maladjustment to those things that were new and foreign. It expressed pain, but hope as well.

Francesco Furci, however, did not stop there. He was filled with resentment and when it was his turn to take the stage, he told the government "big wigs", in a poem he wrote in his dialect, the story of his emigration:

I was desperate living in my town
Married with five children
I worked thirty days a month
I tilled the land.
There were no holidays for me
Night and day I wracked my brain
Because I had no bread for my children.
I asked the town for help
But they offered me no hope

In the meantime vagabonds, bootlickers, and grafters
Filled their bellies alongside the mayor.
Blessed is the German government
You welcomed immigrants by the thousands
You gave us rights
And we are grateful to you for this.
The detachment from our Italy was very hard
We left filled with sadness
In Germany we found jobs
And happiness came quickly.
Italian government, you fill your Gazette
With so many laws
But you only do this for show
Because you are the first to break them.
You made me emigrate to Germany
You made me take that train all alone
And now that you see that I am well off,
Italian government, go screw yourself!

The song that Fabrizio De Andrè wrote, which suggests the grand finale of this poem, was actually written later on. The exhortation, if we can call it that, had been in the air for quite some time. Furthermore, after a century and half, the Italian government does not deserve Mongiana, a champion and metaphor for industrialization in the South, which was strangled by weapons and force.

CHAPTER 6

The Patriarchs

The invasion of the South risked extinguishing a certain species of tree that only exists in the Pollino mountain chain (aside from an area in the Balkans). It has been around since the time of the dinosaurs. On the same cliffs, a little more than three thousand years ago, another tree sprouted, that both mythology and humans believe to be eternal. The meeting of these two patriarchs tells the story of what happened here better than any National Archive. This is the earth, where the destinies of trees and men seem to be inextricably intertwined.

In the South it is said that olive oil is still extracted from the trees that were planted by the comrades of Hector, who fought Achilles, from Aeneas, who founded Rome and from Paris who seduced Helen and doomed Troy. From a comment made by Servius in Book I of Virgil's *Giorgics*, one comes to know of a castle, Gargaròn, (from the name of one of the peaks of Mount Ida in the Troade Mountains), which was built in Calabria by one hundred and fifty Trojans that landed in the Gulf of Taranto after the destruction of their city. It has been proven that the olive tree has been cultivated in Calabria since 1200 BCE: from around the time of the Trojan War. The legendary migration of those who escaped Troy to the Ionic coasts of Calabria rests also on the story of the tormented city of Siris, which was located on the left bank of the Sinni River. The exiled Trojans founded it. A coalition of misfit Achaeans attacked it and conquered it (again!). Taranto (also called Thurii) was renamed the city of Heraclea. The greatest painter in antiquity, the Painter from Policoro (from the name of the modern city) was from there.

In the area surrounding Sibari, where those one hundred and fifty Trojans sought shelter, there is the Garga River (Servius actually refers to it as the Gargaro River while he calls the nearby village Garga). A passionate local scholar, Leone Salvatore Viola, studied the curious formation of the ancient olive groves on the right bank of the river. The trees appear to be in small groups of three or four trees while large spaces, which remain inexplicably empty, separate one stand of trees from the other. They are "domestic" plants, not wild, but no farmer would plant them in that manner.

So what? There is a fascinating phenomenon, according to Viola, that lies behind those odd tree configurations: olive trees "walk". The trees in those strange formations are the product of the "migrant fragmentation" of ancient trees that may even be thousands of years old. What does this mean?

The Greeks used to say that "No tree grows high enough to reach the sky." Even the trees that live the longest, once they reach their biggest size, die because of their enormous size. The dead wood that sustains them increases in size until the discrepancy between the live part of the trunk and the dead part is no longer sustainable. Sometimes the tree's trunk increases to the point where the tree's center begins to hollow out. The wider it becomes (like in the case of the Sequoia tree) the more hollow its center becomes until it eventually collapses under its own weight. This does not happen with the olive tree. It grows and its center becomes hollow, and it continues to grow. However, rather than dying by remaining one entity, it splits itself into more trees (we all knew it was a wise tree, didn't we?). These new trees all begin this cycle anew. This makes the olive tree, the symbolic tree of the Mediterranean, appear to be eternal. "We would like to believe this to be true," says Guido Bongi, a researcher for the National Council of Research in Perugia, who has devised a scientific method to determine the age of these olive trees. "However, the olive tree is not eternal. At this time, the only way to date the oldest "patriarchs" is according to which archaeological site surrounds them and carbon dating. That is really it."

Leone Viola writes that he has studied olive groves of different certifiable ages in the Garga Valley and has gathered reliable data regarding how to estimate the age of the oldest olive trees. The index of growth of olive trees "varies according to the quality and composition of the terrain, its latitude, its height above sea-level, and its irrigation...," states Gianni Pofi, a passionate agronomist, who has studied in detail the plants of the Egnatia archaeological site. Egnatia was an ancient port city on the Adriatic Sea where fleets departed to and arrived from the eastern part of the Mediterranean, Asia Minor, and West Africa. It was then replaced in importance by Brindisi, which became the gateway to the East and is today partially submerged due to the subsidence of the coast. Those olive trees that can be found amongst the ruins, if the studies confirm this hypothesis, could be the same age as the city: over two thousand years old. Pofi warns that a valid index of growth cannot be established everywhere. My objective is not to verify the age of the olive trees in question, but to gather the meaning and behavior behind the human behavior that render what is narrated, plausible.

Viola says that for the olive trees located in the Garga Valley, the diameter of the trunks grows initially a centimeter and one half per year. Then it begins to slow down. After a century, the increase reduces to a few millimeters and after it reaches six to eight hundred years, this reduces further to a half a millimeter. It is at this time, when the olive tree's trunk has reached its maximum diameter that the tree begins to divide itself. The trunk, which is often empty by this point, begins to thin itself out based on where it has injuries, knots, has been pruned, or attacked by parasites. The trunk then dries out and begins to split apart vertically. This can happen in more places and at separate times on the same tree and the trunk can split into three, four, or even five separate parts. Each of these parts begins to live its own separate life around one thousand years because, depending upon where the fractures are, where the trunk dies, its roots also die. The stump divides itself and each "derived plant" takes with it a part of the original tree.

This sets off the mechanism that allows the olive trees to "walk." The internal part of the "new" trees is dead as are the roots. Only the external part of the plant can grow roots to generate and feed new tree bark. However, the more this green façade grows, the more the interior dies. "It is a plant derived by a division," writes Viola "and therefore it is characterized by a part that lives and a part that dies." The farmers use the dry parts of the trunk as kindling. In this manner, mankind assists nature. "Through pruning, man determines and decides the shape of the olive trees through time, "explains Pofi. "After centuries, when the trunk rots and the wood inside deteriorates, it is always man who, with his intervention, determines the fragmentation, thus safeguarding the healthy parts of the tree."

"In this manner, we obtain a tree that 'walks'," concludes Viola, "it drifts in the direction of the green part of its trunk." New shoots grow in the direction of the sun. They distance themselves from the older part of the tree and follow their 'youth.' However, one cannot say that the shoots have been estranged from the tree that bore them, because they are parts of that tree. But one also cannot say that it is still the same tree because it is now divided into parts that have their own roots and undergo their own development. Gianni Picella, an organizer and guide for the Committee for the Protection of Centuries-old Olive Trees, narrates that even in the Garden of Gethsemane in Jerusalem "the old trees, ancient witnesses, seem to derive from one tree, as offshoots of the original tree or from fractures of it. One can even determine their starting point."

Pofi states that, in fact, olive trees also "walk" by dropping shoots from the base of their trunks or from the roots that are farthest away from their trunks, sometimes as far as one or two meters away. Viola limits himself to the notion of fragmentation because it is most useful when attempting to date the "father" trees, and I see no reason to deviate from this route.

Olive trees that have come into existence by division move like the populations of the Mediterranean: they drift away, conserving a common reference point, the memory of their origin: the tree trunk that is no longer there. From which, believes Viola, in the Garga Valley, they distance themselves two millimeters each year, and two meters every millennium. If this is true, that ancient olive grove, deduces Viola, is more than three thousand years old. It was planted while Troy's ruins were still smoking. According to legend, the refugees that came from there, just like the Kurds today, who have fled from the same land, colonized an abandoned town in Calabria.

Don't ask me if the grove is exactly three thousand years old or not. Subsequent studies will prove this to be true or not. The type of olive is actually more indicative of its age than its wood or its current state. Some varieties have been planted recently in certain areas. Others were brought over by archaic immigrations. Still others can be considered autochthonous. This dates them. Professor Bongi takes Puglia as an example where the *leccino* variety, which was not native to the region, arrived recently and is now quite diffuse throughout the area. Olive pits dating back to the time of the ancient town of Messapica have been discovered, which would make them about three thousand years old. Olives of the *ogliarola* variety were discovered amongst the remains of a sunken Roman ship near Brindisi.

I am not competent enough nor am I interested enough to insert myself in such a beautiful and uncertain phenomenon. I can only admire those who dedicate themselves to its study. Only one thing is certain: the olive trees in the Garga Valley are many, many centuries old. The notion that they might be over three thousand years old and that they represent the trust in the future of an ancient people that had been defeated and was forced to wander away from their home offers a ray of hope. Whatever their age might be, they are the proof of the connection between the Southerners and their land. Olive trees are domestic plants. They can live so long, grow, divide themselves, and be reborn from a shoot and start over again only if for the entire time, a man takes care of it. He must trim the branches and lighten the tree's weight. He must keep the area around the tree clear of aggressive weeds and keep it free of dead wood. When this does not happen, the olive tree becomes wild, decays and becomes sterile within a few years. It is almost always suffocated by oak trees that can take over their land and block their sunlight.

Amongst the many olive groves I could have spoken about, I chose to speak of this one to act as proof of the link between the

Southerners and the tree that ties them to their land. Try to think for a moment what it would mean if, as Leone Viola is trying to prove, it were true that the exiled Trojans planted those trees, while in flight from the destruction of their world. They brought with them their code of laws and their gods to act as a pact amongst themselves, and they planted olive trees to make a pact with their new land. Even Pericles made young Athenians swear to consider any land that was blessed by the presence of olive trees, home. This was the pact: I will give you olives for your bread and oil for your kitchen and lamps, and wood for your fires. You will give me water if it does not rain enough and you will clear my roots of weeds so that I can breathe and you will remove the sterile wood that rests upon my shoulders.

If Viola is correct, this means that the pact has never been betrayed: while the Mycenaean civilization reached its apex and collapsed under the Dorian attack; while Athens and Sparta faced Darius and Xerxes in order to decide the fate of the world; while the Greeks built cities on our coasts and fought against the Phoenicians and Etruscans; while Socrates discovered how to reason; while Rome built its empire and destroyed Carthage, crucified the son of a carpenter and fell into decadence for five hundred years; while from Asia, Alaric's barbarians descended upon the peninsula to Calabria or when Genseric ascended the peninsula from Byzantium; while every tribe from Northern Europe in proximity to the Mediterranean coast fought over the Garga Valley and its ancient olive grove (the town is called Saracena, which should be indicative of the outcome of the battles); and the Albanians, Normans, French, Spanish, reactionaries, Jacobins....

Now, if they are effectively three thousand years old or less, one hundred and twenty to one hundred and fifty generations old or only a few dozen (if the plants proved to be much younger), no matter how beautiful or frightening the history in the Garga Valley was, someone pruned those olive trees, cleared their roots, and took away the dead wood. Gods, people, and languages changed. "Wandering" cities replaced ancient ones, but that pact of mutual assistance was never interrupted. Not everyone took care of their own fathers. Some left their fathers to die alone and a statistic on the patricides committed at the time indicates that some even killed their fathers. However, even those who did not take care of their fathers did care for their olive trees.

The proof is that the trees are still there, otherwise they would have decayed and died.

Nothing has been able to uproot, for millennia, the people from Garga and surrounding areas continued to greet and tally blood, stories, refugees and conquerors. Until the Piedmontese arrived. The Pollino Mountains, from where the river descends, recounts the destinies of its people through its trees. The ancient olive trees evolve into fragments that distance themselves from each other, transforming the single trunk into collective memory and independent paths: just like the colonies that were formed from the people of other cities in the Mediterranean, who in the name of their native land, built themselves a greater future. But those who were already here remained and they lived together. With exiled people and colonists, the olive tree reached the Pollino Mountains and found some room at the root of the most ancient mountain plant: the armored pine, a living fossil that was a contemporary of the dinosaurs, whom it resembles with its scaled bark that resembles a warrior's armor.

It is a tree that takes its time to grow, as if it obeys cycles, which are no longer ours. Its seed does not sprout before two years (unlike the ten to fifteen days required for other conifers). It is tormented by beech trees that (due to the climate's rising temperatures after the last ice age) steal its ideal land. The armored pine was forced to seek refuge in the most inaccessible and windy areas, amidst storms, ice and rocky zones. This millennia-old plant survives where no other plant could survive. It is carved by time and lightning. When it dies, it loses its bark and appears as white as the marble used for tombstones. But it remains standing, the king of silence, as a candid monument to itself. This striking feature gave rise to its scientific name, and it is known not for its aspect while it is living, but when it is dead: *pinus leucodermis* (white-skinned pine). Its wood is extremely hard, impenetrable, and in-

vulnerable to the attacks of parasites. This risked to make it disappear forever.

The olive trees of Garga have become patriarchs, because there
had never been emigration, just like in the rest of the South. However, when the Kingdom of the Two Sicilies was invaded, which
brought massacres and misery, the Southerners after having uselessly fought back, fled by the millions. This tied the fate of this
fossil pine to that of the emigrants. The chests made from armored
pine are not vulnerable to termites and safeguarded the belong-
ings of the emigrants from the regions of Campania, Calabria, and
those from the Lucano area, who were forced to flee from their
lands when they boarded the ships that would take them abroad.
My wife happened to find one of these chests that had been used
for thirty years as a woodbin and shelter for chickens. We disin-
fected it with some ammonia and treated it with some oil. It now
sits in our living room and looks as if it were brand new.

There were so many people that were forced to leave after having lost everything after the Unification that the armored pines,
after millennia, nearly disappeared over the course of a few years
because they were used to build chests. Paradoxically, they were
saved because the towns ran out of people before the mountains
ran out of trees. The towns emptied and the pastures were abandoned. Then, a few decades ago, the Forest Rangers (yes, those
Forest Rangers) managed to multiply the few specimens left.

The Pollino Mountains are a different world. The major communication routes of the South are really very few and they are in
bad shape. It is already difficult to follow them without departing
from them to pursue more impenetrable paths. Furthermore, all of
the major roads (the Salerno-Reggio Calabria, Basentana, and the
Ionica) wind around the Pollino Massif. At best, they skirt its border. They seem more like a boundary walls rather than roads. The
mountains have their own time frames, between Albanian communities, Greek Orthodox priests who are legally married, vestiges of
Norman invasions that can be seen in the blue eyes of residents,
Greek last names, Christianized priapistic rituals, and hawks that
live in the deepest gulches of all Europe, like that of Raganello. The

world of the others brushes against all of this and ignores it. It gives me chills to think that those who did not move from there for millennia and saved their ancestral olive trees, by leaving (nearly) marked the end of the witness that has presided over this place for millions of years.

I narrate many things in these pages, yet I think that this (more than the massacres, robberies, or insults) best illustrates the depth of the injury that was inflicted upon us: that people in flight were willing to cancel the existence of the pine tree (which was transformed into chests, almost in the same shape as a coffin) that was as old as the first "father."

CHAPTER 7

The Bad Road

One might look for history in books and actually find it in the road. The Salerno-Reggio Calabria stretch of highway (also known as the SaRc or the A3), for example, tells the story of how the State keeps the South in subordination to the North through its waste of resources in exchange for inefficient infrastructure, thanks to the worst that both the South and the North have to offer. The highway "blatantly divides Italy in two" between a part "that is perceived both by politicians and the general opinion of the public as being capable of great changes and another, that is not," writes Leandra D'Antone, a professor of contemporary history at the Sapienza University in Rome, in her book on the SaRc, *Senza Pedaggio*. She is specialized in public and territorial policies.

The A3 was built with public money that was allotted to businesses in the Center and North who, in turn, delegate the execution of the construction (which is of precarious quality in order to stay within budget) to local businesses that are preferably *mafia* affiliated. The large companies do not believe it is necessary for them to back out of this system: they are there to make money, not fight the *mafia*. Perhaps they do not find it uncomfortable that the alliance between "clean" businesses and not reappears in Piedmont in the work on the TAV (the high-speed train) or on the Milan Expo convention center. These large companies have the management of the system in their hands and are more or less "obliged" to tolerate inconvenient subcontractors that are, in any event, subordinate to the large companies. They are rarely assigned to do anything more complicated than moving dirt and supplying concrete. This corresponds quite well to the notion of the difference between "us, up here" and "you, down there": we can keep you around to do jobs lacking in content and requiring no skills only because we are obliged to and because you are delinquents.

In this manner, the businesses of the North favored the *mafia-run* businesses of the South (legitimate businesses in the South are forced to close due to unfair competition: they are simply unarmed). They raise snakes in their bosoms: they are the slaves that will take over empires. The *mafia*, who has now been introduced into this "game," begins to condition it with the availability of its funds.

Why are the South's roads built by the Center and the North? Because there no companies in the South that are capable of taking on such a large job. The North got a head start building roads, and seeing as they now have more experience, it is more likely that they will be hired to build new roads as well. Their businesses have the facilities, machinery, competence, and have made the compromises necessary to do the job.

Unified Italy cut out the South from industrial production and business. The great infrastructural feats necessary were accomplished in the North. A study dating back to the beginning of the 1900s revealed that by removing the Campania and Puglia regions, in the rest of the South, out of 1,848 towns, 1321 lacked roads. The first highway (in the world, in fact, in many languages the word to refer to a highway is a direct translation of the Italian term *autostrada*: *autopista, autoroute, Autobahn*) was built in 1923-24 in order to transport Milanese citizens on vacation: the Milan-Lake road. The others were conceived to serve two thirds of the country. Nothing was built in the South for decades. Gaetano Salvemini commented, with his scathing irony, on the Conference on Traffic held in Stresa in October of 1954. An announcement was made regarding roadwork for thousands of kilometers of new highways and the enlargement of those already in existence. This would cost one thousand three hundred billion lira (which was an enormous amount of money at the time). This would all be in the North and would stop at Rome. Okay, maybe Naples. "The Southerners interrupted, 'What about South of Naples?'" writes Salvemini, "and the general manager replied: 'Those will be ordinary roads.'" The others requested that they be highways. They did not obtain them. They actually obtained few, almost nothing, of the ordinary roads promised. Gaetano made an example of the fact that Southerners do not know how to ask for things. Either way, those others would very likely not have given them what they asked for anyway.

So those who begin working later on the roads, like the companies from the South, must start from the bottom and ask for little in return. They might even have to lay claim to these jobs with weapons in their hands if they do not have patience, but rather an inclination towards delinquency. However, once they start, they too can grow. (Which is something that the big contractors have forgotten.)

Perhaps the South does not know how to build roads? How about the ones that were already present when the "liberators" arrived? Who had laid those down and built the iron bridges that the rest of Europe only learned how to build half a century later than the Kingdom of the Two Sicilies?

Maybe the South does not have competent engineers? The Salerno-Reggio Calabria has solutions that appear futuristic and daring even fifty years later. The majority of the engineers and people who built it were from the South. The IRI (the Institute for Industrial Reconstruction that financed the rescue of bankrupt companies in the North with tax money) kept Center and Northern highways for itself: it built them and managed them. But when Sergio De Amicis, president of *Italstrade* (a company owned by IRI) discovered what the engineers and personnel of the ANAS office of Cosenza had done for the Salerno-Reggio Calabria, he called his colleague at the ANAS and said, "I will take them all!"

If you had ventured out onto the Salerno-Reggio Calabria highway at the end of July of 2009, the first thing you would have thought, after having driven this stretch in both directions, was that there was a crucial road sign missing at the entrance: "Cross yourselves upon entering." There are 443 kilometers until you reach the Strait. Two hundred of these have been widened and now have two lanes plus an emergency lane. As soon as you enter, those three lanes become two and the speed limit decreases from 80 km/h to 60 km/h. After you pass through the tunnel, the two lanes become three again, but only for seven kilometers, the two again, then three again (except for the exit for Battipaglia). Then there is a short series of movable barriers upon reaching Eboli, where the most sophisticated of the unresolved problems concerning the Salerno-Reggio Calabria resides: the theological one.

In order to say that Italy has forgotten the South, from Salerno down, Carlo Levi, a writer from Turin who was confined to the Lucania area due to Fascism, wrote a book and coined well known phrase: *Cristo si è fermato ad Eboli.*[1] Decades later, the Minister of Public Works of an Italy that had returned to democracy, Giacomo Mancini, father of the SaRc, during a famous meeting in Sala Consilina (a bit further down the road) "turned the metaphor around," according to Pietro Mancini, his son, "Christ went no further than Eboli because the highway ended." Now there is one (since 1973), though it is quite a tormented route. Andrea Camilleri, who invented the *Commissario Montalbano* character, sustains that Christ went no further than Eboli so that he would not have to drive on the Salerno-Reggio Calabria (it is all fine and well that He had to die to save us from our sins, but seeing as He had a choice, He preferred Mount Golgotha....).

The dispute appears to have been solved by Cardinal Renato Martino, after an abominable trip on the A3, he defined it as "the Stations of the Cross." This is without taking into consideration that Christ could walk on water, but did not have a driver's license. Does this close the theological dispute? No.

The clergyman has ignored the fact that the SaRc is not a highway: it does not have the "characteristics ... even though it is classified as such," as it is written in the General Plan for Transportation and of Italian Logistics of 2001, whose regulations our country must meet (the European Union imposes it) so that it can grant the "right to mobility" to everyone. This has been "blatantly and exceptionally" denied by the SaRc, "whose geometry is no-

---

[1] TRANSLATOR'S NOTE: *Christ Stopped at Eboli.*

ticeably below the minimum levels of the standards required of a highway."

But today, after Eboli, a sort of Heaven on Earth opens before our car, with regard to the highway. There are three wide lanes plus an emergency lane, freshly paved roads, and a straight road that leads through a tunnel. Regardless as to whether Christ passed through here or not, this is a miracle. Outside of that tunnel, after a few kilometers, the old A3 appears again. It has two lanes and no emergency lane. There is a sign that states, thanks to the "Law," this will all be improved. For now, the speed limit is 60 km/h.

We would deal with the two lanes of traffic "without" the emergency lane, but three kilometers later, those all turn into one lane. There are always trucks on this road. What is the speed limit here? The speedometer is so embarrassed that it refuses to say anything. There are detours that take you from one side of the highway to another, but there is still only one lane available. On the other side (around the exit for Sicignano) there are many machines and one half dozen workers in orange suits without protective headgear. Then the two lanes plus the emergency lane reappears! This will be the most one will see until one reaches Reggio Calabria because the renovation of the A3 covers the first fifty kilometers South of Salerno with three lanes. The other four hundred kilometers will have two. We are privileged: in the adjacent lane there are cars and trucks that are stuck in traffic for many kilometers. There is a sign that displays the ANAS's call center: 800290092. I call: "Press 1 to signal an accident. Press 0 for information." You just wait and see that no one will answer and after seven or eight interruptions, or the line falling, I will be obliged to just give up. But I have made a mistake! Immediately an efficient female voice answers. I ask "Are there any problems on the A3, going towards Reggio Calabria?" "None," she replies. "How about going the other way?" "Yes, between Sicignano and Contursi." Exactly the traffic I just saw.

But what about the Cardinal, Christ, and Eboli? Where is the conclusion? Give me some more time and I will get there.

The SaRc is not a road, but rather a translation, in asphalt form, of a notion: many things can be done, even well, in Italy with public money. But not (with few exceptions) below Naples. "The Unification of Italy has begun," wrote Arrigo Benedetti when the Milan-Naples stretch of highway was inaugurated in 1964. At best, until Salerno: "The railways used to stop there. Today, the high speed trains stop there, and the "real" highways stop as well," according to Luigi Sbarra, regional secretary of the Cisl (the Workers Union) in Calabria. From there down much less is accomplished, but even that is more than what was intended.

Is he exaggerating? From 1923 onward, all of the highways that have been built are in the North and some in the Center. In the 1930s, our country was the nation in Europe that had the most kilometers of highway. In the South, all we had was the Napoli-Pompei highway, while in the meantime the Fascist regime laid down more than four thousand kilometers of road in East Africa. The South is Africa, except for when it would be convenient to be considered so! In 1952, a new plan for the highways was devised by the ANAS. All of the planned highways were canceled from Salerno downwards, despite the projects that since 1935 called for their construction all the way to Reggio Calabria, on the Tyrrhenian Sea and to the Salento area, located on the Adriatic Sea. The father of the "Losing South" project is the Sicilian Salvatore Aldisio, who did not believe that highways were a priority for the South. It is as if to say: what is necessary in the Center and North is superfluous in the South. This is a notion that can be found repeatedly in many forms throughout history.

We would have to wait until 1955 for the Salerno-Reggio Calabria to see the light of day. Only in its intent, however, because the new Minister of Public Works, Giuseppe Romita from Piedmont, inserts it in the "to-do list" but without allotting money for this project, just as for the "majority of the highways in the South" notes D'Antone in her book. For example, the Naples-Bari highway is also on the list but with a "non-binding commitment." A law imposed that at least 25% of the investments made for highways were to be allotted for the South. But the person who was supposed to respect that law forgot about it and the South, who should have demanded respect forgot about it too. Another law obliged the IRI to have 40% of its factories in the South and that 60% of those should be new constructions. Then a stop sign appeared. Can you guess what law cannot be violated and which two laws were completely ignored without any protest?

Finally in 1961, during the administration of Benigno Zaccagnini as Minister of Public Works, the project arrives that defines the Salerno-Reggio Calabria a "priority" and, besides good intentions, money is also allotted. The year after that, the first stone is laid and the President Amintore Fanfani assured its completion within two years.

The first projects designed for the construction of highways in Italy were made by the IRI. How are these highways? The Geneva Convention established (no, not the law on prisoners of war, even though on the A3, you might begin to have your doubts) the following: they should be usable by cars and motor vehicles and have two lanes of at least seven meters with traffic dividers.... In other words, highways. That is how they were built up to Salerno.

In order to reach Reggio Calabria, the IRI invented "open highways." So how are they built? Well, they do not actually have two lanes per part (we are in the South after all) but actually have three lanes in total. Instead of the standard 3.5 meters per land (the new law actually calls for lanes that are 3.75 meters in width), in certain instances, 3 meters are sufficient: people will just have to be patient if there is one meter less between vehicles passing each other. They will have to deal with a few more accidents, particularly at intersections where the cars skim each other. However, one could follow the same speed limits as on "real" highways (the IRI felt as though it had been invested with the responsibility of a "mission" in the South's favor and it actually put this notion in writing in its plan for the construction of highways in the South, which it never really intended to build).

In these surprising "open highways" planned by the IRI for the South, the insertion of "side tracks" were planned as well for "farm" carts. In other words, if He had decided to stop at Eboli,

He would have been able to take advantage of these "side tracks" should He have chosen to ride His donkey as He did into Jerusalem on Palm Sunday. No one would ever propose that the Messiah do this on a bicycle, but it would have been allowed. He would have also been allowed to travel this "pedestrian-mule" road planned for the South on foot. It would all be for free, eh. We would oblige you to pay for this (unfair privilege, according to some protests).

Do you recognize this? It has been the rule that has followed us from the beginning. When something is done, in Italy, when the time comes to apply it to the South, either it is not done or, if it is done, it is done much later and on a much smaller scale. It is always for good reasons: "So we can save. Sure, they will have to make do, but it is better than nothing isn't it?" Then the IRI would explain that traffic in the South is quite scarce. Of course they would be leaving out three very important factors. Firstly, that is difficult to sell cars where there are no roads. Second, that the presence of a highway would increase the usage of motor-vehicles (in virtue of the fact that there would now be someplace that they could be put to use). Thirdly, the South was in the middle of a financial boom and had registered an increase in the average income. In fact, a few years later, the registration of motor-vehicles in the South actually surpassed that of the Center and the North, despite the poor network of roads and because of the even worse railway network.

Professor D'Antone reminds us to consider the factor of "lateral difference": rather than building roads, perhaps they should build aqueducts or schools.... This is the heart of the issue at hand. If, in the North, something is built, highways and schools, it is normal. In the South, if something needs to be built, the people are forced to choose: do you want the highways or the schools? Why can we not have both, like in the North? There has never really been a Unification of Italy. It is not one country, but two. The Salerno-Reggio Calabria confirms this: the criteria that have been applied to build the highways are no longer the same when they need to be applied to the "minor country."

According to Professor Domenico Cersosimo, professor of economics and vice governor of the region of Calabria, the "Salerno-Reggio Calabria should have a toll as it serves an educational purpose, it creates 'citizenship.' Otherwise, this would be an error and the consequences would all have negative outcomes. If one does not pay for something, one cannot have a say in its construction and maintenance and therefore you take what they give you and cannot protest their inefficiency. In this manner, silence is fueled in the South."

One then becomes used to "considering backwardness as an opportunity, " according to Professor Antone "from which to detract immediate benefits ... that are however short-lived." This is advantageous to everyone, according to Cersosimo: "Because in this fashion, the South can lay claim on funds, perhaps to waste them, while the North can continue to accuse the South and continue to not offer funds due to their wastefulness."

Even the fact that something would be given for free creates a marked difference (you do not pay for something, therefore you are inferior) and a deception: "The flow of merchandise on the A3 is unidirectional. Out of one hundred trucks that are on the highway, ninety-nine carry merchandise from the North to the South, and one carries merchandise from the South to the North," explains Cersosimo. This means that the "discount" applied favors the Southerners once, and the Northerners ninety-nine times.

Shortly before reaching the Polla-Sala Consilina exit, there is a large sign that reads "To Reggio Calabria": if you do not immediately realize that it indicates a detour, once again you will find yourself in the past. There is a brief stretch that only has one lane, then it switches over to two lanes with an emergency lane. Then it switches back to two lanes without an emergency lane, near the gas station, then the two lanes with an emergency lane reappear again for another two kilometers. It goes back to one lane and is detoured onto the other lane then back to the original one. Less than a kilometer goes by when there is another lane switch, which still only comprises the use of one lane. "Drive carefully," a sign says.

After the junction that connects to the Padula-Buonabitacolo road, the future once again stretches before the driver and there are two lanes plus an emergency lane. This continues for three kilometers, and then there is once again only one lane. From this point until passing Lagonegro, there are nine lane detours, though they all still only allow for the use of one lane. There is always at least one truck that determines the speed for all of the traffic behind it and it usually holds a steady speed of 30 to 60 km/h. We started off as being a line of traffic and wound up becoming a family. Then one reaches the "Sirino rockslide" site where the newly constructed road gave out. It had never been used and had never been repaired (they are going to fix it now). At least we are consoled by a view of the lake on the right. Just before reaching northern Lauria, the truck that was in front of us pulls into one of the construction sites. We are free at last! For three kilometers: there is another truck. (Are you getting bored reading this? Imagine those who are living this while driving in their cars.)

The IRI explained that a "pedestrian-mule" road was necessary, but chose to build only those roads that were "profitable" for the Center and the North. It left the other road to be built by the ANAS, which is a public utility company that builds roads. "It was completed in nine years," remembers the engineer Battista Iacino, former head of the ANAS's Cosenza branch. "Now six years are required to build a school." They really performed some miracles, even if it is not mentioned very often. For the first time ever in the world, pre-stressed steel and concrete were used. A path was carved into four very steep mountains (Pollino, Sila, Serre, and Aspromonte). The road goes from being a few dozen meters above sea level to over nine hundred meters then back down to four hundred meters and climbs to reach over one thousand feet above sea level. The road then grazes the Sibari plains before ascending once again to six hundred and fifty meters where it rises along the coast of the Tyrrhenian Sea where it reaches five hundred meters and touches the sea of the Strait of Messina. The road is perched on unstable rocks, landslides, mountains which have the tendency to collapse upon themselves and widen at the base, and finally over wide gorges.

Like the one that stretches across the town of Laino Borgo, the first Calabrian town one reaches upon leaving Salerno. One can see the homes situated in the valley, right on the Lao River. The "Italia" viaduct crosses the river, and still today, it is the tallest viaduct in all of Europe at 255 meters. "When it was built, I was still a student and on Sundays I earned five thousand lira by holding the land surveyor's staff steady so that he could properly measure the distances," says Professor Cersosimo who was born there in Laino Borgo. "It was a great work of modernization, just like the agricultural reformation (which also came out of Calabria) which eventually broke the old feudal system. The highway united us with the rest of the country. This place was its own world. One produced for the local market and each town was its own tailor. I am also a product of this highway's history and its passive modernization that helped many poor people to emerge from poverty. At age sixteen, I bought my first suit from Facis thanks to the A3. Otherwise, a tailor was out of our limited means. The refrigerator arrived as well as the Singer sewing machines. So many possibilities presented themselves, including the possibility to leave. Roads both connect and disperse: they can bring you things and carry people away as well."

Giacomo Mancini wanted the A3 to pass along the mountains and not along the Tyrrhenian coast (which is how it was always planned) so that it might pass through his city, Cosenza, or at least so that some new air could reach the oldest towns of the area. The Southerners call this area the "Bone" as opposed to the "Pulp," which is located on the coastal plains. "Looking back, it is a good thing that this 'backbone' of communication could cross through the 'boniest' areas of the South" maintains Cersosimo. "We used to die of hunger and now we throw out meat." "My father," adds Pietro Mancini, "when he was Minister of Public Works, gave rise to the studies for the bridge over the Strait of Messina which, for him, was the natural continuation of the A3. However, this, along with many other projects, came to a halt when he had to leave the ministry."

"One must not limit oneself to comparisons: how they are, how we are, which implies that one merely looks around. One must look toward the future. It is necessary to compare how we were, how we are, which implies looking backwards" continues Cersosimo, a strange economist who sounds like an afflicted wise man. He has seen the broadening of limitations without losing his old calibers of measurement. "We used to have to remove our hats in front of the parish priest. Now, he is simply another member of the community. Our military draft recruits were ten centimeters shorter than their Northern counterparts. Today they are the same height, while hope still remains higher in the South."

If one exits the A3, one returns to visit a bygone era. To reach the sea, (which at most was fifty kilometers away) one had to travel for an hour and a half to two hours. If someone from Reggio Calabria or Cosenza had an appointment in Catania in the morning, they had to make sure to leave the day before and stay there overnight. The roads wound through woods and towns located on prominent hills overlooking valleys. One could stop to drink from cold mountain streams. Every once in a while one would encounter an impetuous imposition of modernity with neither order nor beauty emitted into an economy that is poor but balanced. It is difficult to say whether the "new" will destroy what is "good" about the "old," or if it will be able to grow thanks to the "new," without losing itself.

"A road can change the structure of development," says Cersosimo. "This not only applies to the industrial sector but for smaller businesses as well. They can connect amongst themselves and form a network with others in the same or complementary sectors. Districts emerge and form 'open-air factories' formed by small businesses that are integrated into a common economic cycle. This is what happened when the Salerno-Reggio Calabria came into existence. It happened all over the South."

Right. How can one not wonder what the South would have been like if the SaRc had been built at the same time as all of the other highways in Italy? If the small and large businesses of the North had not had the chance to accumulate decades-worth of an advantage. What would the South be like with working railways? If the beaches, amongst the most beautiful in all of the Mediterranean, were comfortably reachable, without having to waste two vacations days (one to reach your destination and one to return home)? Cersosimo is right. One must look at the past and then the present, though it is difficult not to wonder what could have and should have been, and never was, and that would have made all the difference. It was desired that it be this way because Italy was never perceived as "one" and the Italians were not seen as equals, with equal abilities, and therefore deserving of the same rights.

Business enterprises that have a brief life cycle, such as in the construction sector, are quite prevalent in the South: the market is simple, the returns are high and immediate, and the risks are low. Many Calabrian construction companies work almost exclusively out of their region, undertaking ambitious projects. They are, however, on the first rung of the economy. This setup is very convenient for the *mafia*, who otherwise would have difficulty emerging in manufacturing and mechanical businesses, explains Cersosimo: "Long-term projects and imposing structures have slow returns. The *mafia* is competitive on the market by complicating the economy."

Mancini was in a hurry to see "his" highway complete. "Many of his biographers have written this, like Antonio Landolfi," his son Pietro recounts. "The Christian Democrats said that the government would not last very long and that they would take back the Ministry of Public Works." Giuseppe Rinaldi was the head of the ANAS at the time, Landolfi remembers. He had demonstrated that he was very efficient when it came to the construction of the Milan-Naples highway, while the SaRc stopped at Eboli. Mancini removed him from his post and the Christian Democrats protested, but the A3's construction continued. (Mancini was a great decision-maker. He stopped the plundering of the Valley of the Temples, Agrigento, Rome and Capocotta, on the shores of the Lazio region. As Minister of Health, he understood the impor-

tance of the polio vaccine, and called Borghi, yes, the man of refrigerator fame, and commissioned him to deliver a large quantity
so that the vaccine could be distributed throughout Italy. Polio
was practically eradicated from one year to the next.)

Now we are on the old stretch of the road, which has two
lanes without the emergency lane, with few interruptions where it
returns to having one lane until we reach Tarsia where the modern part is located. It will have an emergency lane until Cosenza.
This part was actually confiscated by an anti-mafia judge.

"The A3 actually follows the same route as the ancient Roman
road called *Via Popilia*. Their idea behind building roads was that
the various parts of the empire needed to be connected to one another and that the territories along the roads would also grow,"
according to Iacino (who was accused and acquitted because he
was the head of the ANAS during the trial investigating subcontracts given to *mafia* gangs). The first to realize the advantages of
this situation was the *mafia*. They immediately demanded protection money and the assignment of contracts. Immediately, they
went from being violent shepherds to businessmen. The Calabrian
highway made the '*ndrangheta* the most modern and international
of all of the *mafias* (it was also the oldest). The large businesses of
the North did not waste any time: they paid and continued their
work. "The '*ndrangheta* is a protagonist that knows how to take
advantage of an opportunity," explains Cersosimo, "if you look
on the surface, it is a business that is among those who best know
how to remain on the market. If you look a little deeper, you see
the aberration of an economy supported by violence, abuse of
power, and archaic social systems."

"The current renovations were preceded by a *mafia* war. Twenty-
four people died in the area surrounding Cosenza," according to
Doctor Eugenio Facciolla, of the District Attorney's office in Catanzaro. He previously worked as the head of the anti-mafia district. He and his colleague Roberto Di Palma, in Reggio Calabria,
conducted investigations that yielded a limited number of convictions, but allowed them to comprehend the mechanism behind the
subcontracts. The gangs united into one cartel and a businessman

represents them all at the contractors'. He then subcontracts the job to the 'affiliates' according to the stretch of A3 that pertains to them."

"Dino Posteraro laid down telephone cables (you know, the small ditches dug at the sides of the road?): he had a shed, a pole, a shovel, and even a wheelbarrow. He instantly became a leader in the highway construction sector by acquiring a bankrupt business" remembers Facciolla. In the Reggio Calabria area, the businessman who represented the cartel was a union leader, Noè Vazzano. "It struck us that all of the business representatives of the largest companies addressed him, a former locksmith and fourth level worker," states Di Palma.

The investigation of the stretch of highway near the Cosenza area was referred to as "Tamburo" (drum) and that for the area surrounding Reggio Calabria was called "Arca" (the ark) because of the cartel representative's name Noè (Noah) and because all of the *mafia* families were "on board," Facciolla explains. "Bids for the contracts were sent from competing companies, *Asfalti Sintex* and *Astaldi*, from the same fax number." And from the same studio in Rome, the contracts were drawn up for the various companies in the South. The Calabrian investigators forwarded their findings to their colleagues in Rome. They never heard back.

In theory, the contracting companies could only delegate a certain percentage of their work, and should execute the rest with their own machinery and employees. In practice, however, "*Asfalti* came here with the contract and subcontracted it on site," adds the judge. The *Asfalti* company does this, but so do many others. The judge's investigation began because the head of the *Asfalti* company's yards, despite many intimidations and attacks, did not understand how he should communicate with the locals. Or perhaps he chose not to understand. He asked to be transferred. Someone more intelligent came to take his place and everything ran smoothly. The gangs profit, they are all allies, and make 3% off the final sum. This is called the "Calabrian tax." As long as you pay it, nothing happens to you.

Pino Aprile

The first jobs were assigned in December of 1997 and the tasks were scheduled to be completed by 2009. The assignment of the contracts, however, was such that total chaos resulted: bankruptcies, price revisions, updates for unforeseen obstacles, and payment delays. In 2001, it was decided that the seventy-seven lots would be combined to form fewer than ten lots and that they should be assigned to general contractors. This was done to ensure that the time frames would be respected as well as the quality and budget. This solution could almost be believable if one were to forget about the subcontracts. "The jobs that were assigned in 2008 that were to be completed in 2000 were actually started in 2009," Doctor Facciolla cites as an example. "Litigations, disputes.... This is how we proceed." Well, if you can call that progress.... In 2004, the CGIL (Federation of Italian Trade Unions) calculated that at this pace, seven kilometers of road were laid down every year. The ANAS assured that the funds were on their way and that the job would be finished by 2011, then 2013 (then the date was pushed to the end of 2013; the day after it was pushed further to 2014).

But with the assignment of subcontracts, the problem did not change at all because the lots were once again repartitioned. In 2005, a report issued by Fillea (CGIL's construction union) revealed that the CMC, a large company that was at the head of the "red" Cooperative societies, had been assigned to lay down thirty kilometers of highway. They had subcontracted to one hundred and seventy four different companies: on average, a different company for every thirty-three meters of road. The record was held by *Leonardo Costruzioni*: they had received a subcontract for less than a gross of 1,500 euros.

The companies that obtain the contracts are always the same. In the magistrate's investigation, they were able to reconstruct how the companies are able to receive these contracts: excessive price slashing. "If we assume that tar costs 90, how can one estimate its cost to be 60?" reasons one of the investigators. The ANAS then writes to the company owner inquiring about this anomalous estimate and the company responds. And the deal is done. If I ask,

"But what was their answer?" they look at me strangely. At that point the winner of the contract goes to Calabria and subcontracts the tar to a company that must, therefore, logically spend less than 60, otherwise how can they generate a profit? One can only imagine that they must save on quality and quantity of materials. The stretch of the A3 that is near Vibo Valentia was initially planned to comprise a double layer of roadbed, but in the phone-tapped conversations, the order was given to only lay down one layer. In another phone call, the instructions are even more explicit: "Put down some garbage, then put down a thin layer of tar. That's all." The final quality check, however, did not reveal any irregularities (with some embarrassment later on, when it was too late, one of the men in charge of the quality check was revealed to have previously been convicted for his affiliation with the Sicilian *mafia*, just to give you an idea of how difficult it is to determine whom you are speaking with here). In July 2009, the DIA (Antimafia Investigation Unit) confiscated over sixty million euros worth of assets from the Mancuso gang, based out of Vibo Valentia, who was a subcontractor in the SaRc project.

Is it possible that there is no way to carry on business, how can you say it, in a normal fashion? Eugenio Facciolla, who is entirely intolerant to delinquency, opens his arms out of frustration: "Calabria does not have an economy. It only has jobs in the public sector." These are clearly not enough for everyone. People kill for these jobs. There is nothing left for the shy, the honest, and the poor people. Here, to open a business, one must be a hero, be very wise, or be a delinquent. There are few entrepreneurs and those few that there are do not last very long. In the end, nearly all of them go elsewhere, if they don't actually leave this world. The wise are those who use their intelligence to guide their desperation.

If the large Northern companies pay and remain quiet it is because they are obliged to do so. If someone from the South pays "protection money" to the *mafia*, then they must rebel. Someone occasionally does. The Sicilian Manufacturers' Association expels members who pay "protection money." The National Manufacturers' Association encourages and sustains this behavior. However, it is careful before it expels a group that is of international caliber that notoriously in Calabria (and not only here) let themselves be extorted so that they can "work."

Judge Di Palma has tried to place a distinction: "Is it really a free market when one is obliged to pay the *mafia* 3% of one's earnings in order to enter it? The answer is no. But this does not offer an acquittal because one has no choice but to be subjected to this behavior, and then one becomes an accomplice when one accepts that the quantity and quality of the materials is low."

However, during the trial, he was unable to condemn this behavior as fraudulent. The fact that the companies that supplied gravel did not have gravel mines, but rather collected pebbles from the sides of the road could not be considered fraud. *Mafia* trials are curious: the truth of the matter is always evident, the truth that is to be proven before a court of law becomes contorted and sophisticated, with such a well studied interpretation of the law that the details often kill the evidence. "In the desperate search for the smoking gun, the fact that fifty people saw the gun go off is ignored," according to the district attorney.

And what about the *mafia* attacks? "Sometimes, they serve to illustrate the fact that not everyone is in agreement with one another," hypothesizes Di Palma, "or perhaps to signal trespassing into one's territory." Sometimes, intimidations, the destruction of insured trucks, and machinery (perhaps the older machines, if what they say is actually true) can justify the company, who is the victim in this case, for delays in the completion of the job and requests for revisions of the prices previously agreed upon. But Di Palma, a Neapolitan turned Calabrian, suggest another reason for this as well, that has something to do with the character of this land: "I imagine you are familiar with the story of the sheep." Actually, I am a vegetarian.... "Sir," said a man from Aspromonte, "my neighbor has a sheep that is just perfect, a beautiful sheep." The next day he comes back and says "Sir, my neighbor's sheep gives much wool." The day after that he comes back and says, "Have you seen how much milk that sheep produces? How about the delicious cheese made from that milk?" Finally, the man cannot tolerate these comments any longer and says, "Fine! I will give you a sheep too, but stop mentioning the sheep!" "No, sir, you have misunderstood me. Kill that sheep."

Sometimes, these attacks are preventive measures. Between 2005 and 2006, in the town of Barritteri, which only has a few hundred inhabitants, an epidemic breaks out: death by murder. It is a fraction of Seminara, and perhaps Seminara is the only place that has actually heard of Baritteri. So? In that small town, in the area of Aspromonte, a project was drawn up that would station the base-camp of the *Condotte D'Acqua* company, which was hired to build the nearby stretch of the highway.

The local magistrates suspect that the job will be done poorly, in order to continue to ensure work on the part of the company. As soon as it was discovered that the A3 would be renovated, "we all went to order a new Mercedes," a collaborating witness confided in Facciolla. "We would pay for it with the money from the highway, which would become our life's investment. By contract, the companies then have the right to perform maintenance on the stretch of road they built." From recorded phone conversations, a project was already being formulated that would call for a simulated rockslide onto the highway. This would then give rise to a new contract for road maintenance.

I know that I must appear naïve, but sometimes I just exaggerate on purpose. For the second time in forty-five minutes the person I am interviewing looks at me perplexed, almost wondering if I am really this ingenuous or if I am faking it. So I ask my question: "Pardon me, but why would the companies build the road properly when it is far more profitable (both in the long and in the short run) to build it badly, as long as they have the right to perform maintenance?"

What the magistrates do not say is the pressure they have been forced to endure. Especially Facciolla: he has had to face numerous inspections and accusations. In the end, he left the anti-mafia organization. It seemed as though they were finally able to create a breach in the mafia-business alliance operating on the Salerno-

Reggio Calabria, through a series of trials. But one of the men convicted in the trial, Carmelo Pirillo, "Minister of War," as he was nicknamed by the gangs of the Cosenza area, hung himself in his jail cell. A *mafia* boss, Antonio Di Dieco, repented and began giving names, including several important employees of the ANAS (though his words are never confirmed). Then he regretted having repented and when the trial was over, Francesco Amodio decides to repent. He was the driver for the *mafia*'s accountant, Vincenzo Dedato, who also repented later on. He was the second in command after the *mafia* boss.

The trip continues from Cosenza, there are two lanes with brief stretches that have only one lane open (due to the pruning of some shrubs). Shortly before reaching Altilia, important work is done to secure the mountainside from rockslides after one occurred in January and killed two people while injuring five. There are yards that are kilometers long that are adjacent to the riverbank up until Falerna. Then there are two lanes with an emergency lane with the exception being a few short reductions that leave one lane open, until one reaches Gioia Tauro. Gioia Tauro is the longest stretch of renovated road and is located in the most heavily *mafia* populated area. Does this mean something? "The *mafia* is a business," explains Doctor Salvatore Boemi, the head of the newly established "Center for Contracts" in the Region and a former judge, who demonstrated great courage ("Inspired by Giovanni Falcone's teachings, we began to nurture a dream: to make the *mafia* understand that they were on a losing path. We were not few, nor were we stupid or ugly. In 1995-1996 we began to see some positive signs. Then something happened...The declarations of witnesses were demoted and the hard jail time given to convicted *mafia* bosses was subdued. That initial burst of springtime that we had experienced received an unexpected freeze.") "Don't believe those who say that the *mafia* blocks businesses and progress. Gioia Tauro is the Calabrian equivalent of Corleone in Sicily. Look what they have done. There is talk of building a regasification plant, which would involve the investment of one billion euros." This is as if to say, "And this would be the *mafia* that is trying to maintain economic 'backwardness' so that it can detract advantages?"

From the highway you can see the cranes of Gioia Tauro, the biggest port in the Mediterranean for containers (it was constructed for the Fifth Metallurgical factory, which was ultimately never built. It was taken over by Ravano, a businessman from Genoa. The *mafia* now profits from it.) It is the third largest in Europe and the fourteenth in the world. You already know this if you read the newspaper. The A3 crosses Calabria without actually acknowledging it,

"Elsewhere," according to the union representative Sbarra, "transportation is a system that connects, at the regional level, with highways, railways, ports and airports. We act in isolation and any possibility for transportation ignores the other." Then again, how do you connect a railway that dates back to the 1800s with a newly renovated highway ("While the rest of the country is busy planning their fourth traffic lane and their fourth highway, we are worrying about building our emergency lane," adds Sbarra) or ports that operate on an international level? Gioia Tauro's port ceases to exist once one steps out of the shipyard. The merchandise that arrives (aside from cocaine) does not create any opportunities for development. They are taken elsewhere and return to Calabria, transformed, and at a higher price.

This is another page of history written about the Salerno-Reggio Calabria. In the end, something is accomplished in the South as well, but not as part of a project that takes advantage of opportunities and uses energy productively. Each job is done for its own sake, without a larger concept of a system behind it. If something is done, the system is not contemplated. If the system is contemplated, the job is not done. From time to time, a cathedral emerges from the desert: a metal works factory, a road, an airport.... "What sense does it make to build a highway, if you don't build it around a secondary network of roads that render the entire territory reachable?" asks Iacino. "The Salerno-Reggio Calabria should not be a highway built for 'racing,' but rather as a means to reach certain stops along the way," he adds, quickly, after seeing the expression on my face. "The Pollino is a beautiful and majestic mountain that is begging to be discovered. Yet, I don't know it, and neither do the Calabrians."

After Gioia Tauro, through to Scilla, is the most tormented section of the highway: it has one lane and is extremely narrow, and is perched a few hundred meters above the sea. If a truck driver sneezes, a tragedy could occur. How does one interpret the sign that reads "Beware: Possible sounds of exploding mines"?

In 1994, on the stretch of road between Vibo Valentia and Mileto, during the attempted robbery of an American family who was on vacation, a seven year-old child was killed: Nicholas Green. This particular occurrence stirred a great deal of emotions because the parents of the little boy donated his organs. The dignity with which they dealt with their pain in such a positive manner left its mark for years. Attention was given to the security on the A3 and many more people began to donate organs after this event. Today, the SaRc is not among the most dangerous roads for accidents, but truck drivers concur that it is far more dangerous in that one is vulnerable to armed robberies then in Milan, Naples, and Rome.

The last part of the highway upon reaching Reggio Calabria goes back to having two lanes, but they seem enormous.

Have we earned the right to visit the bronze statues of Riace or not? They exemplify beauty and strength (for the Greeks, strength was not brutal or monstrous: Achilles, not King Kong!) Statue A is nearly in the dark. "The light bulb went out," states the guard. "Just today?" "No, six months ago." "Well, if you give me a ladder, I'll change the bulb myself." "It's a special bulb that does not emit heat. In any event, in September we close." "But it's July." "Right, they were supposed to close in October last year, but then...."

Should I return to the SaRc, or has this been enough? I have no other choice but to take that road to leave this place and I have an appointment, somewhere between the best and the worst that the Italian highway system has to offer, concentrated in the same kilometer. Here they are, shortly before reaching Bagnara: the Paci 2, otherwise known as the worst tunnel built on the continent according to the European Tunnel Assessment Programme. It consists of a tunnel that stretches for over one kilometer, without aeration, with only one lane. Immediately, I find myself in traffic, a truck has stopped on the Sfalassà (it is the best, most ingenious viaduct constructed and is 245 meters tall). The country is split into two parts. In 15 minutes, two policemen on motorcycles from the highway police arrive and allow the traffic through, one direction at a time. Good job.

Cosenza's Special Division of the ANAS governs security and traffic on this part of the A3, and it is headed by the engineer Salvatore Tonti. "We are not restoring a highway, we are building a new one on top of an old one, without blocking traffic," he states, citing the president of his company. He shows me a panel from which they monitor the flow of traffic. The "garrisons," whose placement was determined with the collaboration of the prefectures, are ready to intervene when necessary. They have also established a call center, where 98% of the one hundred and fifty thousand calls received throughout the year are answered within twenty seconds. They also have a location set up where they take note of the five hundred thousand notifications of accidents on the road as well as other information. They are brimming with pride and are satisfied with having accomplished a "job well done."

How about the most disgraceful highway in all of Italy? What about the emergency lane? "There could have been fewer difficulties, and they could have been diluted for over the course of several years or they could have had considerably more difficulties concentrated in a shorter span of time. The latter was chosen. But then we would have a wider highway with anti-seismic technology. It is not how you believe it to be, believe me," states Tonti.

They have nothing else. "The railways want to reduce the number of ferry boats on the Strait of Messina. Not one euro is being invested," protests Sbarra, a union leader. "President Moretti told us that he has little money available and that he chooses to spend it where he believes it will be best put to use: where money has already been spent for renovations. Where we are, since something was not previously renovated, it makes no sense to renovate it later! Then they speak to us about the bridge across the Strait of

Messina: what sense does it make to build it, if they ever do, after they have reduced the surrounding area to a desert?"

Boemi, a former judge, makes a serious comment: "The renovation of the A3 is actually a project of political marketing. Aside from Christmas, Easter, and *Ferragosto*, the Salerno-Reggio Calabia should be sufficient to satisfy all needs."

They say that it is the *mafia* that does not want the Reggio Calabria-Taranto to be built. Boemi almost does not let me finish my sentence: "It's the politicians that don't want it to be built!" He proceeds to paint a picture in which the *'ndrangheta* is ready to take advantage of the opportunities that present themselves, and not block them: "When the Calabrian *mafia* understood that agriculture had no possibility for further development, it immediately looked elsewhere. Its men were already inserted in the secretarial positions of the undersecretaries of the State since the 1970s. Saverio Mammoliti already sold drugs in Rome. It has all been recorded in documents, one can read the verdicts, but no one does."

How does that phrase go? Ah, Yes: "The *mafia* knows how to take advantage of opportunities." In fact, "The Salerno-Reggio Calabria gave rise to the period of kidnappings because it was now possible to carry a victim from Milan to Aspromonte in one day," continues Boemi. "But in the long term, that criminal undertaking generated much criticism. (This was illustrated by the solidarity of the Calabrian women with Mrs. Casella, who presented herself in various towns of the South in chains, begging for the return of her kidnapped son.) In the meantime, the *mafia* sought approval, and so the *'ndrangheta* changed business. They moved from their small towns on the Ionian Sea (the gangs from the Tyrrhenian Sea had already found their own business in dealing with the South's highways) took planes, and began making agreements with the whole world and, with the money obtained from the kidnappings, they became drug traffickers. In this activity, according to what one hears, there are no victims, but clients that request a service at an acceptable price."

Boemi speaks on the edge of a paradox, but perhaps not even as closely as one might initially think. This means that these men have demonstrated notable skills in an environment that is extremely difficult (international crime) starting from the pieces of feudalism forgotten in the mountains, and turning it into, in a few years, the best in the world. The activities of the *'ndrangheta*, criminal and not (from finance to construction to the service industry) was governed by little towns like Platì or San Luca, and extended to include twenty countries on four continents. It is not sufficient to be merely criminals: others are criminals as well. One must compete with intelligence in an economy that moves exactly according to the same rules and means as the legitimate one (calculations, risks, banks, alliances) with the addition of savagery. If you make an error, you don't merely fail, you die. A sort of Darwinian system of elimination of the weakest is established which leaves only the most savage and most skilled people standing. "Of intelligence that is considerably superior than average" report both Elio Veltri and Antonio Laudati in *Mafia Pulita* and (according to the secret services) Vincenzo Morabito, "*U Tiradritto*," as he was nicknamed after the name of his gang, the head of the *'ndrangheta*, created an empire from the town of Africo. His men, along with computer engineers, committed fraud and stole billions from foreign banks in the 1990. The big bosses of the *'ndrangheta* were "found living in the caves of Aspromonte with laptop computers with which they directed the international traffic of drugs and managed their respective fortunes." This is a perfect summary of the most ancient of *mafias*, who, however, was the first to use the Internet and to be globalized. It is the most powerful in all of Europe after the Russians. It has the ability to "face the challenges and changes that global modernization imposes, in the most surprising and unexpected ways: they manage to remain true to themselves," writes Francesco Forgione, former president of the Parliamentary Anti-mafia Committee.

This is a very dangerous interpretation of the *mafia*, but it is not without foundation: to those protagonists who are ready to do anything if it will allow them to emerge, can do so by the only route left, crime. In that world, they proved their worth. Perhaps if they had had other opportunities, they could have proved their worth in other sectors. Pantaleone Sergi, who for decades was a reporter for *"La Repubblica"* newspaper remembers a famous and heavily criticized interview with Giacomo Martini. This old Calabrian politician "spoke of the *'ndrangheta's* leaders as a sort of precursor to a ferocious version of capitalism, a primordial one, that would comprise all of the skills and intelligence of the 'civil' one. He intended that, in a few generations, they would become indistinguishable from the Milanese 'commanders.' I was absolutely not in agreement," says Sergi, who is now the spokesperson of the President of the Calabria. "Now, I've changed my mind."

The least that one could say is that the Calabrian members of the *mafia* today are at least "colleagues" and sometimes competitors of Milanese finance and business, that seemed light years away from the shepherds of Aspromonte who stole herds of sheep (sometimes, they still do this). The true capital of the *'ndrangheta* today is Milan and Buccinasco. It is there that Frederick Forsyth went, upon a suggestion offered by the FBI, to "understand the *'ndrangheta*" better, in order to write a very successful spy story. He wrote a bestseller on cocaine. Everyone knows that even in Milan there are those people whose pockets are quite full, yet they only see their own money with an ethical distinction. The crime lies in how those people make their money, but the money itself is not a crime. It is merely money.

This notion is valid in the courts as well, as is illustrated in the verdict of a trial in Milan, as reported in *Mafia pulita*: the office of the accountants Enrico Cilio and his son Sebastiano (who graduated from the Bocconi University) had conducted, according to the plaintiff, a series of money laundering operations for the Morabito gang. First, the accountant confessed, then he withdrew his confession. The Morabito clan had its power and while the court acquitted Cilio "emphasizing in its verdict that for fifteen years he had favored and endorsed 'methodical practices' of tax evasion, written contracts intended for tax fraud, written false sale contracts to obtain funds from a bank involved in the matter, and used sums of money deposited by clients to pay his own taxes." In other words, he had committed a series of financial crimes for which any other court elsewhere in the world would have sent him straight to jail.

But the *Mafioso* was Morabito. Cilio was only the accountant. Milan is full of accountants because it is where one finds the most business. And one knows how it is with business. Accountants like Cilio, Michele Sindona's son-in-law, are only doing their job.... Every once in a while some famous Milanese lawyer is arrested for his affiliations with *Cosa nostra* or the *'ndrangheta*. There are a few lines published in the newspapers. You read the names and you can also find those same people on the administrative boards of large multinational banks.

When the first part of the highway was built, Andrea Barbato wrote in the "*Il Giorno*" newspaper that, in the end "between Milan and Salerno there would be something like a city that was eight hundred kilometers long with motels, and parking, restaurants, scenic overlooks, men in jumpsuits, hospitals, police stations, and cafès." But from Salerno going South, if by chance you happen to pull over into a rest area, often you are overwhelmed by the stench of feces and urine due to the lack of gas stations and relative rest stops with restrooms: when one has to use the restroom, and it is not available, one must adapt to the surroundings. But now, climbing up from Cosenza, and having to pass by the first rest stop due to traffic, I start to hallucinate and envision mirages (the temperature is about right, the latitude is as well, but I still have not come across an oasis): bottles of water that are dripping with cold condensation, tables set with copious amounts of food, shady palm trees. About one second before I seriously contemplated taking a bite out of my steering wheel, near Castrovillari, beneath the rocky buttresses of Mount Pollino, I saw a rest stop, complete with sandwiches worthy of any famished truck driver. The young man who waited on me proudly stated, "We make everything here. Even the bread. Well, we don't make the *'nduja*[2] but we buy the best." He cuts the bun open and I point to my personal cocktail of Calabrian delicacies to fill it. It is a true "bomb"

---

[2] TRANSLATOR'S NOTE: a very spicy, spreadable Calabrian sausage.

of delight, especially due to the fiery hot peppers, which pay homage to the fiery temperatures outside.

"Sir, if you pass through this area, will you come back here? Do you know Mount Pollino? We get all of the vegetables you have eaten today, locally." All of a sudden, you don't feel like you have come to a rest stop, but rather as if you have been invited into someone's home and that they are anxious to please their guest. I was quite disheartened. The people that work there are all so young and work so hard because they know what it means to be lucky enough to have a job at all. They are conscious of the nature that surrounds them (one can see a beautiful waterfall from the highway as well as the majestic armored pine trees that only grow here). You sense their powerlessness when it comes to illustrate, communicate, and transmit what they know, and what you do not perceive, because you pass through this place too quickly. You don't ask questions about this place because you are uninterested in them or in their glorious mountain, which you only see from the A3, cursing at it for all the time it takes to traverse this land due to the many interruptions, detours, and solitary highway lanes. You can read what they want to say in their faces, "Sir, we have something worth knowing about. There is so much here that is worth knowing, why do you not care to know it?" They saw the photographer who travels with me and understood I was a journalist. They have seen themselves described as being lazy or as delinquents. This insult hides everything else including their efforts to improve the world by doing their job well, even if it only means preparing a sandwich. I left that rest stop with a coating of their obstinate and melancholy hope and wish to eventually break through this wall of suspicion and indifference.

Di Dieco, the *mafia* boss of the gang who oversaw the construction of the Salerno-Reggio Calabria and who repented and then withdrew his repentance, is from this area: Castrovillari. The repentance that tore apart *Cosa nostra* doesn't exist in the Calabrian *mafia* because it is deeply rooted in families and individuals would have to accuse their own fathers and brothers. "Here, unlike in Sicily, where the *mafia* clans are called "the people from

Corleone" or "the people from Catania," they are called the "Pesce family," the "Piromalli family" or "the Morabito family" explains Roberto Di Palma. "That is their strength."

"This is true, but it is also their greatest weakness," adds Salvatore Boemi. "Having understood how the *'ndrangheta* works, we now know how to deliver the death blow." In other words, if you discover a member, you have consequently discovered the rest of the clan as well: his closest relatives. Boemi knows what he is talking about because he did a large part of the investigative work done to uncover the identities of the *mafia* families: "From 1994 to 2001, sixty-four families have been discovered in the province of Reggio Calabria. I speak of verdicts: this is all documented information. Now we have discovered eighty-three. The map of the province is dotted with the penalties inflicted. With one verdict, twenty-two families were condemned. We obtained four hundred life sentences for homicide. We could control them, if only we truly wanted to. We could induce them to change their way of life." In those words, the anguish of this man is detectable. He is a man of the law and he sees that the end could be very near: we know who these people are, where they are located, how they operate, and where they invest their money. What else do we need to know? And instead....

"Instead we limit ourselves to the application of a Fascist law: don't go out before dawn, return home before dusk, check-in twice weekly at the military base. I have heard people mention that the weapon of the future to use against the *mafia* is the confiscation of assets! Pio La Torre (killed) spoke of it years ago, as did Rocco Chinnici (killed) in 1981, who was Falcone and Borsellino's boss (both killed). We have been doing this since 1983!"

No one seems to have an explanation as to why we are not able to unhinge the industrial-financial-political-*mafia* alliance that has not only taken the Salerno-Reggio Calabria hostage, but the entire region as well, including its future. Perhaps even that of the country. Or perhaps there is no desire to seek a true explanation. But if you ask a Southerner what they think, they reply: "I am a Southerner who feels betrayed by the State's institutions" for which he has worked his entire life, in the trenches. He still does not quit: only the trenches have changed.

I express an opinion, though it is not even my own but that of Giovanni Falcone, when he was asked if it would ever be possible to defeat the *mafia*. He answered by stating that since man made the *mafia*, then other men could defeat it.

It had never happened that the State possessed so much information on whom, where, and how to strike the *'ndrangheta*. But the act that could definitively put an end to the *mafia*, which would be the product of a political decision, is not visible, or at least not clear. This could be because that which is not done, is not done out of volition. In the preface of Arcangelo Badolati's book, *'Ndrangheta eversiva*, Peter Gomez writes that it seems that "by now, this has become the century of Calabria's organized crime." In this region, 27% of the population is somehow affiliated with the clan, as opposed to 12% in the Campania region, 10% in Sicily, and 2% in Puglia. These are perfect conditions to maintain the economy that has risen in the South: the South produces money without producing goods and therefore cannot interfere with the North's business endeavors. For now, the North, and those involved with the North's business, manages the money produced (did you really think a Northerner would transport those billions of lira in cash in briefcases to the notary with a van to increase the capital of some of Italy's most important companies?). "One must learn to live with the *mafia* and the *camorra* and resolve the problems of crime as each sees fit" stated then Minister of Public Works Pietro Lunardi (he is the same man who said, when the Salerno-Reggio Calabria was blocked, that it was the Southerners fault for not putting chains on their tires. Perhaps in August?) He must have been right, with his Lombard sense of practicality: they never had any problems with the *mafia*. The intertwining of strings of magistrates, policemen, *carabinieri*, and Libero Grassi who, in order not to pay the "protection money," gave his life, should serve as examples of unsuccessful cohabitation due to incompatibility of character. If Roberto Saviano speaks of the undertakings of the Casalesi family in Parma, the city revolts. Even the prefect attacked the writer. They accused him of inventing things. Then, it turns out that everything was true: 20 million euros worth of the *camorra*'s assets were confiscated in Parma. Everyone is quite surprised when the District Attorney of Modena, Vito Zincani, accuses the businesses of the *camorra*. In Reggio Emilia, the Calabrian *mafia* is more active while in Bologna, the Sicilian *corleonesi* are more active. "There are businesses owned by the *'ndrangheta* that have been in operation for over thirty years in Turin" according to Rocco Varacalli, the only "repentant" of the Calabrian *mafia* in Piedmont. "Every area of the city is covered by a *locale*: a nucleus formed by at least five people." When a *camorra* war broke out in Naples, it was the Venetian businessmen affiliated with the clans who assisted in the hiding of the *mafia* boss Pietro Licciardi and his men. As the minister wisely said, "one must solve the problems of crime as they see fit." Well, technically there is a penal code that delineates the solutions to these problems, but we are amongst practical people who "live with" this situation out of convenience: the *mafia* removes money from the South and invests it in the North. This is not any more or any less than what the banks, or Tremonti for that matter, do. Why would the North find this inconvenient? "Every hour, two million three hundred thousand euros pass from the hands of businesses to the hands of the *mafia*," according to the book *Il pedaggio dello sviluppo*, which was written by three economics professors and researchers, Centorrino, Limosani, and Ofria, and was published by Palomar. This means that, with the "protection money" collected, "each year organized crime subtracts twenty billion euros from the commercial system" according to the sixth report issued by *Sos Impresa*.

This is only one of the treasures that would stay almost entirely in the South and that the Center and North would lose if the country should win the war against the *mafia*. Are we really that surprised as to why there are people who prefer to live with such a reality? "Italy is with you," said then President, Carlo Azeglio Ciampi to the Calabrians when Francesco Fortugno was killed. After the attempted assassination of Reggio Calabria's District Attorney, Mimmo Gangemi, a writer from Aspromonte commented: "Italy is not really with us. Only we are with ourselves."

Greed and business: it is according to this scheme that an explanation can be offered with respect to the business opportunities available to the South: crime and the black market, which makes up about 17% of all the wealth produced in Italy, according to the Insitute of Statistics (ISTAT) or 27% according to the Organization for the Cooperation and Development of the Economy (OCSE). This comes with an additional advantage: crime (like the subordinate politics of the Southern *ascari*). This has the same need to keep the South in subordination as the economic system of the North. The mechanism functions by using Southerners to keep other Southerners in subordination. I spoke of this matter with an important colleague of mine from Milan: who "reproaches" the North for being absent in the fight against the *mafia*, aside from reminding the Southerners that they are the *Mafiosi*.

"Do you know how many points of the Gross Domestic Product the *mafia's* proceeds come to?" he said while looking at the other diners before him. He ended up not stating the exact amount of points, or at least I do not recall this number, but he gave an estimate of one hundred and thirty billion euros, seventy-billion net profit. This comes to 7% of the wealth produced in the entire country in one year.

"If this enormous sum of money were to disappear from one day to the next," continued my fellow diner "Italy would find itself quite behind, but the South would utterly collapse. All countries, advanced and not, have an illegal portion of their economy." Perhaps he only wanted to amaze us (I hope). I, both stupid and stupefied, said nothing. What I could have said, of course, came to my mind much later. For example: if it were such a simple concept, how come Chinnici, Falcone, Borsellino, Livatino, Ciaccio Montalto, Dalla Chiesa et al. did not understand it? But, most importantly, the *mafia's* economy is sick and it holds back the real, healthy economy. It is discouraged from growing in a place where it finds its competitors armed with machine guns or in collusion with banks and with enough power to strangle it. But that day, at that table, no one said anything. Some even agreed with what was said. Otherwise, the *'ndrangheta* would take all of its billions and invest them in the Frankfurt stock exchange or in Gazprom (Russian gas) stocks or that of other multinational companies, like it has already begun doing.

The war declared on the *'ndrangheta* would block work on the highway, perhaps, for years. This would be inconvenient for the ANAS (the former director of the Cosenza branch, Iacino, was put on trial, because "according to the magistrates, it was not possible that the ANAS was unaware" of the *'ndrangheta*). The defeat of the *mafia* would also be inconvenient for large national companies (in the end, they only cost the companies 3%, which can be recuperated in other ways). It is not convenient for the politicians either: jobs mean votes and the clans indicate their favorites while large companies fund electoral campaigns. It is inconvenient for the financial world because the money collected from the clans are used to fund investments managed by specialized offices in Rome and Milan. It is even inconvenient for the Calabrians themselves: little by little, this highway is being built. This is like the Fiat company: half of the region lives off of it. If the "factory" closes, what will they live off of?

"Perhaps there is a collective interest in not finishing the highway," says Domenico Cersosimo. Maybe.

The truth has many shades to it: there are the facts, which are not always easy to reconstruct or even to recognize. There is the legal aspect, which cannot coincide with the factual side and, in fact, when the *mafia* is involved, which happens often, it actually betrays the facts. There is the matter of perception: that which one "knows" because one lives the situation. Sometimes, this last aspect is the truest out of all the others.

The latest and most bitter lesson imparted regarding the Salerno-Reggio Calabria pertains to that last category. Southerners know that any time something needs to be accomplished in the South, the State assigns the job to the most stable and efficient organization around. An organization that is ready to welcome modernity, is prepared to compromise, and has political affiliations:

the *mafia*, "who does not impose, but rather participates." The first alliance was formed by envoys sent by Garibaldi to Sicily in order to prepare for the invasion. Garibaldi validated the *mafia*. Every once in a while someone comes along and tries to break this tradition. Their names wind up on commemorative plaques (during the legal proceedings to establish the damages to which Paolo Borsellino's widow and family were entitled, the State's lawyers intervened in opposition, without even having the right to do so.)

Roads, according to studies on the histories of nations, are indicative of the development of a population. They summarize the method of government as well as the skill level and organizational capacity obtained and that which is to come. Briefly, roads reveal the abilities and intentions of a country. If our country ignores or neglects those of the South, it is because they ignore and neglect the South as a whole. Even when roads are built in the South, they always ponder whether they are really necessary. The Salerno-Reggio Calabria, read in this manner, is a national and local instrument for education on how to be inferior.

"But I do not want to speak of this," says Boemi, the man who is building the organization that will take the corruption out of the contracts and subcontracts in Calabria (assuming that he will be allowed to effectively do so).

Aside from the A3, what is left? "The best, abandoned by the rest of the country: all of Ionic Italy. This is something I do not understand, I hope that I do not understand, and am not obliged to understand given that I am no longer a magistrate. I believe that the Gulf of Taranto is amongst the most beautiful places in all of Italy. This is an opinion, and therefore subject to debate" states Boemi, born "by mistake" in Reggio Calabria to a Sicilian family. Calabria does not geologically belong to the South as it is connected to the Alps. It detached, along with Corsica, from the Ligurian-Provençal region and migrated until it was caught between Sicily and the Pollino Mountain range. In 20 to 30 minutes you can go from seeing larchwood pines (and in the winter, ski slopes) to the sea. "Tell me what the economy and lifestyle of the Ionic coast would be like should it to become reachable by the highway that was never built and that would have been less costly to build than the A3, not to mention easier. What if there were airports? What if it were not as difficult to travel by train as it was decades ago? " When economists went to analyze the flow of tourists in the South, they discovered peaks, regarding foreigners, in the provinces of Bari, Lecce, Catanzaro, Vibo, Trapani, Sassari and Nuoro. "These are all cities that are connected by airports and in those years they became destinations along low-cost airline routes from other European cities," summarizes Viesti in his work *Le sfide del cambiamento*. This allowed the Anglo-Saxons to discover Sila. In this Calabrian mountain chain, many Anglo-Saxons have begun to purchase houses and build colonies that are more or less stable. If you give people the means to reach these places, they will come. Even Italians would come here: "But to reach Catania is usually much less expensive for an English or a Spanish tourist than for someone from Milan or Turin," states Cersosimo.

From Reggio Calabria to Taranto, it is as though the coastal railway did not exist. If two brothers left from the Strait of Messina and one took a plane for New York, while the other took a train to Bari, the first brother would be able to call the second and (rightfully and worriedly) ask him "Have you arrived?" The second would respond "Almost," if the train were running according to schedule (this is nothing to laugh about: there is a possibility that the train might arrive on time. We live in a quantum world, after all.) A cousin of theirs could prove to be even more unlucky should he choose to go from Trapani to Siracusa. If there are no delays, he could make it there in fifteen and one half hours. For 400 kilometers. It seems as though one is reading a complaint from 1911, for "the inadequacy of the railroad network and the slowness of the Southern trains" (there are similar statements dating back even further). But, upon being interviewed concerning the complete abandonment of the South, Mauro Moretti, the managing director of the Center-North Railways (they are illegally called the railways of the "State") declared, ineffably: "We are a company and there are stretches of railways that have a market and others that do not.... Please tell me why I have to install a train that travels from the South when no one ever travels North?" He was not even graced by the idea that the correct question the head of the railway company should ask himself actually was: "Please tell me why anyone would ever want to board the filthy trains I allow to circulate in the South?" His words are the product of that idea of the South as being inferior that one takes for granted: Southerners, you wouldn't happen to want trains like we have, would you? In this manner, you have protests from the people of Puglia because the ETR 500 high speed trains obtained are taken away and reassigned to other destinations, all located in the North, and are substituted by "old intercity trains that have been improved and renamed Eurostar City trains. However, the restaurant car has been eliminated." In the meantime, the bishop of Locri heads the protest against the elimination of the Intercity "Pitagora" line and rings the church bells.

In the North, the railway companies spend the equivalent of a half a dozen bridges across the Strait of Messina for their high speed trains in order to gain a half hour on the Milan-Rome route, while "in Calabria the only investments made consist of the elimination of a half dozen grade crossings" according to Luigi Sbarra. It is a mechanism that is both perverse and efficient: the railway lines of the South are poorly served with filthy trains and unacceptable travel times. Who would ever take a train from Catania to Palermo when it takes six hours and eight minutes to travel one hundred and ninety kilometers? How about with the threat of a fine, because there are no ticket vendors in numerous stations and the automatic ticket vendor machines, once broken, are never fixed? The train conductor knows this but tells you, "But you have boarded without a ticket, and I must give you a fine."

"Italy does not need to amaze people with trains that travel at speeds of two hundred kilometers per hour. Instead, it must get rid of those trains that travel at twenty kilometers per hour which represent the only gift the State ever gave to Southern Italy." Well said. Who said it? The director of "Il Mattino," the newspaper of Naples, Paolo Scarfoglio, ninety-years ago when the announcement was made of a marvelous new technology (at the time this referred to electricity, which many people in the South are still waiting for) reserved for Lombardy, Piedmont, and Liguria.

The head of the Railway company (the primary requisite for someone in this position is not to have a sense of shame, otherwise they could not say certain things without an "extra" face) explains that he only invests money where money can be made, in the Center and the North. He does not mention, however, that he receives money from everyone, both in the North and in the South. But that isn't all: in order to have better service, the Regions transferred four hundred million euros to the Railway company according to the coordinator of the Regional Councilors for Transportation, Ennio Cascetta, from the Campania region, in 2009. These were funds taken from the FAS (those that were allotted for under-utilized areas): these were designated largely for use in the South. Instead, they were given to the Railway company that only invested in the North to compete with the airlines. In the South, they tried to compete with mules. The governor of Sicily, Lombardo, states that the unions complain, "because in addition to abolishing long train routes, the trains used exclusively for cargo were also reduced. This is a dramatic decision that penalizes our products" (Salvemini had already documented, over a century ago, that the Railway company asked that a tariff be placed on products from the South that was ten times higher than the one placed on products from the North). On certain trains ("Scrap metal," according to Lombardo, "no one would accept such derelict wagons, not even in Congo") one might not even count a half dozen people. You do not ask why there are so few people, but rather why there is still anyone at all that is willing to board such a train. Sooner or later, "for budget reasons" dry branches must be pruned. Those dry branches are the South. Just like "Gelmini's meritocracy": always more money for the North's universities and always less to those of the South, until it would be "just" to close them. Or one could refurbish "fourth class cars" (these are train cars that have no roof and no seats) that united Italy used only in the South because they were branded as "uncivilized" in a Parliamentary debate.

But then an eighteen year-old Calabrian girl, Maria Perrusi, is elected Miss Italy and they discover, in 2009, that to arrive by train from Calabria to Salsomaggiore, for the final round, she traveled for twenty-one hours (according to European studies, a city that is located five hours from the capital is considered to be on the outskirts). This is the same amount of time it takes to travel to Australia, though on a plane. They are all amazed. But this passes quickly. Perhaps it is necessary to remind them that when Italy announced that it wanted to extend its railway network in the South, the construction of the Massaua-Asmara in Eritrea was launched, in 1887. The train finally arrived in Reggio Calabria in 1895. It never reached Matera: a piece of Italy "that is not well known, and certainly less explored than the Eritrean colony. Certainly they were luckier than we were because at least they had a steam locomotive! (...) A country becomes a stepmother, and not a mother when one part of the population reigns and the other languishes in poverty," wrote Giuseppe Zanardelli in 1902 as mayor, to the President of Italy. He was originally from Brescia, in the North, and was one of the first people to seriously concern himself with the South. "When I was a young boy," narrates an old farmer from the Lucania area to *Viaggio nel Sud* a television segment conducted by Sergio Zavoli (with whom I have worked) "and I listened to the radio as they announced: 'the Italians have conquered East Africa and they built roads. The Italians built a railroad for East Africa. The Italians built hospitals and schools in East Africa.' I thought, how fortunate! If only the Italians had conquered us..." The mayor of Matera, today, could copy the letter of his colleague from 1902 and mail it exactly as it is to the head of the government and to the managing director of the Railway Company of the Center and North (inappropriately named for the State). Nothing has changed. Still today, Matera is the only capital of a province that is unreachable by train. But when the railways wanted to publicize themselves, they used Matera as a destination in their television commercial. ("An illuminating slip," I said to a colleague from Matera "I wonder what Freud would have to say about this." "If he were from Matera," my colleague replied, "nothing: he would immediately have resorted to using his hands for something violent." Managing Director Moretti need not get upset: it's just an expression.)

Now we will travel the straightest part of the A3, the part that crosses the bed of an extremely wide lake, in another geological era, it was called the Vallo di Diano (Diano's Wall). On the left hand side, we have (or at least in theory: in practice, this area is not reachable) the enchanting coastline and beaches of the Gulf of Policastro and of the Cilento. On the right hand side, we have mountains and forests that stretch for hundreds of kilometers in one of the least inhabited regions of the country. But how does one get here?

Further ahead, in Sicignano, you will cross the Basentana road which leads to Metaponto. The Romans, in order to punish the Lucanians, who were unyielding and resisted being ruled, cut off the land from their great roads thus condemning the city to isolation. From that time, the only difference is the presence of the Basentana road and a layer of asphalt on the old mule roads. The Salerno-Reggio Calabria is a lesson on how to be inferior. The isolation of the Ionic Coast is a lesson on how to be annihilated. Salvatore Boemi is 66 years old and is obstinately optimistic on the possibilities of redeeming a land that so many people find convenient to maintain unredeemable. He is moved by a burning passion (It gives me the shivers when he says, "We are those people who had the honor of sharing the dream of Falcone and Borsellino."). He is a man who measures his words and who knows much more than what he said in a court of law.

For this reason, it is disheartening to listen to his "sentence" pronounced amidst rage and pain on the wasted paradise that faces the Ionian Sea: "This land has been willingly detached from the rest of the country. Its backwardness is due to its poverty." The goodness of what you produce is determined by the market, if you can reach the market. In this vein, "there is no market in the South" according to Viesti. The few infrastructures of transportation that there are, from the railways to the roads, are from the South to the North, ignoring the rest of the surrounding South.

The paradox is that the markets that are the farthest away are the ones that are the most readily accessible. Calabria is not the only place farthest away from the port of Gioia del Tauro, but all of the South is entirely too far from its merchandise, the fruits of its own labor, for which only one way out has been prepared: towards the North. "Ask yourselves why one cannot send a freight car filled with iron from Naples to Campobasso (one hundred and ten kilometers)," people asked themselves this question a century ago because that freight "arrived from Sesto, in the province of Milan, first."

"This poverty," states Boemi, speaking of the Ionic coast, (he could even avoid the strict referral to such a distinct part of the South) "is a choice."

He means by others, and perhaps not only others.

In the long run, it is convenient even for the victim to remain as he is. It is the role he knows best, what he has always been and what he is. He has been educated to consider himself inferior, as nothing, until he makes this character his own.

CHAPTER 8

Teaching Inferiority

Students in the South are less brilliant than those in the North, and their professors are less prepared (rightly so: of the tens of thousands of short-term teachers "sacrificed" by Mariastella Gelmini, the current Minister of Education, in order to save money, seven out of ten are from the South). Universities in the North are more efficient than those in the South. The pro capita productivity rate of workers decreases based on latitude: it is lower in the South. The quality of administrators in the South is inferior. Civic education (ranging from obeying traffic lights to proper garbage disposal) is inversely proportional to the distance from the Alps (in the direction of the Tropics): it is minimal in the South and in its most degraded form, results in a social system that is supported by unlawfulness and *mafia*. Attention to personal hygiene and nutrition is more precarious right where the climate would call for additional care (the "stench of the South" was intolerable, and disturbed the noses of Massimo D'Azeglio, that leftover of pro-Hitler youth in the *Lega* party: Matteo Salvemini, and Professor Gianfranco Miglio, already in Florence). The people in the South want a "steady job" and a salary, preferably in the public sector, while those in the North have a "religious" work ethic. The Southerners cheat at everything, from undeservedly high grades in school to public contests....

Let us conduct an experiment in interactive writing: you continue the list begun above. It can be as long as you like. But, when you reach the end, go back to the beginning and ask yourself the question: *Why?*

One can debate many of the aforementioned topics of discussion: the North tends to hide its unlawfulness (when it is large, it also becomes known as politics, finance, and business) and to magnify and define as intolerable that of the South. Curiously, it does so more often with the smaller examples rather than the larger ones: it emphasizes the number of people on disability pensions rather than the billions of euros made by the *mafia* (perhaps this is because the North does not profit from the former). There is a doubt that the South's social fabric has been torn, the cities are dirtier, the public administration is more corrupt, micro and macro crime is more deeply rooted and diffuse. The question still stands: *Why?*

I also have more questions that need to be asked: why do the Southerners continue to put up with being insulted by the likes of a Minister Gelmini? (Try to imagine a Minister of Education from the South that says, "Professors from the North are all racist and need to be re-educated.") Why do they allow for such disparity (in funding and services) that, were they to occur in the North, would block the entire country with its protests on the part of those discriminated against? Why do they let themselves be identified as thieves only because they are from the South? (Try to imagine that, at the announcement of the creation of a "Northern Bank," a Southern representative expects to be placed on the bank's board of directors in order to check that nothing dishonest is done. This is exactly what Calderoli asks of the South, should it proceed with Tremonti's plan for a "Southern Bank." This is the same man that wound up in an investigation regarding the Fiorani Bank as well as the same man who was the director of the *Lega* party that decided to found their own bank. It ended up failing miserably due to its indecent balances and documented operations, all in record time. This is to demonstrate the abilities of this aspiring "controller.") Why do the Southerners bow their heads when their Northern brethren accuse them of something?

The answers can be narrowed down to two possible ones:

1. The Southerners simply are this way. The difference "lies in the fact that the Southerners are Southerners," writes Viesti. To summarize, quite simply: "Man is what he is."

2. The circumstances induce the Southerner to behave in this manner. (For our mutual tranquility, I would avoid, for now, to include the alternative "middle" answer: "this is true, but the answer also lies a little bit in the idea that they are also the way they are" because the quantitative and qualitative definition of that "little bit" would constitute the greatest success ever in the fields of psychology, perhaps biology, anthropology, and sociology. Providing of course that we would be able to find an agreement between all of the specialists in these fields regarding the definition of that "little bit.") In other words, "Man is what he is allowed to be." This was stated by Amartya Sen, a Nobel Prize winning professor of economy and ethic philosophy at Harvard University.

Now I will embark upon a dangerous topic of discussion, because it regards the reasons and qualities of human behavior. This is one of the slipperiest topics in existence because it is the most subject to "explanations" based on prejudices, our personal experiences, hearsay, and even our characters and moods at a given moment. I will not do so alone and, obviously, what I write will be subject to debate (but perhaps less so than a topic that begins with "My cousin once told me that, one time, a friend of his from Naples...."). It will certainly be questioned by those who do not doubt the existence of three hundred thousand riflemen from Bergamo and the compatibility of the *Lega* member Borghezio with the parameters of decency.

The first type of answers, upon developing them further, amount to: "They are not like us, Madam" and they intend to say: "They are inferior." The idea is diffuse in both the North and the South and it does not matter whether it has some element of truth or not. If one accepts this explanation to be true, one must also accept the consequences that come along with it. The inhabitants of the South innately carry the ability to steal as well as have a penchant for corruption, laziness, indecency and filth. They are unable to govern themselves alone or at least do so honestly. In other words, they belong to a human species that is degraded or incomplete, as though during the course of evolution, it regressed or stopped at the threshold of civilization, unable to cross it entirely. Otherwise, how would you explain that despite what is done to help them, they continue to remain behind, one hundred and fifty years behind. All this while others progress in spite of the dead weight that is the South (the leper that one was obliged to go to bed with, according to D'Azeglio).

It is also nonsensical to say: "they are like us, but they do not want to behave like us." In other words, that they prefer to live amidst the garbage, to board trains that take five hours to travel one hundred kilometers, to have running water that only functions for three hours a week, to receive inferior treatment in filthy hospitals, to be "taxed" by the *mafia*, to live badly with a handicapped pension rather than well and with a good salary, to drag oneself around as long as it means not tiring oneself, to send one's children to school in buildings that collapse upon them.... It is the same topic as before, simply stated in a different manner: do you see that they are not like us?

It could effectively be this way: on the staircase of evolution, whereupon we place ourselves on the top step, there are beings that possess a different cerebral development. This limit constitutes a biological niche in which some species find their environment. But why then were chimpanzees, gorillas, and other anthropomorphic creatures unable to make that final evolutionary jump and become "men" like our ancestors, who were at their same level? Because we are the most ferocious predators to ever appear on the Earth, was Carl Sagan's answer in *The Dragons of Eden*, and we could have carried out a limiting function regarding intelligence, by destroying all of those beings that, like us and those after us, were at the conquering point. Considering what the *fratelli d'Italia* did to the South from 1860 onward, this theory could stick. Even if we had ever had the possibility to evolve to Borghezio's level, ethnic "pruning" imposed on our people (or species, or race?) broke our knees just as we were beginning to run.

Is this discussion a paradox? So is the topic of the South's inferiority, but nonetheless it is still in use. Therefore, let us for a mo-

ment suppose that it is true: Southerners do not suffer from an inferiority complex, Southerners are inferior. But if this is true, then
they must remain so wherever they are (after all, a chimpanzee
can't obtain a college degree just because you take him to college).
Otherwise it would become necessary to admit that they are not
inferior and that their status of presumed or real inferiority is due
to different causes: excluding themselves, these causes must be external. Right? (Perhaps Bossi will understand this concept upon
receiving his fourth degree in medicine, or perhaps he will only
say he received it, like he did for the previous three.)

For example: why is it that the Southerners that have moved
to the North don't litter but recycle, work like everyone else, have
interesting careers, create new companies, give students grades
that they deserve that are not based on favoritism, don't run red
lights (any more than anyone else), complain about taxes (just like
everyone else) and try to evade them when they can (just like everyone else), and, without even the help of glottologists from the
valley, are able to comprehend the meaning of the word *cadrega*?[1]
There are those who become as civilized as Borghezio, well-
cultured as Bossi, humane as Salvini, well-balanced as Calderoli,
and as friendly as Gentilini. They also vote for the *Lega* party and
say: "Those people are not like us, madam" and mark their accents to signify their conquered distinction from those others.

I really tried to reason like the worst inhabitants of the North
(the most honest of that lot are the *Lega* party members: they say
what they think) but the argument, as you can see, does not hold
up.

Again why, if one changes location, do behaviors change, and
the unredeemable person from Catanzaro or Caserta is no longer
the same person in Monza or Pavia? Would you believe that the
answer is of the second type: it resides in social psychology and
not in anthropology (or rather than within mankind, it lies in his
condition)? We begin to bounce from "they are different" to "circumstances make us different." In the first instance, we would be

---

[1] TRANSLATOR'S NOTE: "chair," in Lombard dialect.

a subhuman species (or worse: sub-*Padanian*). In the second, we would be beings whose actions are induced by the environment.

How does one's will figure into the equation? "One must find a space amidst the conditions in which the individual lives his life. It is not a large space and not many have the interest and ability to do so," states Professor Piero Bocchiaro. There is embarrassment in his voice because he is aware that he has just opened a can of worms (free will, predetermination, personal responsibility, consciousness of one's actions....). "One's genetics and predisposition to certain disease count. The education that one's parents give, financial stability, nutrition, as well as social, religious, and political conditions all matter. There is very little space left. In any event, the perimeter in which one can exert his will was not designed by the individual. The structure of the field in which one moves does not depend on that individual."

We speak of normal situations, not of exceptional ones. This should be obvious: the child of a happily married, well educated, billionaire couple who is in good health, who lives in a large house in a healthy environment, should avoid calling another child a "filthy ignoramus," if he are the child of a violent drunkard and an HIV positive prostitute who live in a shack that has no water, whereupon he does not go to school, but rather out to steal, because he is hungry. I give an extreme example so that everything is very clear. One tends to perceive those merits that derive from the advantage of a better condition as one's own. This is wrong, but it is extremely gratifying.

Piero Bocchiaro is a young scholar who studies human behavior. He has been a researcher at Stanford University, taught at the University of Palermo, and is now teaching at the Vrije Universiteit of Amsterdam. He wrote *Introduzione alla psicologia sociale*, but the book that prompted me to ask him for assistance is *Psicologia del male*, in which he analyzes a series of famous experiments, through which he tries to understand the basis for our actions.

"A role." He states. It is the role which is assigned to us and that we accept (consciously or not) or that is imposed upon us, that ultimately determines our behavior. This is to the point where, according to social psychology "it does not matter *who* acts, but rather in *which* context the action takes place." This means: tell me what condition you find yourself in and I will tell you what your actions will be. What about me? Does it not matter what I decide to do or not do? Little, "It is that 'deviation' of the single from the role that, when it manifests itself, is suppressed and normalized by social and psychological mechanisms. In the most extreme cases, the deviant is eliminated," Bocchiaro explains.

The first experiments that yielded these conclusions were first conducted half a century ago. Since then, these results have only been further confirmed by additional studies conducted and the news reports.

Do you remember what happened in the Iraqi prison of Abu Ghraib? The guards woke the inmates at all hours. They obliged them to clean feces with their bare hands and to do push-ups naked, while others were made to sit on their backs. They were made to "screw" a hole in the floor and to take showers while hooded and in chains, with hands on each other's shoulders while the guards tripped them and made them fall. They were forced to prostrate themselves so that other prisoners could sodomize them.

The question that the world asked itself was how did the American authorities manage to concentrate such a large amount of sadists in uniform in one prison? "They were not sadists," assures Bocchiaro, "but rather normal people who were brought to such extreme behavior by an extreme situation. Some were actually described by people that knew them to be sweet and sensitive. Two clinical psychologists, who were given the task of evaluating the personalities independently from one another, deemed them to be perfectly normal. It was their role that led them to be completely unrecognizable."

You don't believe this? Well, you should know that the evil things done that you have just read about also happened in Abu Ghraib, but that I copied them from the results of an experiment that was conducted decades prior by Professor Philip Zimbardo at Stanford University.

Pino Aprile

It was during the years of the protests against the Vietnam War and people were putting flowers in cannons and shouting, "Make love, not war!" Out of dozens of volunteers, eighteen candidates were chosen. The most "normal" of them did not know each other and they included pacifists and well-educated students (in fact, they were students at this well known university), and they were all in perfect psychological and physical health. By lot, half of them were assigned to be prison guards, and the other half were to be the inmates (the prison seemed real and was constructed in the basement of the Department of Psychology). Everyone was free to leave whenever they wished. However, their roles took over the personalities of these human guinea pigs so quickly that within forty-eight hours, both the inmates and the guards were convinced that they were exactly what they were assigned to be. Whatever those students were when they walked into this experiment, within a matter of hours, they no longer were. In their places appeared "other" people, generated by their roles.

This experiment remains one of the most dramatic ever conducted and was one of the reasons that that type of experiment was eventually banned. They even made a movie about this, called *The Experiment*. It began on a Sunday, and was supposed to last for fifteen days. On the Friday of the first week, Professor Zimbardo was forced to interrupt the experiment. The nearly complete destruction of the physical and psychological conditions of the volunteers had generated such excesses of violence that it was feared that further extreme, even criminal, developments would not be able to be controlled.

(I have some objections too, but I will save them for later.)

When Eichmann was brought before an Israeli court and was accused of having slaughtered six million Jews, it was discovered that he was not an evil genius, but rather a very average man. He excelled in nothing, if not in his own average existence. ("He is far more normal than I am after I evaluated him," one of the psychiatrists said).

"There are common individuals who perform extraordinary actions," Bocchiaro writes. This is because the situations in which they find themselves are extraordinary, and therefore so are their actions, for better or worse." In his book, Bocchiaro cites the example of Giorgio Perlasca, an Italian who saved five thousand Jews in Nazi-occupied Budapest, by pretending to be the Spanish ambassador. He was discovered thirty years later. When he was asked why he did what he did, this hero answered, "Opportunity can turn a man into a thief. Well, it turned me into something else."

(Objection: Why was there only one Perlasca? It is a question that I am about to ask.)

First, I must cite the mechanisms that have been studied through a series of experiments like that conducted at Stanford and with an analysis of events taken from the news, through which evil becomes an everyday occurrence, dangerously, without guilt. It is the *transfer of responsibility* to the authority whose orders the individual executes (the Fuhrer, the State). It is the removal of one from oneself (I am no longer Pino Aprile, but a Nazi) that causes their consciousness to atrophy because it renders one anonymous within a larger group. It is reinforced by conformity (everyone is doing it) and the diffusion of responsibility in the group to which the individual belongs (it is not I, the German in uniform, that is killing the Jew, but the Nazis, the Germans, the Aryans).

The action is facilitated if one describes the victim in such a way that diminishes them as a person and renders them different, inferior beings ("They are not like us, madam"), through insults and derision ("Neapolitans, you stink"; "Earthquake victims"), their metaphoric elimination ("Power to the Etna"; "Send the emigrant home"; "Let's use non-European immigrants to replace the rabbits during hunting season") until they reach the extreme: dehumanization ("The Jews are rats, and this is an extermination," the Nazi's used to say. "Naples is a sewer that is infested with rats and needs to be decontaminated," the *Lega* minister Calderoli once said.).

By providing a justification for everything, more traps are revealed. I will cite only three of them: the attribution of guilt to the victims ("They are all lazy thieves") that therefore deserve the punishments inflicted upon them. Moral justification: ("I act this way to ensure a superior common good, the Unification of Italy, that unfortunately imposes the need for some sacrifices"). The belief in a just world, "that all of us," Bocchiaro guarantees, "innately harbor" ("If I am better off or worse off than you are it is because I deserve it") and it is the strongest drive. The victims themselves, due the power of the roles imposed and of the circumstances, convince themselves: "I must have done something for this to have happened to me. Imagine the murderers. "It does not matter how you justify your superiority (race, civility, salary, culture, and religion) what matters is that the other is never your equal. He is not playing the same game," states Bocchiaro. Vito Teti, in his anthology of "studies" on Southern inferiority, best sums this up in one splendid phrase: "The inventions of racism are insidious because they end up creating the reality that they imagine and the corresponding feelings."

What about the Neapolitans? "They have no other aspirations besides that of serenely enjoying their misery," writes Renato Fucini, a Tuscan, shortly after the Unification, "let them wallow in their own mud" (Luciano Salera cites this phrase in his work *Garibaldi, Fauchè e i Predatori del Regno del Sud*). "Oafs," "Bedouins," "Worse than Africans," "Degenerates," "Retards," "Savages," "Degraded people" (this last one is a true revelation!): these are how the Southerners were referred to and described, with animal-like features, by their Northern brethren who descended to free them (in other words occupied with a praiseworthy cause to benefit unworthy people). These are expressions that spring forth from one of the most powerful and uncontrollable drives of the human spirit: disgust. Marc D. Hauser, a professor of psychology, evolutionary biology, and biological anthropology at Harvard University, explains the reason for this in his work *Menti Morali*: disgust "possesses a certain degree of immunity to conscious reflection and it is as contagious as yawning or laughter and infects the thoughts of others at stupefying speeds." It changes you before you are even aware that you have been changed. Disgust is diffused at an epidemic rate of speed. It generates racism and ever more violent behavior as it takes root in the spirit of an individual and society. The language it generates is that of disgust and derision until it reaches levels of dehumanization. I cite Borghezio, Salvini, Calderoli, and so many others as examples, and this is only in Italy. There are specialists of this particular field that have recognized their skill and expressed their appreciation: "We like your country very much," said the former head of the Ku Klux Klan in the 1970s, in an interview published in "*La Repubblica*" newspaper in 2009. He now runs the operation's website. "There is much excitement on our website regarding what is happening in Italy." In this manner, the KKK opens a branch in Italy: we have finally earned it! (One cannot choose one's own name, so pay no mind to that of the chief defender of the white race in the KKK: Don Black).

To be clearer in his book, Hauser adds: "Disgust appears to be the most irresponsible of emotions. It is a sentiment that has produced radical divisions between members of a group and outsiders whom they subjected to cruel treatments. The trick behind disgust is quite simple: if one declares that those one does not like to be similar to a worm or a parasite, it becomes easier to consider that person disgusting and worthy of being excluded, avoided, or annihilated. All of the worst cases of human abuse imply this type of transformation, from Auschwitz to Abu Ghraib." Parasites, worms, rats ... this was how our local racists, whose ancestors came to unite Italy, referred to us Southerners.

This was how the invasion of the Kingdom of the Two Sicilies was prepared. From those who left the South to go to Turin, to Lord Gladstone, the Kingdom of the Two Sicilies was presented as the "negation of God" (but the King of Naples was the most Catholic monarch at the time, even too much so; his accusers included both Italian and British, grand master masons and "priest-eaters" as well as the King of Piedmont, who was actually excommunicated). The Southerners were described as slaves of an oppressive regime (yet they fled abroad only after the arrival of their liberators). Their monarchy was depicted as being obscurantist and backward (yet it was at the forefront of many fields both in the civil sciences and science proper; Naples was a top contender in

Europe for cultural excellence. Their schools, however, were closed by the Northerners.) Freedom of press worked like a dream and while republican newspapers were printed and foraged so were Pro-Savoy newspapers (this liberty was left intact: even after the "liberation": the newspapers that were in favor of the new king continued to be published. How about those who were against him? Well, no: the offices of those newspapers were closed and their printing presses destroyed).

If the matter begins in this fashion, could one imagine that Italy in 1860 was like a laboratory in which a social-psycho-logical experiment was under way? "Sure," Bocchiaro states. "Let us imagine that in this enormous space, one hundred and fifty years ago, prior to the commencement of this study, the participants are arbitrarily divided into two groups and they are induced to interpret a role, just like in the theater: the Southerners will be the "prisoners," and the Northerners will be the "guards." A prison, so to speak."

This is exactly what the entire South became, not only because of the tens of thousands of people that were imprisoned without formal accusations, without a trial, without a verdict or with self-serving accusations, farcical trials, terrible sentences, mass executions, but also for the state of siege, the suppression of all liberties, the power given to the occupants concerning the lives and assets of the conquered, the instatement of concentration camps for tens of thousands of people.

"Shortly after," continues Bocchiaro "the Southern-prisoners began to feel powerless and depressed, while the Northern-guards acquired destructive values that transformed them into persecutors. At the beginning of the experiment there were no differences between the two groups. After some time passed, there were no similarities. The role had substituted the person. There were oppressors and the oppressed. In order to justify the continuous abuses, the latter needed to perceive the former as inferior beings. The Northern-guards took possession of the power of collective action, which reduced their sense of personal responsibility. In other words, none of them felt as though they were liable or guilty to have taken part in the actions of a group."

In the Stanford experiment, a few days were sufficient for the volunteer prisoners to convince themselves that they deserved to be in prison and they continued to stay there even when they were free to leave at any time. Those few days were also sufficient to give rise to the guard's preconceived notion of superiority and of their right to rule over the prisoners "so as to maintain order."

A few days. Here, that experiment has lasted for one hundred and fifty years. The moral and ethnic superiority of the North and the equivalent inferiority of the South are matters of faith by now.

Are these observations sufficient to explain the incredible period of violence that was unleashed, for years, in the South that brought to the planning of the deportation of the Southerners to Patagonia or other deserts? I refuse to believe that history concentrated the worst beasts in Europe in the city of Turin. Those who believe this are refuted by statistics.

"It is the *distance*," says Bocchiaro. "One's sense of guilt diminishes with distance. That which is far from you, even if it has been decided by you, does not touch you, or at least not very much. In Stanley Milgram's experiment on obedience towards authority figures, the volunteer that had the role of persecutor had difficulty inflicting punishments when the person who received them was with him. He had far fewer problems when that person was somewhere else, and it was even easier when the person was out of his field of vision."

None of the "fathers" of the *Risorgimento* (from Garibaldi to Cavour to Victor Emanuel, a relative of the Bourbon monarch) had ever been to the South prior to the invasion. Some did not even set foot in the South even afterwards (like Cavour). They decided the fate of a population based on "hearsay." After one hundred and fifty years, when a massive mudslide caused a disaster in the province of Messina, the Milan-centric government forgot, as opposed to other national tragedies, to observe a minute of silence for the victims and to declare the state funerals (which were conceded only after many protests). This was the expression of one of the worst Lombard souls: the newspaper "*Libero*," participated to this moment of grief with an article explaining why this disaster "does not warm our hearts." As though this event occurred too far away for them to be affected by it. In newspapers, the importance of an event to common interest is signified by its proximity to the first page. "*La Padania*" newspaper published the news of the death of many residents of Messina on the last page. One more step away, and the story would have fallen out of the newspaper, amongst the news that was not even worthy of note (But at least they did not write "Let's go mud!": after "Let's go Etna" and "Let's go Earthquake".... Or, perhaps, they did write it, to respect their beautiful *Padanian* traditions?).

(I started off with objections, now I begin to have some answers.) It no longer seems to be a coincidence that several "liberators" of the South had some serious second thoughts about how the situation really was, once the distance was eliminated. There were those who deserted their side in order to help the Southerners defeat their invaders. There were those who wrote that they had initially gone there to help their brothers and were forced to oppress them and deprive them of everything. Garibaldi himself regretted having been the cause of so much pain.

Even in the psycho-social experiments described in Bocchiaro's book, "a minority of the participants acted in opposition to the others. Social psychology, however, is not very familiar with these figures except for the fact that their personalities happen to be identical to that of the other participants."

It cannot say much else regarding these exceptions, of the rebels, of those like Perlasca: they are the subject of his new research project.

Actually, there is something more to be said: they are few and there are social mechanisms that can be employed to re-incorporate them with the others or to eliminate them. In the Italy-1860 laboratory, "as in the Stanford experiment, if a guard wanted to act in opposition to his group," explains Bocchiaro, "he would be pushed to re-align his conduct with his group by a very powerful drive: the sense of belonging. This emerging law required ruthlessness with the threat of losing psychological, financial, or social benefits." More or less: if you are a guard, you must behave in a certain fashion, otherwise you become a prisoner or, in the best case scenario, you remain isolated. If you are a "soldier blue" and refuse to kill the Indians, you will be treated as one of them. Simon Wiesenthal told me about a Nazi soldier whose uniform did not condition his behavior. He was shot because he was unable to torture people regardless of whether they were a Jew or not.

"Mercy will be considered treason," they told their soldiers, those liberators that came from the North, when they ordered the reprisals against the population of the South, like at Pontelandolfo and Casalduni, with the murders of children, rapes, and all of those innocent people that were burned alive in their homes.

The Southerners bent to their will. But some opposed those weapons with weapons of their own. They were called "brigands" and some of them actually were. "Even in the Stanford experiment there were signs of rebellion by a prisoner," narrates Bocchiaro. "But he was not supported by his companions, either out of fear or *perceived powerlessness*. The revolt was then easily sedated and an image of power and unity was restored to the Northerners, in the Italy-1860 laboratory, while it re-invigorated the fatalistic spirit of the Southerners. This was because the failure of the revolt appeared to be a confirmation of the superiority of the Northerners and the inferiority of the Southerners."

What is *perceived powerlessness*?

"It is the experience of the defeated. When you are in a situation of difficulty and you try everything to free yourself and all of your efforts reveal themselves to be futile, you accept your condition: your role of a "defeated" person. You convince yourself that a system that would allow you to prevail does not exist. You understand that you are powerless to change circumstances, which affect you negatively. Therefore, despite what you do, the effects are always the same, and are dramatically negative."

You dedicate yourself to industry and they close your factories to favor the North. You dedicate yourself to specialized forms of agriculture and you are ruined because an agreement with France is recanted. You start over again and war breaks out. You cultivate vineyards that are destroyed by a parasite. You oppose the invaders with weapons and you lose. You offer to reason with the invader and address themes of common interest, and the invader does not listen to you. You put your money in the Discount Bank, which then goes bankrupt. You seek comfort and support in the laws, but they all favor another part of the country, to your detriment.... Now each one of these episodes has a reason, but lined up in this fashion, the reason appears to be quite different: it's you. They want to convince you and you convince yourself that it is an inadequacy on your part, an inability, which is at the root of your defects, of your backwardness. According to the theory of a "just" world, you have what you deserve because you are the prime example of an incomplete species: *homo sapiens sapiens minor atque terronicus.*

But if you go away from your South, it happens that your previously unknown (even to yourself) abilities are revealed and you are able to reach results that had previously been denied to you. Then, you convince yourself that you are not an *inferior* species, but that the term pertains to the location. You are not *inferior*, but rather the South is. Or perhaps you are, when you are in the South. If you remain there, you abandon yourself to uselessness, which is imposed and accepted. You stop pushing yourself to change, improve. You are in the laboratory at Stanford, and your role is that of an inferior being that slides into further decay. This is because "populations and individuals who have been blessed with natural beauty are not inclined to carry out the difficult job of earning a living for themselves. They believe that everything is owed to them and that it rains upon them from the sky. In this manner, they avoid tiring themselves (...); they become chatty, vain, narcissists and reduce everything around them to good luck and bad luck. Since they are not accustomed to working, they live for free out of inertia, always proceeding downhill.... Beauty becomes uglier with the passage of time, until it finally turns completely into ugliness": this is Naples, a summary of the South, in the book <u>Sud</u> by Marcello Veneziani. He is a good colleague who also knows of the superhuman tenacity carried out over the course of the centuries that transformed our region from a desert to a garden. This was accomplished by men who were moved by hunger and willpower alone. But Veneziani described how the South appears, how people say it is and, effectively, how sometimes it actually is. He forgets, however, why it is this way. It happens to the best of us to turn ferocious out of a sense of powerlessness in addition to disappointment and to acquire the ability to see with the eyes of others. At times, however, our own eyes are more sincere.

No other opportunities were left for the Southerners. Their society, beautiful or ugly as it was, had its referral points (the king, priests, small plots of land, large landowners, opportunist bourgeois). The invasion and war of annexation cleared them all away and did not substitute them with something as certain. The brigand and guerrilla formations re-conquered the towns and punished those who had joined the Piedmontese. They restored authority to the poor pro-Bourbon people. When the Savoy troops returned, they took away any authority given to the loyalists and re-established theirs. Perhaps even more than once. With the nobles and bourgeois that flattered and betrayed each other, power floated amidst uncertainty. The people learned one thing: no matter who came or went, they were always the ones to lose. Is this the meaning of *perceived powerlessness*?

"It is this. I would also add that even those who picked up their rifles and chose to react, lost. Those who did not, saw them lose," continues Bocchiaro. "In all of this, those who could intervene do not: the authorities, (even when one knew with certainty who they were) with their silence, only served to facilitate the implicit acceptance of the situation that was created. In order to justify this, they diffused ad hoc ideologies that were aimed at blaming the victim. Blaming those who suffer is the tragic outcome of the belief in a just world. This is the conviction that one obtains what one deserves in life and deserves what they obtain. If you are subjected to abuse or you contract AIDS etc. you were obviously 'asking for it.' It is those who cause the suffering that tend to transform the victim into the culprit most often. The guards feel that they can legitimately abuse those who suffer because they believe that their superiority is innate. The two groups that were initially equal are now at opposite ends of the spectrum. They are divided by a gap that has been created by strong psychosocial mechanisms, even if they are predictable, just like our psychology laboratories have demonstrated. People of different ages, socio-cultural levels, status, and sex are all victims of such mechanisms."

I had asked Professor Bocchiaro if one hundred and fifty years of an Italy that has been united and guided by the concept of the South's inferiority could be interpreted according to the psycho-sociological mechanisms that have been studied. We now have that answer: a part of the country restricted another in a prison whose walls and bars were made of prejudice. The authority that designed such a system of power came down from the North. The South was subjected to it and accepted it. Both convinced themselves that it was true. There were still some amongst the "prisoners" that did not accept these conditions (and some amongst the "guards" that doubted). But every rebellion has been suppressed. "These people," continues Bocchiaro, "have no choice but to devise an escape plan. Some are able to carry out their plans, fleeing as far as they can in order to get away from their persecutors."

Some did escape: at least thirteen million Southerners escaped over the course of the century, though that number may have been over twenty million. This is the largest flux of emigration that Europe has ever known. It has been estimated that it was this emigration, and not the Savoy weapons, that ultimately brought about the end of the "brigands" and their armed resistance. Once they had left, all those who could have been an obstacle to the "Superior Northerner/Inferior Southerner" system had been removed. "Those who remained behind were those who were able to tolerate abuse, those who could not or did not possess the will to fight, those who accepted apathy, or those who were in power," according to Bocchiaro "thus creating, in this last instance, significant cracks within the group it belonged to."

Those others were the guards, but amongst the prisoners (or colonized people), in the name of the guards (or colonizers) several of them took on powers that would become very strong and would bring many benefits to those who controlled them. This power might even confer an apparent independence, but it could never compare to that of the guards (or colonizers) from which it descended. The Southern representatives voted for, with few exceptions that almost always lose anyway, in favor of laws designed in the North to the South's detriment. Today, they support government that is influenced by the *Lega* and Tremonti, who spend the money designated for Calabria's roads in Lombardy. In 1863, the most frightening repressive law, that basically subjected the South to the invaders' will, was presented by a representative from l'Aquilia, Giuseppe Pica.

If it were possible to apply principles of physics or biology to social psychology, one could say that these changes always happen when the cost to apply them is at the lowest level possible. It is the acceptance of a condition of an inconvenient inferiority that, in certain cases, could be more convenient and "less costly" in terms of emotional "energy," than to attempt to refuse it (like the "brigands" and emigrants found out).

"It is said that the defeated do not write history," comments Luigi Zoja in his book *Storia dell'arroganza*. "But the defeated accept the spirit of the victors." To fully feel this spirit, they adopt the ideas and ways of the victors, even if it is to their own disadvantage.

Professor Bocchiaro cautions that those "shared visions" hide more than one trap. The behavior of those people involved adapting to the dominant idea and aimed to reinforce it. To simplify things, let us call these "shared visions" prejudices: the society that harbors them will act in such a way that will serve to confirm them. "This is a self-fulfilling prophecy," Bocchiaro states. He cites an example: "In the Sixties, some social researchers approached various teachers and pointed out among their students, those who appeared to be (based on careful observation) the most gifted as well as those who were not cut out for learning. At the end of the year, the grades of these two groups of student mirrored the results of the researchers results perfectly. It is a shame that there were actually no careful observations performed, but rather the "gifted" and "poor" students were chosen randomly. It happened that, under the influence of that prejudice, the teachers had dedicated themselves more to those "gifted" students and neglected the others." (Don't tell this to Mariastella Gelmini, poor lady.)

But that's not all. "In the United States," continues Bocchiaro, "there is a stereotype according to which African American students are less intelligent than others. They are aware of this, and out of fear of strengthening this stereotype they are under an enormous amount of pressure that negatively influences their grades. So, psychological pressure, in addition to the difficulty of the task at hand, induces, in the vast majority of instances a clear drop in performance. Even the teachers are influenced by this stereotype. It just so happens that, even if the students are at the same level of intelligence, the African American student will receive a lower grade than his Caucasian counterpart."

In this manner, on the basis of scholastic results (data that are "objective," according to the Minister) some American scientists have established that African Americans are less intelligent than Caucasians. In other words, they are an inferior race. No one has adequately commented upon, with a good old Bronx cheer, this discovery (they have not done so in Italy either, with the Southerners replacing the African Americans). One of those "tan" human beings of inferior quality, Barack Obama, became President of the United States. This means that anyone could aspire to anything in that country! A professor from Ulster University in Ireland has recently verified, with a similar method using scholastic grades, that Southern Italians are less intelligent. Here's someone else who wants to be the Minister of Public Education in Italy!

This social and psychological mechanism hides a very powerful trap: "Shared visions," continues Bocchiaro, "mean that all must function in such a way as to reinforce this common vision. In the "I am superior/You are inferior" scheme, not only will both parties act as though this notion were real, but also in such a way as to bolster the positions in question. Let me explain myself better: if I had two friends, and one was known to be fun-loving and the other to be disagreeable, and I asked the former to tell me a joke and greeted the other with a strained "Hello" that elicited a rude response, this response would prove his disagreeableness. This game, however, is always lead by the "superior" and followed by the "inferior," who does nothing to improve his condition because he retains, even unconsciously, that the evaluation that penalizes him is just, and that it is unjust for him to rebel against it."

Within the families and minds of the Southerners, the memories of relatives and fellow citizens that rebelled against this condition have been erased.

"Sure. It is the shame of the victim that prompts them to remove the memory of what they had to endure as though it were a misdeed. When one is taught to be inferior for one hundred and fifty years, like in our Italy-laboratory, there is no need to demonstrate it: everything around you tells you that the situation has developed in a certain manner. The "superior" knows it, as does the "inferior." It is a fact." (If even a powerful free spirit such as Norberto Bobbio reaches the point at which he says "the 'problem' of the Southerners is the Southerners' problem"...)

Conduct an experiment: say something trite with a Lombard accent, complete with a tiny furrow between your brows and tighten your lips like an intelligent person would under pressure (imagine Cota, Calderoli, or Gelmini!) and then announce the discovery of cold fusion in a Calabrian or Barese accent (just like Lino Banfi). Want to bet that the Nobel Prize for physics will go to the Northerner?

Let me summarize: it has been one hundred and fifty years since Italy was united by brute force based on the idea that the South and the Southerners are inferior. This is a vision that is shared by both the North and the South. It is based on this shared vision that the State places different emphases on different geographical areas. A civil gap emerges from this vision, in the sense that the behavior of the Southerners in the South is, on average, more disorderly, disrespectful, and illegal. In one word: uncivilized.

This is only so that the "shared vision" might come into existence?

Not only for this reason. Tragedy breeds tragedy.

Wars are both daughters and mothers of a backward civilization because they reduce the relationship between men to a primitive power struggle (any roman legion with a dagger is worth more than Archimedes). The social fabric of the South was torn by a war of invasion and occupation. But this happened in other countries that were able to reassemble themselves (some were able to do so better than others) in time. While in the South, the unified country applied discrimination, obstacles, and weights in order ensure that it remained in a state of inferiority. In a constant state of "illness," as it has been referred to, where the patient "does not die, but does not get better either."

These elements, though they are well known, appear to be insufficient to explain the destruction of civil order that one encounters in large areas of the South, where one's sense of community is limited to one's town, family, or *mafia* clan (a phenomenon that, after the Unification, acquired powers that it had never before possessed).

Strangely enough, the consequences of the most serious loss that the South was subjected to as a result of its invasion and its centuries old discriminatory politics, was never analyzed: the loss of its fathers. Hundreds of thousands of them were killed either because they were resistant or merely annoyingly existent. This happens in all wars, but the natural wisdom of demography puts everything back in its place. In the South, after the massacre, the only way that was left open to the Southerners was to flee, and in a century's time (in other words, for three consecutive generations) fathers were forced to emigrate by the million, without considering the other hundreds of thousands that were swallowed by the two world wars and the colonial ones as well.

This had never happened before. The South had always had its reference points, in its families and society, visible. It did not matter if they were backward or not, nor if they were handsome or ugly. The only thing that mattered was that they were strong and present and that this had lasted for such a long time that it had been considered unchangeable. The South might have appeared to be a society that was anchored in archaic values. (Still today, in part, it is. This is not an obstacle for development: Japan, India, and China are examples.) It did not matter how bad the poorest members of society were, they still believed that they were better off staying rather than leaving. This is the opposite of what happened at the same time in the North.

A society continues to exist as long as it has a moral code to compare to others. Troy did not die as long as there was one person, Aeneas, who could plant the seed of his civilization and reproduce it. A social system remains intact as long as its values and the ability to transmit them are saved. Its size does not matter. Even a cell is enough. It is for this reason that Aeneas was a world, while a million men without roots and memories could not be. He was an idea of good and evil and was aware of the importance of contributing to the thoughts and needs of others. It is the willingness to leave one's door open, not upon perceiving who one's neighbor is. He was the dispenser of the right amount and type of good manners. It is what one understands and transmits, without even being conscious of it, just by existing in one's own family. It is this element that one uses to determine one's own self-worth and can use as a means of comparison with others. "Now I know everything," says Telemachus, the son of Ulysses, to the Proci, when he realizes that he is a man and the reason for which he is: "I can distinguish good and evil." He managed to do so without his father, but thanks to that aspect of Ulysses that lasted throughout his prolonged absence. A social system can withstand many mutilations and remain itself. But if the community is destroyed and the generational cycle is interrupted and the reference points are removed from the new generation and are substituted with incompatible ones, a sense of order is lost. It is not necessarily true that another is proposed, or if it is proposed, that it will be accepted.

In family and in society, fathers are the law. They are the guardians of rules that are the same for everyone. Mothers are love: they are those who make exceptions in order to favor their own children and this makes them more willing to make requests that override the rules, "even when these are in direct contrast to the law and principle" writes Mario Alcaro in *Sull'identità meridionale*. A father must protect society even if it means giving up his home. A mother must protect her home even if it is at the expense of society. This distinction between the roles is the basis of our patriarchal system. I recount this system by summarizing Luigi Zoja's book on paternity, which can never seem to gather enough praise, *Il gesto di Ettore*. In English this book is simply titled *The Father*. If the authority of the fathers weakens, the system of rules upon which a community is founded unravels because the guardian that oversees the limitations of one's behavior goes missing. Therefore: "Any loss of paternity is a loss of civilization," according to Zoja. It is true even today, with fathers present, but with a much weaker role. Imagine being a part of a society that sees its institutional, legal, and family reference points destroyed by an invader. Imagine that it sees its fathers err either by opposing or by conforming. Then for a century, this society does not even see its fathers, because they leave.

The hemorrhage was so violent that a serious demographic problem emerged: the South became a predominantly female population. The system of rules veered towards the matriarchal system: that which favors my children, even if it means damaging the community, is what is right. One can see the reasons behind the success of the *mafia*, whose root is feminine. This is despite its machismo: the *mafioso* is the product of the maternal "exception," not of paternal "law."

Friedrich Vochting summarizes different reports on this subject (by Faina, Arias, and Marcozzi): "Even morale suffered. In certain towns in the Abruzzo area (author's note: *where certain specific studies were conducted*) according to reliable sources, it seems as though only one twentieth of all of the women and ladies have remained chaste. Not only were the cases of adultery numerous, but one was forced to take note of how the sense of honor, which was so tangible in the older generations to the point that it was often defended by gun and dagger, had become relaxed, almost to the point of destruction, due to the prolonged absence of the men."

Vito Teti (author of *La razza maledetta*) cites the study conducted by Lionello De Nobili that "starting from the reports and the sentences pronounced by Calabrian judges, he links the increase of crimes of "indecency" and those against the "family's honor" that saw women as protagonists, to the phenomenon of migration."

In this manner of viewing things, "there were, without a doubt, moral prejudices" observes Ercole Sori in *L'emigrazione italiana dall'Unità alla seconda Guerra mondiale,* that "focused overall on the family, where the disruptive effects of mass emigration can be measured best. The signs appeared to be quite explicit: the diffusion of the "two homes," one in their native town and another abroad, the disappearance of husbands along the winding roads of emigration, the increase of separations, the increase of idleness and the infidelity of "white widows" who in the fight against the gossip of their neighbors also raised the number of public quarrels noted in the local courts, the diffusion of syphilis (which was imported along with the emigrants), the precocious emancipation, insubordination, as well as the loosening of 'moral inhibitions' of children."

And even if, in some cases, "a new morality emerges, where a family fortified by emigration is at the center," the corruption of woman (and consequently of the family) and emigration seemed to go hand in hand with one another. In this manner, "the number of adulteries increased along with illegitimate births and abortions. These were all attributed to male expatriation," reports Andreina De Clementi in *Di qua e di là dall'oceano.* (Can I ask you to remember this when I speak of the "broken window theory"? Thank you.) "Especially in the first fifteen years of the (author's note: *last*) century, the men were almost always absent. The South needed to deal with a drainage of the male adult population, the likes of which it had never seen before." This "undoubtedly affected the entire socio-economic structure." One had a civil wedding, the husband emigrated with the dowry of the wife and when he returned with the money he had made, they married again in

Church and consummated their marital vows. In Calabria, one out of every three families was "headless."

The root of what we feel to be still passes between the legs of women. Up until yesterday, (and to some extent even today) the responsibility of female decency was the responsibility of men. In the most traditional civilizations, the father and brothers of the adulteress faced the task of killing her. While in Western civilization these practices became a thing of the past, the meaning behind what "justified" this behavior remained, albeit in a milder and more farcical form: the derision of a cuckold is a sort of social punishment for that man who was not able to control his woman's sexuality. In the recent civil war in the Balkans, the population's identity was a target. In order to destroy it, ethnic rape was used as an instrument where women were used as passive carriers of another race. This further served to breakdown in men the notion of having DNA that was worthy of being passed down. All of the literary works produced before the Unification of Italy identified the honor of constructing a country with defending a woman's purity; sometimes this is recovered through death, a suicide, if rape was committed (Banti provides a rich anthology in *La nazione del Risorgimento*).

To those fathers that did remain in the South, guardians of a residual authority that was no longer heeded, it happened that they were often disobeyed and derided in public by those "Americans," the emigrants that returned home. By now, these emigrants had acquired financial opportunities and ideas that were no longer comparable to those of their severe relatives, who administrated the little, antiquated wealth that was left behind. Southern society was that which did not allow one to emerge, but also did not allow you to sink either. The richness that bounced back home from overseas destroyed the proportions of that world. The "American" that returned home came back "transformed from clothing to conscience" and this "return home unleashed small earthquakes. Once freedom had been tasted," summarizes De Clementi "it was difficult to once again subject oneself to paternal authority. On the other hand, this authority had also lost its luster. This ability to manage money endowed the son with a power that was unknown to the father."

One received the derision, from a new winning world that was rich (it was even brighter because it was far away, and therefore glorified by one's imagination), towards the last remaining shadows of a world that was defeated. In order to fully comprehend the importance and meaning of this: one often makes fun of that which is deemed to be beneath oneself, even a confrontation. Derision is equal to spitting upon one's enemy that is already on the floor. It is the cowardly Achaeans that dip their spear tips in dying Hector's blood, from whom they used to flee.

The South was called to choose between two evils: brigand or emigrant. Or, first a brigand and then an emigrant. "When the wrongs one receives are many, and render it impossible for one to stay in a given place, one does not resort to justice. One does not have faith in justice and therefore chooses to emigrate. In other time periods, one resorted to crime," writes Pasquale Rossi in *Carattere del Mezzogiorno d'Italia*, where "never had virtue been so solitary or so negatively inefficient."

In the time in between the collapse of governmental order, due to the invasion, and the establishment of a new one, homicides, and crimes against individuals and their wealth were rampant and there was no control over this situation. This was also partly due to the sort of permission to "commit crimes" granted to those who favored the Piedmontese in exchange for political support of the new regime. The arduous recuperation of order was then maimed by the mass exodus prompted by poverty. And "in the first decade of the century," notes Teti, "at the same time as the social turmoil brought about emigration, one witnessed an increase in the phenomenon of crime."

Once the fathers are away, the children are out of control.

Immoral women, delinquent children, and mocked fathers: this is the undoing of a civilization. What remains of Troy are slaves and refugees. The new rules are those put in place by the victors and it is they who govern. The old rules disappear, and even if some of them resist, they are the rules of a defeated people.

With their avidity and cynicism, "the statesmen of Piedmont and partisans have corrupted the Kingdom of Naples as far as what was left of morality. They stripped the people of their laws, their bread, and their honor (...) and discredited justice.... It is true, they united the country, but they rendered it a miserable and vile servant, a courtesan." It was November 20, 1861 when these words were pronounced in the Italian Parliament by Duke Carafa of Casoria.

In nearly one hundred years, in the South, due to the massacres carried out by the North's army, for the more selective war from 1915 to 1918, (six hundred thousand people died and just as many were wounded, with half being from the South, who comprised only one third of the population. The divisions from the South were sent forth to be massacred. The North passed over their dead bodies. The "Catanzaro" division mutinied) and for the mass exodus, fathers were taken away from their sons for three generations. The South emerged from this situation in a debilitated state. It was deprived of its most profound convictions: its moral code had been amputated. Its strength and laws disappeared, and since they had been deprived of their best values, they believed that those of others had a stronger base and therefore a future. Their values no longer did.

"The moment people decide to leave and seek their fortunes elsewhere, the social fabric is torn from where that emigrant was inserted into society," writes Goffredo Fofi, picking up on an observation made by Giuseppe Galasso. "One can then speak of individual returns, but no longer of a reconstruction of that psycho-social balance that existed previously in the places from which those individuals departed." Here, they are specifically referring to the post-war emigration to the North, which cost the South over a quarter of its population.

They say that numbers talk. This is not true. Do not be offended if I tell you that you have not understood something when you believe that you have. I will try to explain: the South witnessed the laceration of its social fabric by the massacres of the Unification, then by millions of emigrants at the turn of the century, then by millions of "internal" emigrants and "clandestine" emigrants during the Fascist regime, then those who emigrated during the "economic miracle." Today, it witnesses the flight of its college graduates. Do you realize how much a quarter of the population is? Look around you, amidst your family, friends, and colleagues. Single out the most resourceful people, the ones that are the best at their jobs, who have talent to offer elsewhere. Now remove them from your world. One-two-three, take that one away! One-two-three, remove the other one! Do this five million times. You will see your intelligent boss disappear, followed by the young person who would have taken their place, the one who works continuously without ever stopping to look at their watch. You would see that person who always succeeds at whatever they do, disappear along with that person who was always able to mo- tivate even the laziest people…. Do this millions of times, three or four times in a row for a total that reaches anywhere from thirteen to twenty million people over the course of a century. Those that remain behind are those who have resigned themselves to their fate, the losers, the whiners, who expect others to provide for them, the bully that takes advantage of others. I know a place that is described in this manner, that once was not this way, and that I refuse to believe cannot be transformed into something else.

That place is my home. This was done to us.

Out of this emerges "'an inferior caste' in the South, like for the African Americans in the United States," Zoja explains. "The anthropologist Margaret Mead has conducted numerous studies on this topic. The life of the African Americans, one century after the abolition of slavery, still felt the repercussions of a condition that they were subjected to. The slave traders did not buy and sell families, but individuals. The sturdiest men became fathers, be- cause they were purchased for breeding purposes to increase the 'assets' of the owner. There was no paternity for slaves, only in- semination. There was no family, only reproduction. Still today, in the United States, a tragically high percentage of black women, very often underage, are teen mothers, like their own mothers and grandmothers were. Even in Scandinavian countries there is a high percentage of children born out of wedlock, but there (due to the emancipation of unmarried women) it does not make much of a difference. The father is absent as an individual, but is very present in the culture, with not only emotional values, but social values of which the mother is a carrier. This is not the case in Southern Italy in the nineteenth century, where the roles were quite distinct and women were prepared to protect their child from the treacherous world. The father figure is a creation of culture, not of nature, like maternity is. Mead says that it should be taught to every generation. The miseducational power that lacking a father can have is frightening, even if only for one generation. Imagine for more than one, like in Southern Italy."

Professor Zoja already knew about some of the misdeeds that were done in order to unify our country, and his curiosity is piqued by other aspects. He does believe that the parallel between the conditions to which the Southerners were reduced and that of the African Americans is forced. The African Americans were condemned to a freedom without paternity that was acquired with the abolition of slavery. This also brought forth degraded social behavior, such as alcoholism, crime (like in South Africa after the end of apartheid) and weak family ties. The African Americans wound up in the North, in Detroit, in automobile factories. The Southerners wound up in Turin.

"All of this did not happen because of a conspiracy, out of an evil mind that delineates the destinies of men," warns Zoja (and he is right to do so). "It is the historical circumstances that prompt marginalization. The trouble is that there are few ways out."

This is true: needs (Piedmont's debts, the interests of the superpowers of the time, a diffuse romantic Unitarian ideal, the political weakness of a country to take advantage of) create circumstances. Facts and behaviors are determined by these, and these in turn generate convictions, such as the existence of the South's inferiority. Perhaps one can see an extension, an adaptation to what John Davis says in *Antropologia delle società mediterranee*: "The subjugation to an authority figure is more common and more diffused in the Mediterranean than bureaucracy, Fascism, Communism, and any other type of democracy. It does not need any of these to exist and can co-exist with any of them." Even if that authority figure is imposed through the use of weapons and discrimination, that figure can be identified in the coupling between Northern economic power and the political power that holds our country together. In this manner, the South is subordinate and seeks subordination.

"In the North," writes Isaia Sales in *Leghisti e sudisti*, "economic power attempts to become political power. In the South, political power is economic power." This is the chain of power between a mother-country and its colony.

Upon the ruins of a country that, in the South, had been united for over thirteen centuries, no order of fathers established itself strongly enough to reconstruct a common dignity comparable to that of the victors. Numerous tears in the social fabric favored egotism, corruption, and abuse. The public officials governing the South were the worst that the South and the North had to offer. They were the most incapable and dishonest people available. From the North, they arrived to govern the South as a punishment. From the South, they came to demonstrate their subordination. In the Parliament in Turin, the echoes of a Garibaldininan and Piedmontese civil service reform reached the South. In Messina, once the Bourbon employees had been killed, their assassins took their place. In Siracusa, the hospital employees equaled four times the number of patients. The number of public employees, on the entire island, increased to the point that the expenses reached nearly one million lira at the time as compared to the Bourbon regime (which established a limit as to the number of public employees that could be hired). And what about now? They continue to grow.

When today, while forgetting their origins, one judges that type of behavior (Ask me if I like this behavior. What a question! Of course, I don't), it is appropriate to remember Professor Zoja's words: "Any loss of paternity is a loss of civilization." Such a loss also tends to prevent recovery as well. "The shattering brought about by the emigration phenomenon necessarily resulted in less homogeneity of interests between individuals," explains Giuseppe De Rita in *L'emigrazione italiana negli anni '70*. The ability to understand and desire to do something for the common good, and not merely one's own, is lost.

"One cannot live here," one of the millions of Southerners who fled to the other side of the ocean justified their departure with this phrase. "The Lord does not send us what is Good. Our lands are dry. We have unripe mountain land, and our men tire of this land that yields nothing. They leave to go to America. Let them go."

The South was oppressed, the Southerner was humiliated, and the order that once prevailed was dissolved in a shameful and spiteful manner. "Its revenge lies within its own degenerative process," wrote Ettore Ciccotti, a representative from the South, a century ago. He knew the consequences of the damage that was done and would repay those who had done this with the same token of disfavor that those who were subjected to this damage had been paid: "The bad examples it offers, those sad instruments that supply the forces of evil are a deaf reaction that is both objective and inevitable."

The disorder that was created remained. It grew and continues to grow still today, and it supplies itself through a phenomenon known as the (here it is!) "Theory of the Broken Windows." It explains why the Swiss throw paper on the ground and run red lights when they come to Italy and why the Italians no longer throw paper on the ground and cease to be color blind at traffic lights when they are in Switzerland. It can best be summarized in this fashion: dirt attracts dirt while cleanliness attracts cleanliness. According to G.L Kelling and J.Q. Wilson, who studied this phenomenon, "the presence, in certain areas, of graffiti, overgrown weeds, broken glass, and abandoned cars and homes fuels the notion of general disinterest on the part of the residents and local government," writes Bocchiaro. "If no one seems to care about what happens, the level of vandalism and crime in that area is destined to grow."

If this did not occur everywhere, in the South, or at least not with the same virulence, it is due to many factors.

To continue with the theme of "lost fathers": Puglia resisted the temptation to emigrate longer than any other region and only after World War II did it undergo an exodus comparable to that which had emptied the rest of the South nearly a century earlier. In the ten years spanning from 1906 to 1915, Abruzzo lost 43% of its inhabitants. Calabria lost 40%. Basilicata lost 38.5%. The rules, in Puglia, lasted for a longer period of time. This could have something to do with the fact that the region (in the eyes of the North) presented itself in a less "Southern" manner than the other regions. As a result, the *mafia* was never able to establish a strong foothold there, despite its repeated attempts.

"The deterioration of a given environment reflects the internal malaise of its inhabitants," states Bocchiaro. "But it is also one of the causes," suggest Kelling and Wilson "because it gives rise to behavior that is increasingly less civil which is accompanied by a "secondary pleasure": the impression that one can do whatever one wants, even if this notion eventually backfires. Is it really chance that cities like Naples or Palermo, which are submerged in garbage, register higher crime rates?"

Rudolph Giuliani, as Mayor of New York, obtained great results in crime reduction. Everyone remembers his slogan: "Zero Tolerance." They have forgotten, however, that by following Kelling and Wilson's advice, he was able to fight off all of the effects of the "Theory of the Broken Windows." In the most deteriorated neighborhoods, he substituted those broken windows and cleaned the streets. One time ... two times ... many times. Finally, the windows remained intact and the streets stayed clean because the people who lived there had finally been convinced that they were a part of the city, and not excluded from it.

A chasm has been dug in our country. It has never been filled. Those who found themselves within it were made to believe, and then subsequently believed, that they deserved to be in this state. They no longer claim the same rights, or rather "extraordinary interventions" (in the sense that it is extraordinary that every once in a while, someone intervenes). Those who are on the outside continue to draw whatever they need from these places and toss in their contempt along with their toxic waste, all the while believing that they have the right to do so.

Yet, "all of the studies converge around the observation that the increase of production and the rise of income in the South automatically yields significant macroeconomic benefits for the North," Viesti notes. But it is preferable to continue to depress the South, even if it means losing something. This is not rational.

"Roles, the diffusion of responsibility, dehumanization, the loss of individuality, conformity, the belief in a better world, broken windows: these are the psycho-social principles that are responsible for the rift created between the North and the South of Italy," according to Professor Bocchiaro. "It is a question of underestimated factors that are neglected in favor of explanations that are decidedly more convenient for those whose sole interest is in maintaining the *status quo*."

What was that person saying before? Ah, yes: "They are not like us, madam."

CHAPTER 9

Fortunately, the South Has the Plague

Southerners learn this lesson when they are still young: the South has the plague. It is covered in sores that it must keep. Already in 1861, President Bettino Ricasoli asked the Chamber of Deputies "not to hold useless discussions. Promoting the plagued provinces of the South is a waste of time." Prior to him, Liborio Romano in his letter to Cavour listed the "ten plagues" of the South. While growing up, Southerners learn to recognize these "plagues." Emigration? A plague. Unemployment? A plague. Rusty railroads? A plague. Inadequate roads? A plague ... until the final conclusion was drawn: Southerners? A plague.

But despite the "proven" inefficiency of teachers in the South, the "certified" stupidity of their students, the (denied) "inadequacy" of the remaining (at least for the moment, right Mrs. Minister?) schools, sooner or later someone will read a book and discover that there is such a thing as ancient Chinese wisdom. The ideogram that means "crisis" or "plague," if you will, is composed of two characters: the first means "disaster" while the second means "opportunity." This means that, no matter how unfortunate a situation might seem, it can also be interpreted in the following manner: Emigration? An opportunity. Unemployment? An opportunity. Rusty railroads? Etc.

Emigration can be a reservoir of values (even economic ones), a treasure, if one is able to take into consideration those people who have demonstrated their abilities in so many fields, elsewhere. This could be further enhanced by engaging them in projects that would bring them back to the South, along with the myriad experiences they have acquired over the years.

Today, technology brings them closer.

The last of my mother's three brothers, Uncle Cosimino, died in Torgiano, near Perugia's gates, where he had moved (as Massimo Troisi would have said) as an emigrant. The Southerners are those people who disperse themselves around the world for the sole purpose of reuniting for weddings and funerals (it is a custom that was invented to ward off family arguments). The native town of the Punzi family (my mother's side of the family) is Laterza, near Taranto, approaching Matera. It is infused with a French-laced dialect.

Uncle Cosimino had a kind, warm personality. In fact, along with Aunt Anna, they brought eight kind, warm-natured children into the world. If Torgiano's population has reached five thousand, they owe it in part to the Punzi family, which has since expanded into neighboring towns.

For Uncle Cosimino's funeral, members of the Punzi family arrived from Switzerland, Lombardy, Puglia, Basilicata, and Lazio. The town's main church was so full that some people were obliged to stand outside. There were many family members from the town, but there were also many family members from elsewhere, intent upon whispering their personal information (in their newly rediscovered Southern accents, laced with Umbrian, Lombard, Roman, and German accents as well): "Are you Aunt Anna's son, Nino?" "No, Pino. Nino is my older brother." "Excuse me! But you know, after all these years...."(What does my uncle's funeral have to do with the ills of the South? A little patience, I'm getting there....)

At the cemetery, while they sealed the grave, my wife approached Aunt Anna: "I am sorry to finally meet you in such an awful moment. I am Rossana, Pino's wife." My aunt replied, "If this situation allowed us to know each other, then it is a beautiful moment, my daughter. Cosimino would be happy." (Can you believe that?)

The reacquisition of those lost elements in my family portrait found me quite guilty in my happiness. But it was a funeral, how could anyone be happy? I noticed that I was not alone in my reaction. The collective discovery of all of those family ties ("That's

Memena's son? No way!") radiated so much joy that the funeral became a party.

"Let's all go home now," ordered Aunt Anna, in a sweet but irrefutable tone. "Everyone." There were those that said, "My train is leaving...." and those that showed logs of their travel times, but they were to no avail: Aunt Anna had spoken.

In the home of the deceased, one room had been adorned with refreshments: sandwiches, drinks, coffee. There, the many loose ends were once again reunited into a knot amidst all of the eating and drinking. The pleasure of having rediscovered affection that had almost been forgotten already became intertwined with the sad realization of being on the verge of losing it once again.

In the South, those who are not emigrants, or do not have any relatives that have emigrated, are in the strict minority (A phrase that referred to the Cretans is also applicable to the people here: "They make more history elsewhere than they could ever hope to by staying here."). Along with Maurizio, the youngest son of Aunt Anna and Uncle Cosimino, I began to take note of all of the family members that were bustling about the house. There were so many of us. "We should get together more often," reasoned Maurizio, "otherwise when all of our parents pass away, we will become so distant that even funerals will not constitute enough of a tie to bring us back together."

This was true. So we thought to organize a "Punzi Family Day" in Laterza, perhaps in May during the Feast of the *Madonna di Materdomini* so that we could unite every year and meet any "new" family members. The feast day, the band, the epic banquet: we will probably have to reserve an entire hotel if not an entire farm. If whole families came, we would be hundreds of people.

For Laterza, this would mean jobs and money.

A town with many emigrants would find itself with much business if it declared a "Welcome Home Day" for each family: registering people, grouping them by family, reconstructing family trees. It would allow the town to get back some of its people. It would allow many people to get back their hometown.

Emigrants are no longer starving, which was the original reason they left in the first place. They are lacking the town from which they came. Many come back for vacations, weddings, and funerals. They would meet with whoever chose to come back. Perhaps it could even be on a day that was particularly significant for a given family. On that day they could greet close relatives as well as those whom they believed to be lost. Many people would willingly spend some money for an experience like this. The towns most affected by emigration would benefit the most from these "Welcome Home Days." They would receive new ideas, money, and connections. Is this merely a hypothesis? Not really: emigrants returning home, in past years, have been the ones to prompt the creation of new industries, especially in the Abruzzo and the Salento areas.

So Uncle Cosimino's funeral does have something to do with the South's plagues? Does it really seem so difficult to transform a "plague" into an "opportunity"? Can't the same be done for what is missing or inadequate: roads, railways, schools, airports...? These are all jobs and therefore opportunities.

With what funds? When one reaches this point of the discussion, the discussion dies. Isn't the heart of the "Issue of the South" here? Yes and no. Money does not solve problems if those who manage it do not desire them to be solved. Aside from the beginning of the 20th century, and in the first years of the Fund for the South, in a century and a half, the South has been considered the place where money (and not even much of it) was brought in order to be redistributed elsewhere.

The rift between the North and the South was constructed purposely and people strive to maintain it. Those who fought to eliminate it, despite their good will, often committed two errors. The first was in thinking that decisions and "extraordinary" interventions were necessary. These became instruments and alibis, which those in bad faith, in order to pretend that they were doing something when they were actually doing the opposite, gave very little "extra" while taking away much of what should have been "ordinary." Pasquale Saraceno stated the most obvious notion, which of course no one wanted to hear: in order to balance a country that has been split into two parts, one must apply two different policies. If the country is divided into those who have more and those who have less, the "more" must flow into the part that has "less," especially if the "more" had been removed from the part that has "less." It is for this reason that those who truly wanted to mend the rift, and those who said that they did (but made sure that they actually did not) turned to "extraordinary" interventions, that were additional. In one word, they were "territorial" in the sense that they were directed towards one part of the country. In this manner, the first group was satisfied and then the second group stretched the exception to include those who really did not need the added benefits and thereby actually widened the rift.

It was Gaetano Salvemini who revealed this glaring error (one takes notice of it only when someone else points it out). The Fascist regime forced this professor from Puglia into exile and as a result, he was more appreciated abroad than in his own country (in order to receive the honor of his presence in the United States, Harvard University created a position for him as Chair of the History of Italian Civilization). He came back to Italy after World War II. There were many discussions held concerning the "extraordinary" interventions (the Fund for the South emerged from these) to help solve the "Problem of the South." He stated that the solution could only be to provide the same things for everyone. He cited elementary schools as an example. Once the number of illiterate people had been determined (at that time the problem was still a serious one) the new classrooms were to be built where this phenomenon was the greatest, then where it was of medium importance, and finally where it was a small problem. This was to occur wherever it was necessary: North, South, mountain or sea.

Now imagine applying this criterion to the remaining problems: the railways, highways, universities.... The country would finally be unified. At that point one could truly compare who could govern well or not.

This solution is too simple, balanced, and equal. It must be wrong. It leaves no room for political discretions (look at how many the *Lega* wants for the North, Sicily for itself, and Trentino-Alto Adige as well....): if I am owed a hospital, I should not have to thank a local politician for it. This excludes criteria that are convenient, from time to time, to someone: "But we pay more taxes," "But we have too many unemployed doctors," "But we are hosting the Alpine Troops." At that point, if we have a hospital that has been constructed in the correct need-based proportion and equipped in the same manner as all of the others, but is a disgrace and the people continue to seek medical care elsewhere, it would be our own fault, and not of the North or of the Communists.

Naturally, the "extraordinary" interventions were adopted as the preferred means of distributing wealth so that someone in the South could boast about their acquired gain, which would still be less than one could find, obviously, in the rest of Italy. This would also allow for those in the North to say, "Again?" The State designed the system in this fashion and considered the South as a sort of "lesser" country by offering it "extraordinary" assistance. This is the opposite of "equality for everyone."

The second error was that even though the South received benefits, it did not have decisional power over them. Salvemini had proposed, in the 1920s, that Italy should become federalized, to prevent the South's resources from continuing to migrate to the North and that the South continue to be subjected to the decisions of others. This would have resulted in the two-fold damage of the South that would have meant it was deprived of its resources and would no longer be accustomed to being responsible for its own actions. He was not the only person to have proposed something similar, but since this brought no benefits to the North, it simply was not considered.

I then understood where both Salvemini and Giustino Fortunato had gone wrong: "Fortunato placed too much hope in the Northerners and I placed too much hope in the 'filthy people' (fifty years ago, the Northerners referred to the Southerners in this fashion)." Both men, however, expected both parties to work together to find a solution. They did not consider the fact that it was more likely that the stronger party would prefer benefitting from

its advantageous position, while the weaker of the two would settle for the meager fruits of its labor because it was convinced that
it could not aspire to anything beyond receiving the table scraps
of the wealthy. If the South attempts to reorganize itself, the North
intervenes like a "foreign state," according to Salvemini, "intent
upon defending its small, rotten bourgeois delinquents": its allies.

Guido Dorso, a researcher from Avellino gifted with the ability
of analyzing situations to the point of near-clairvoyance, reached a
very different and more radical conclusion. The "Padanian struggle does not embody an Italian issue, but rather is a negation of
the country," to the point that "the 'Pro-*Padania*' movement could
always be the base upon which the successors of Fascism construct their ideals for governing a future State" (*La rivoluzione meridionale*, 1925: written over a half century before the *Pro-Lega* and
Pro-Berlusconi movements e-merged). The South, by itself, had been
given the task of "waking a dead population" and ridding itself of
the "crooks from the North," whose oligarchies "were able to create a tried and true dictatorship geared towards damaging the
South."

Today, the South is in the same state that Lombardy was in
prior to the Unification. When the Austrian intellectuals attributed
"the Lombard's lack of energy" to racial inferiority, it happened
that "Austria received tax money from Italy and deposited these
funds beyond the Alps," according to Salvemini. "Lombardy, when
placed in favorable conditions, amazed the world with its progress. The South will do the same," when Lombardy ceases to behave like Austria did at the time and the South ceases to behave
like Lombardy at that time as well.

For this, according to Guido Dorso, "the solution to the 'Problem of the South' can therefore not exist if not in a state of autonomy. Any other attempt will either result in the old system of
'charity' on the State's behalf or threaten to throw us into a state of
separatism."

Today, I am not sure if Dorso himself would stop at a condition of autonomy or would fall into a separatist state of mind after
seeing a North that is hypnotized by the *Lega* party (and yet "if

one puts aside marginal folkloristic notions, there has never been any cultural hostility between these two parts of Italy" wrote Luciano Cafagna, a modern history professor, in 1994 in his work *Nord e Sud*).

There is a Zen fable that has guided me through many difficult situations: the story of the Birds of Paradise. The Birds of Paradise lived happily and peacefully until the Birds of Prey arrived and began to kill them off. The Birds of Paradise had never fought before and did not know how to defend themselves. They helplessly fell at the claws of their aggressors. One of them declared that he had heard about a Wise Man who lives on a mountain far away that knows the answers to every problem.

They decide to find him. Millions of them darkened the skies while flying towards this remote destination. They were ravaged by the Birds of Prey, storms, hunger, exhaustion, and sickness, but they finally reached the mountain.

"Sir," the boldest of the Birds began, "what is the name of the One who will save us?"

The Wise Man said, *"Trend'acìjdd."* The oldest of the Birds translated: "It is an ancient language (author's note: *in my town, Gioia del Colle's, dialect*). It means 'Thirty Birds'."

They counted themselves: there were thirty of them.

"Outsiders will never bring about the resolution of the South's problems," writes Domenico Ficarra in *Le ragioni del Sud*.

Do you remember the experiment conducted in the prison recreated in the basement of Stanford University by Philip Zimbardo? It mirrors the situation of the Birds of Paradise with the arrival of the Birds of Prey/guards. Initially, in their country there was only one role to play: the happy bird. Afterwards, there were two: more and less. The Birds of Paradise numbered in the millions, but were helpless. Despite their number, their role would have remained the losing one.

The story states: one must subtract oneself from the role that condemns them to inferiority. It is necessary to leave the laboratory. Later on, one might want to come back to this game, but on a level playing field. In the North-South experiment conducted in the Italy-laboratory, is this what the South must do in order to free itself from the losing character that was imposed upon it due to the split that occurred one hundred and fifty years ago? Venture out on its own (or almost, like Dorso suggested)?

"Yes" answers Professor Piero Bocchiaro "but...."

... [I]s there another option?

"Yes. One could free oneself from their condition of inferiority without splitting from the rest, by 'remaining in the laboratory' so to speak. It is essential to be aware of the arbitrary nature of the separation of the North from the South and to learn to recognize the psycho-social mechanisms that prevent the South from freeing itself and that the North needs in order to assert its sense of superiority. This would be a good start and would serve to question many things. Then, one must train oneself to oppose discriminatory procedures and behaviors. For example: if I am aware that the people from the North treat us as though we were inferior beings, at the very least I can label this behavior. In this fashion, I have already distanced this concept from myself rather than accept it as being true. I also maintain my dignity by not submitting to this abuse and I show my adversary the pettiness (and prejudice) of his reasoning. Reaching such an objective requires some time, but it is possible, as long as the concepts expounded begin to infiltrate everyday language, particularly that of the young generations." Needless to say it would not help the cause to propose that the Alpine troops of the North receive a 500 Euro bonus while those in the South do not or that anyone who tosses paper on the ground should go to jail, but only if they are Neapolitan. Like in psychoanalysis, one heals when they stop trying to hide their illness. Instead, they admit it and recognize it.

It seems to me that Professor Bocchiaro not only believes his own words, but he believes *in* them as well. However, if he says that this is all possible, it must mean that it is true, even if it is difficult. Here we fall into another little story, that of Gianni Rodari. He tells of a man who wasted his life looking for a country without defects. He would have rendered his life more useful if he had only done his part by eliminating one defect from any place he chose. I know I cite these stories too often, but it is because I believe the entire human condition lies somewhere in between the two.

It is possible to obtain the knowledge of the mechanisms that determine the North and South's different behaviors if information reveals them. Training oneself to avoid them presupposes the willingness to do so. The majority of information available tends to justify the increase of exceptions in favor of the stronger party. A quarter of a century's worth of education under the *Lega*'s influence has stripped the worst aspects of this behavior of the shame that kept them at bay. One adopts racist notions by invoking one's freedom of opinion. One advocates insulting those whom they consider to be inferior by invoking freedom of expression. "If politics is a system of consequences," observes Agazio Loiero in *Il patto di ferro*, "the consequence is that Italy has entrusted the task of organizing the structure of the State to the one person that in one hundred and fifty years of Unification hypothesized seceding from Italy." Appointing Bossi to the position of Minister of Reform is like appointing Dracula the director of a blood bank.

Perhaps the *Lega* party really does want its independence. The socioeconomic powers that support the North, in reality would be content if by law (federal, astral, weight, and military) a general decrease of the South's rights were ratified, with respect to the North: healthcare? More for us, less for you. Schools? More for us, less for you. Roads? More for us, less for you. Railways? Almost everything for us, nearly nothing for you. Any other words that are used to describe the heart of this issue are merely like gold-wrapping around a bludgeon: it covers the weapon but does nothing to weaken the blow. Having shifted the benefits in their favor: "the descendents of those rhetoricians that advocated the Unification of Italy have become those who advocate its dissolution," wrote Professor Vito Teti in his 1993 book, *La razza maledetta*. Ilvo Diamanti, from the University of Padua, in his book, *La Lega*, points out that the *Lega* area "is the location where the added industrial value registered the highest average per inhabitant and showed the largest amount of growth in the Eighties." Giuseppe

Berta (professor of modern history at the Bocconi University) recounts in his book, *Nord*, the feelings that Milan has towards its region, on one hand "proud to sustain (...) a large part of the nation" and on the other hand they feel impatient at being "the ones supported ... often by being idle and ungrateful." This is what happens when one forgets in what manner and at whose expense Milan and its region are who they are today. In order to confirm how deeply rooted this Milan-centric view really is, states Guido Piovene, "[t]he only way out that is offered to Milan in order to live with the State in Italy's current condition is to take it over." It was successful with Fascism and with "Berlusconism," but it is still not enough. They aim higher with the *Lega*.

This type of politics (the strong receive increasingly more while the weak always less) breaks countries apart because sooner or later a breaking point is reached. What the boorish *Lega* members shout now was initially whispered about in living rooms and shops. Voices become louder when civilization wanes, and the measure of decency is lost. They want to go from an apartheid that is evident from its actions to one that is ratified by law. Laws erect walls (they determine limitations to actions), and walls divide. It is a good thing if they separate assassins from possible victims. It is a bad thing when they do so by separating areas and rights in the same country. In the long run, there will no longer be one country, but two or more. Or none. The Unification of Italy was irremissible in a world that was split between two superpowers. Once the Berlin Wall fell, it was no longer the case. The wall was erected here, within us.

Superiority claimed out of more merit, from which more rights would be derived, is not a fact, but rather an idea. A wrong idea. Inferiority that justifies social disorder and fewer rights in exchange for more assistance is not a fact, but rather, an idea. A wrong idea. For anyone who might wish to insist upon this notion, I can offer another valid one of the same caliber but with more substance as reported in the first volume of *Le leggende degli ebrei* by Louis Ginzberg, a great scholar and professor of the Talmud's interpretation of the Bible.

A legend concerning the first day of Creation states that God did not touch the North, on purpose, in order to make the difference more apparent. "God left the North unfinished," writes Ginzberg, "so that anyone who proclaims themselves God can be asked to complete what is missing. In this manner his fraudulence will be revealed."

I am convinced of the legitimacy of what Professor Bocchiaro has explained. Due to a series of historical circumstances, convenience, and prejudice, roles were defined that, in turn, generated certain types of behavior. This different way of acting has become our sick way of co-existing. Psycho-sociology, however, also says that recognizing the arbitrary nature of one's roles is the way to free oneself from the improper and unequal behavior that those roles impose. It can be done, and I believe in it. India continues to remain a unified country despite its centuries-old caste system.

"The Italians from the North and South came to know each other through the crosshairs of their rifles" wrote Salvatore Scarpino in his book, *Indietro Savoia!* The prison of the "inferiors" seems to favor the guards and it deceives them, because it imprisons them as well. They too are deprived of the sun. The Stanford Experiment shows that one can emerge from this situation. The door is not closed.

If the task were simple, I would be certain of one thing: we would never be able to pull it off. The fact that it is nearly impossible, gives me hope. We are that strange country that manages to accomplish something only when we are told that we cannot.

If there is no desire to leave the prison together, the prisoner will have to escape: the door is not closed. Some have already begun to peek outside.

Amongst the Southerners, the revolution against imposed, and no longer universally accepted, inferiority trickles down many currents. It can be seen in political and cultural movements of territorial reclamation, personal eccentricity, or even "economic" secession (In Sicily, the first supermarket that sells only products from the South was constructed. A half dozen of these stores are planned for the rest of Italy, including one in Udine). When analogous movements emerged in the Alpine valleys, the daily newspapers followed their developments, analyzed them, and published reports about them. In the South, this movement is conducted in silence: all of the major newspapers are headquartered in the North and one is located in Rome. All of the private television networks are based in Milan and the public ones are strongly influenced by the owner of the private ones and his allies in Milan. All of the editors of the most important magazines (besides "*l'Espresso*") are located in the North. Their sensitivity to certain news stories is influenced by the environment in which they operate. What happens in the South is less interesting to them because it does not interest their readers. They do not consider a story that questions the prejudiced concept of the South's inferiority for publication. A website that was known to promote progressive ideas refused to publish a study conducted on the management of funds allotted for the development of the South by an economist of unquestionable scientific rigor, Viesti, because it proved that the money was not wasted. "It was not convincing," they said (but perhaps they simply did not want to be convinced). For a similar reason, Viesti was forced to discontinue his collaboration with a national financial newspaper. Vittorio Scacchi, a knight, who was the director of the Tax System and Land Registry for the Kingdom of Sardinia, who was sent to "fix" the finances and bureaucracy of the Kingdom of the Two Sicilies, allegedly ruined his career by praising its organization and proposing that the rest of the country adopt its methods. That which is in contrast to prejudice does not sound credible and is considered suspicious. Sacchi was considered to be the authority in his field. But....

In addition to the desire not to know about a certain North (while others, after initially being surprised, appear to have an insatiable desire to learn about unspoken truths), there is a corresponding growing need, in the South, to rediscover the identity that has been denied to them. "Even in history, as in science," believes Ficarra "for every action, there is an equal and opposite reaction." The episode that concerned the *Controcorrente* publishing house (which is specialized in publishing books on the real story behind the *Risorgimento*) surprised even its founder, Pietro Golia. The first volume, published in 2001 revealed the existence of a market of unexpected proportions. In nine years, they have published one hundred and fifty titles, each with a very interesting number of copies sold. "It is quite revealing that their sales continue," says Golia, "and that there is a sort of ripple effect: when someone reads one of these books, they tend to seek out the others as well." The same thing has happened with the publisher *Il Giglio* (like the Bourbon's lily symbol, you understand), which has published around twenty titles as well as DVDs that address the same topic.

This new knowledge generates a need for discussion. People seek each other out and meet. "There are anywhere from seven hundred to one thousand conventions per year," Golia informs us. From the reacquisition of one's memory, new organizations spring forth: local committees (always more numerous and active), demonstrations, booklets, books on recently rediscovered "brigands," the massacre suffered, and forgotten local history are published. It appears that, counting classic texts as well as more recent publications, there are over one thousand titles available that have been republished and have received the critiques of a network of media. These include the main monthly publications *"Due Sicilie," "l'Alfiere"* (which happens to be the oldest publication, dating from 1960), *"Il Brigante," "Nazione Napoletana,"* as well as a myriad smaller publications as well, like the *"Nuovo Sud,"* a monthly publication that is available both in print as well as on the web, which has adopted very modern notions coupled with graphic design. On the web, one can find a network of websites and blogs where all relevant news stories are commented upon and through which there is a sort of spontaneous lobbying movement. If the usual cartoon/movie about Garibaldi is aired on television or an article is published that contradicts a re-established truth about the *Risorgimento*, a wave of protests, letters, and emails is unleashed. When Mario Cervi reviewed my book, *Il trionfo dell'apparenza*, in the newspaper *"Il Giornale,"* he only objected to my allusions to a need to rewrite the story of the Unification. Obviously I thanked him for his kind attention and we discussed a great deal about the *Risorgimento*, without reaching an agreement. That, however, was sufficient to elicit an avalanche of protests directed towards Mario, some of which were quite violent. Mario has strong shoulders and replied gracefully with clarity. However, he was surprised and said he never would have expected such a response. "I did!" I responded. "The silent approval of the South is, perhaps, ending." I told him a few more things, upon which, again, we were not in agreement. Do take notice of the pages of the newspapers that publish the readers' letters and comments and you will have a better idea of what I am speaking about.

For years, by now, in the Lucania area, the theatrical season of the *Grancìa* (Italy's first rural and historical park) is centered around *La storia bandita*, a reconstruction of the epic tale of the "brigands" through the narration of its most famous story: that of Carmine Crocco Donatelli. The well-known actor Michele Placido, one of Donatelli's descendents, lends his voice to the character. Attendance is based on curiosity and often evolves into a sort of mission, conducted with a sort of militancy. It is like taking part in the commemoration of the surrendering of Gaeta. Every year in February, it is reconstructed with a historical procession, followed by a church ceremony, which then continues on the highest peak of the *Montagna Spaccata*. Here, shots are fired by people dressed in the traditional uniforms of the time, complete with historic rifles and naval cannons. It is interesting to observe the change of emotions that can be seen on the faces of the new "arrivals." These emotions range from withheld mockery to embarrassed participation, once they realize that they let themselves get carried away by the scenery (the amazing panorama definitely plays its part). One is no longer surprised by Teresa De Sio singing *Sacco e fuoco* "which speaks of the betrayal committed by the Savoy monarchs in order to damage the South" and that Eugenio Bennato and Carlo D'Angiò compose the "Brigand Anthem." One is no longer surprised that Federico Salvatore launches an invective on the monument that was never built to commemorate the Southerners that died for the Unification or that Pasquale Squitieri shoots a movie that narrates the story of the South's armed resistance (which the RAI television network airs only in the middle of the night, uselessly, when only vampires are awake, who already know everything there is to know about bloodshed).

Do you remember the *Lega* party's contrived Celtic past? In the South, there is no need to invent such things because it is sufficient to remember them. The Commander Antonio Romano (who is neither a relative of Alessandro nor of the Romano family involved in the epic history of the South, Domenico and Liborio) while on the ferry from Terracina to the island of Ponza flew the Bourbon flag, one that was truly worthy of respect, next to Italy's tricolor flag, just like when one sails in the territorial waters of another country. To be honest, this flag does not resemble the Neapolitan one. It has the shield of the Bourbon Navy. Prior to setting sail, he blared the national anthem of the Kingdom of the Two Sicilies. The Argenio family (a family of haute-couture tailors from Naples that is in strict opposition, when comparing the classic styles of attire, to the English style) were the official tailors of the Royal family and of the Bourbon Navy. The silk scarf with the golden shield of the Navy of the Kingdom of the Two Sicilies with a navy background is so valuable, that my wife refused to wear it and framed it instead. But the article of clothing that has had the most success is the tie with the reproduction of all of the units of the lost naval fleet (complete with a little horn as a good-luck charm to ward off evil). Their attention to detail is maniacal. The city where the largest number of these ties is sold is not Naples: it is Milan, followed by New York. A tie is not merely an article of clothing, but rather the last remaining frill of man's vanity. It has no practical purpose and winds up acquiring one of identity. Its colors can signify one's yacht club, soccer team, one's lost country or one's desired one. It is a symbol of membership for reciprocal acknowledgment. The Neapolitans in Milan and in America wind up attributing the continuity of their history to that strip of silk out of that pride that only emerges when one is far from home. "What nation has these colors?" narrates Salvatore Argenio about a man who asked him this question at the Pitti Fashion Show for

Men in Florence. "Where are you from," I asked him. "Naples," he responded. "Then they are the colors of your nation," I said to him. "Months later, he came to visit my store. He had begun to read books about the Kingdom of the Two Sicilies and had begun telling his family about them. In turn, they became interested as well. Now we are used to this. One tie can open the doors to history. As businessmen, we have discovered a new market. So today, we also manufacture a line of houseware with the Bourbon colors as well as watches with the Neapolitan Navy's coat of arms … and there never seem to be enough. It was not like this before. People used to be ashamed of anything affiliated with the Bourbon monarchy."

The drive to act according to a "role" in the Italy-laboratory would seem to be easier to execute in the South (where the "brigands" chose their pride between "living on their knees or dying on their feet") than in the North because it is easier to convince oneself that they deserve more rather than less. In reality, explains Bocchiaro, the difficulty faced is the same. The Southerner, by ridding himself of his inferiority, carries with him the emotional baggage that includes resentment, a desire to reclaim what was his, and built-up aggressiveness that has accumulated over the years. The Northerner does not possess these things and exits his role of "more for me and less for you, because it is right" with some leftover generosity, almost in anxiousness to give something back (was this the underlying source of the Pro-South movement?). If we can make it as a unified country, but as equals, it will be because the Northerners acknowledge the existence of discrimination that has benefitted them more than the Southerners realizing that it was damaging them (even if it is necessary for them to realize this). I know a great many Northerners who seem to disappear behind the shouts of the *Lega* party, and am lucky to consider some of them my friends. I am not "committing the error of expecting too much" as Salvemini said of Fortunato, "because I know of whom I speak." Must I remember that the Pro-South movement actually began in the North or that it emerged later on in the South? I have not forgotten the bitter conclusions of one of the most serious and honest advocates of the Pro-South movement, the Lombard, Pasquale Saraceno: "Italian experience indicates with certainty that once a dualistic situation develops, it no longer seems possible to correct it." But social movements are alive and are constantly changing, condemning us to be optimistic. If we are at the dawn of something, then it is not out of place to quote the verdict (recently dusted off by Enzo Bettiza) of a man who was in love with our country, Gregorovius, who pronounced it at the beginning of the *Risorgimento*: "Italy, as it was, could not continue to exist. Italy, as it is, cannot remain this way. Unfortunately, it will never become what it should be."

If we are not able to stay together as equals, the South could leave only to recover its dignity. In the meantime, the North already thinks of seceding to save money ("The separation, which we hope will be consensual between Padania and the South," according to Bossi, the secessionist, "...is also an economic necessity": that "also" means "only").

Where the fracture appears to be inevitable, the correct question to ask would be: should we wait for this decision to arrive out of the desire of both parties so that it finds us unprepared and we must yield to it or should we foresee it and at least make an attempt to govern its execution? As soon as it is given the opportunity, the *Lega* of the North will split the country. It attempted to do so when Italy decided to adhere to the Unified European Currency. It sustained the notion that Italy as a whole would not have been able to join the use of the euro, but that the North alone could manage it quite easily. It proposed entering the European Union in phases: the North would go first while the South would sink further into the Mediterranean Sea under the depreciated Lira that would be weighed down by a considerable portion of the national debt. Then, if it is in the state to join the rest of Europe.... They failed, and we joined the European Union as one nation. But what about the next time? The *Lega* has become more powerful and the tie that binds us to them has become more fragile. If a scant minority in the North is favorable to the secession, then a solid minority feels that the South is "far away." For Giustino Fortunato (in *Le due Italie*, published in 1912, and *La questione meridionale*), federalism "would not lessen any evil, but rather would carry many benefits with it. Any weakness in the bond of unification would signify the beginning of our shared perdition." But the world has changed and Italy could exist as two or three countries. Bruno Luverà, in his book *Il confine dell'odio*, explains that "micronationalism" emerges out of fear (particularly in the strongest regions) so that "the freedom-security duo tends to overlap the freedom-equality duo." One could even add that equality safeguards freedom, while in the name of security freedom is sacrificed sooner or later.

If we are unable to react by taking a lesson from Rodari's story about the country with no faults, we will have to learn instead from the story of the Thirty Birds, and we will have to act alone. It would be quite a disaster, but less so because it would be our choice to leave rather than to be driven out. It could actually be the beginning of a series of separations. In the South, Sicily would seize the opportunity to free itself and to finally become an island state conveniently located in the middle of the Mediterranean Sea with free ports and the possibility of having uncontrolled commerce, like the *mafia* demands. It would be like a sort of Cuba under Fulgencio Batista (with disasters and casinos, and businesses of all sorts as well as few taxes and impunities) but instead located in between Europe and Africa. In the North, Lombardy's tendency towards hegemony is not well tolerated by the other regions. Within the more deeply rooted communities, like in the Veneto region, the Milan-centric governing policies are not appreciated. Imagine if they were given a reason to do without it. The Venetians do not identify themselves in the *Padania* area, but rather in the Venetian Republic, which historically has been one of the oldest states. There is another trap that is often ignored: the *Lega* has based the heart of its policies on the concept of egotism. It is based on "me, and my money. I refuse to give my money to those who have less than I do." But the North is not homogeneous. Even if the South were removed, there would still be areas where the income is inferior to other areas. Therefore, the notion of separation, even if it were to occur in an environment where there are fewer differences, would present itself again. There are regions that have special statutes that if the State that guaranteed them were to disappear, would mean they would lose the privileges they have. Where would the South Tyrol area and the Aosta Valley wind up? Giuseppe De Rita, who has studied our country like few others, remembers that already in 1845 it was said that Italy was a "nursery of nations."

Even other countries within the European Union risk splitting up. Spain is constantly threatened by turmoil in its Catalan region and the bombs by the Basque population. Scotland aims toward a similar solution, without resorting to causing such an uproar, and is quite close to solving its problem. The Czech Republic and Slovakia split, and nothing really happened.

A few years ago, the English-speaking and the French-speaking parts of Canada were on the verge of a split as well. I remember reading that someone proposed to proceed towards the split, but only after calculating how much the poorer area should receive as compensation. Perhaps it was not this that ultimately held Canada together, but.... Belgium would probably have already divided itself amongst its French-speaking and Flemish-speaking populations, which seem to no longer be able to live together amicably, "were it not for their common debt that continues to bind them," according to Professor Gianfranco Viesti. "Who will pay it?" It is a question that one can legitimately ask us as well. Perhaps it is a coincidence that Belgium and Italy have the highest deficits in the European Community.

If it ultimately came to a split between Northern and Southern Italy, calculations would finally be in order. They should include the damages and robberies incurred by the invasion as well as the one hundred and fifty years of one-sided favoritism. Perhaps these calculations should be made anyway, so at least we would know for sure whether the Southerners should stop complaining or whether the Northerners should start paying compensations. In either case, a little bit of truth would do everyone some good. For example: one could calculate how much the railways only invested in the North and how much was (not) invested in the South. The difference should be made up (with interest, you understand, and if one truly wants to be proper about things, the damage of such inequality should also be taken into consideration). The same should be done with the roads, schools, swamp drainage, hospitals, ports, electrical power ... one could subtract what was spent for the Fund for the South, but also calculating the portion that had to be spent to pay for ordinary requirements that should not have been paid with the money from the Fund. One should also calculate that portion of the Fund that bounced from the South back to the North.

"It is better to be poor in a rich country," according to Vito Peragine. But this implies that one accepts to remain poor and actually running the risk that one's situation could worsen. If the country arms itself with laws that condemn you to always be "inferior" with respect to the others, you will never be free of your "inferiority." When the Berlin Wall came down, "the general opinion was that the East Germans were the luckiest former communists," remembers Frederick Taylor in *Il muro di Berlino*. They had a powerful brother while the Czechs, Slovaks, Hungarians, Poles, and Balkans would have to make it on their own." In reality, this revealed itself to be a disadvantage. West Germany transferred a considerable sum of money over to the East and invested in infrastructures of all types so that those territories could be equal to those in the West. However, the "Syndrome of the Wall" remained (it is thought, or perhaps it is hoped, that this might disappear within another generation). It consists of the shared notion, on the part of both the West and the East, that the latter is inferior. The unification brought about a nearly equal economic status to both parts. The people in the West accepted to have a certain amount of money removed from their salaries for the East. Those in the East, in agreement with their Unions, agreed to receive salaries that were twenty percent lower in exchange for both the quantity and quality of services that they would receive. And yet ... "[s]mall, ancient, splendid little towns, though they were rebuilt with money from the West are declining and are losing their youths. The population is aging at a frightening speed," according to Taylor.

What happened? The funds allotted skipped over East Germany and ended up creating jobs in those Eastern European countries that seemed to be drifting away after having lost their big Eastern brother without having created one in the West. Slovakia is quickly becoming the European country with the highest number of employees in the automobile industry, ahead of Germany, France, and Italy. Another important piece of information could belong to this category: Southern Italy recorded one of the most interesting economic comebacks when, at the end of the year 2000, it lost its Fund for the South and for a few years did not receive any incentives from the State.(This means that politics did not insert itself between businesses and their money because the power that elsewhere belongs to big businesses or high finance "instead was attributed, in the regions of the South to those classes that manage public spending" as Adriano Giannola confirms in *L'economia e il Mezzogiorno*. It would be sufficient for this class to reveal the essence of that power, which is subordinate and colonial, in the South, which emerges from and is supported by the management of "granted" resources, which are to be extorted and redistributed).

How much is the South worth if it were to be detached from the rest of Italy? Very little. We would be the last country in the European Union, and perhaps we would not even meet the requirements to be a part of it (While when the Unification was forcefully completed we were in third place behind Great Britain and France as far as industry was concerned. We were in first place considering our technological innovations and civil liberties and were considered behind only in infrastructures and roads).

But, alone, we would have the chance to transform our delays into opportunities for development without having to give them up, like we do now, while waiting for those in power to decide whether we "deserve" them or not. Take the railways as an example. We would no longer have to beg those who manage them not to prune the "dead branches" (which they caused to die). Instead, we could assign them to the French railway builders, which are amongst the best in the world, for a certain number of years, with advantages for both of us. What about the Bridge over the Strait of Messina? The biggest American companies (including those responsible for building the Golden Gate Bridge in San Francisco and the Verrazano Bridge in New York) had already offered to build it, by contributing funds in exchange for its management for a certain period of time. The IRI (the Institute for Industrial Reconstruction) allowed for this proposal to fail and then took over the task itself, while biding its time, you know, for a few decades, because it did not believe it was a priority. What about the highways? The Japanese are experts in building roads in areas of elevated seismic activity. We would only have to pay them tolls, rather than Benetton.

And then, since our income would no longer have to be "averaged" with that of the North, we would immediately be eligible as a European country for those economic incentives allotted for development. This would come along with a considerable additional advantage: that Europe's funds allotted for the South would stay in the South, because Tremonti would no longer be able to use them as a piggy bank for the North. They would be forced to build the Milan Expo Center with the money allotted for Milan, and not those allotted for underutilized areas. They could continue to offer abatements on the ICI property tax, but without using the funds that are allotted for the highways in Calabria and Sicily. They would no longer be able to barter with the investments made for the "Adriatic Corridor" in Southern Europe (this is the highway that would have linked the South to the rest of the European continent) for the umpteenth, useless, detrimental airport in the Padania area, like Malpensa. The Bari-Malpensa flight with Alitalia costs more than the Bari-New York flight, to the extent that many people from Bari heading to Milan purchase tickets for New York and when they reached Malpensa to catch their "connecting" flight, they simply throw out their other ticket. To go from Palermo to Tunis, it is necessary to pass through Malpensa Airport. Approximately 90% of travelers from the South are rerouted through Malpensa Airport. If a location were to be selected to house the headquarters of the European Authority on Nutrition, perhaps the home of pizza and the Mediterranean Diet could stand a chance.... Need I continue?

The South, alone, would immediately sink in a dreadful situation. It would seriously risk to drown, but also to learn how to swim. It would be a new beginning. It would be the onset of a strong personal identity and the awareness of such a challenge would provide it with a considerable drive. When it was not hindered (either openly or subtly) from doing something, the South has demonstrated its ability to accomplish things. Once the Fund for the South was abolished and the "extraordinary" interventions on the part of the State were stopped, it was believed that the South would crash. This was not the case. In fact, in an unplanned reaction, the South had never produced and exported as much as it did in the second half of the Nineties. It can do that again, maybe even better, if it were not conditioned by the directions of the *Lega* and its undeclared affiliates. Where it would fail, it would receive what it deserved. But at least it would know what it deserved, without having to trust the wisdom and fairness of Calderoli.

No matter what direction we move in, we always reach the same point: where our history was interrupted. We must start from there, even if it means undoing what was done and going back to being alone. And what then? Well, we could always reunite, but as equals. Perhaps it would take a few generations. Hollywood, in a well-known movie, already reminded us that Renaissance Italy, which was divided and at war, gave the world Michelangelo, Leonardo, Dante, Machiavelli, Galileo.... Switzerland, in its five hundred years of peaceful existence, managed to give us a cuckoo clock. I can already see some fringe benefits: it would be much easier to find someone who took their exams in Reggio Calabria in order to assign the Ministry of Public Education.

On January 16th, 2010, the newly "resurrected" Parliament of the Two Sicilies convened. There were one hundred and thirty people that convened in the Barons' Antechamber of the Anjou

Tower in Naples (the castle located by the port). "We want to establish a new ruling class in the South comprised of competent and motivated experts that represent the South's will as well as its interests. It also needs to represent the South's dignity in order to ensure that this part of the country is no longer a pawn that is moved at the convenience of others" stated Gennaro De Crescenzo, the president of the Neoborbonic Movement that launched this initiative. "Our 'government' has few 'ministries' with which to control the works of those Southerners who have been elected to the European Assembly, as well as the national, regional, and municipal governments. It proposes to analyze laws and legislative measures in order to evaluate their impact upon the South, and to denounce them if they are not observed. We propose to suggest corrections and alternatives. In our Parliament, rather than include well known personalities, we prefer to have professionals, artisans, lawyers, experts, university professors, and businessmen who are in a position to understand, criticize and propose notions."

So this would be the Shadow-Government of the South.

"No, no. This would be the Light-Government, to diffuse information and to make sure that everyone understands what has not been spoken about or that has been neglected. Our history has never been thoroughly investigated and we have never witnessed such a desire to know about ourselves."

He proceeds to explain that the term "Neoborbonic" does not mean that they desire the return of the dynasty and the regime. "We opted to call ourselves in this fashion because all that is affiliated with the Bourbon dynasty has been denigrated. We decided that we needed to re-conquer respect, starting with our words. We only want to succeed in educating a ruling class that is not subordinate. In this manner, anyone, according to their own ideas, could represent the South, and not some delegate from somewhere else. It does not matter if they are on the Left or on the Right. That Italy could be one, divided, federalist, a republic, or a monarchy could be pleasing to some and not to others. But we would no longer be followers. We have no affiliations with any political parties, which is both our weakness and our strength. The *Lega* tried to infiltrate itself because we share some common beliefs. Then you hear the likes of Salvini ("Neapolitans, you stink") and Calderoli ("Naples is a sewer" whose rats must be exterminated) and your hands begin to get itchy. Rocchetta, from the *Liga Veneta*, came to visit several times to advocate federalism. 'This means we choose the companies that will build our infrastructures as well as the automobile industry, perhaps even Spanish or Japanese companies.... We will also tax *panettone*.' 'No way,' was his reply. 'Well then we aren't interested,' we replied, and we never saw him again."

De Crescenzo says that they are most interested in safeguarding the dignity of the people even if it means not adhering to proper legal form. If they can salvage that, the rest will be what it can be.

The inferiority of one part of a country would eventually come to a breaking point anyway. Unbalanced social systems don't last forever, even though they can last for a long time. A universal law that I learned late in life, states: no one can hurt you more than you allow them to. For the South, the question is: to what point, for how long? Something is happening. It could be another jolt that is then placated (like a sort of release of accumulated social tension) or it could be the turning point. I don't know.

But I have witnessed some negotiations in the market in Calabria. I have understood when the seller marks off a price limit below which he is willing to forego the client: "*Ni bulìti u cùariu i' mia?*" he says. Are you after my skin?

At that point, no means no.

One day I read a phrase by Francesco Saverio Nitti and I felt ashamed: "History and life are composed of things which are forgotten." Forgive me for everything (for having learned things late, the tones I have assumed, any excesses I have allowed for, and any errors and lapses I have made) in my attempt to remember and to understand what I did not know that I am.

The Southerners happened to lose their past, the world from which they came. They are exiles from their own history and their own memories. They are exiles in their own home. They are simply exiles. This happened from nearly one day to the next, and all that they were was declared to be extinct. Some of their behaviors remained amidst the ruins, and not even the best of these. The best was either stolen or destroyed. That disfigured level of quality has its weight, and it is further emphasized by those who disfigured it. Remember what Predrag Matvejevic wrote in *Mondo ex*: "It is necessary to read a page before turning it." We are trying to recover the pages that were torn out so that we can finally know something about ourselves. If anyone is annoyed by "the nauseating stench of dead words," it is their own problem. In order to find itself, our center (I am borrowing and adapting a concept conceived by Joseph Roth) must temporarily migrate to the outskirts of history. That which we learned from the false past that was handed to us by the victors is not useful in a future that still wants to view us as foreigners. The recovery of our memory and lost pride will not be sufficient if we do not accept the full responsibility of our fate, which no one should blame us for while claiming the right to rule it for us.

"A learned and virtuous man, whose holy words nourished wise men," Firdusi underscores in *Il Libro dei Re*, "once said, 'He who does not obey reason will be destroyed by his own deeds.'"

It is impressive to discover in the book *Il Cigno nero*, by Nassim Nicholas Taleb, that what we call history is actually a sequence of events that are almost always unexpected by its contemporaries. It is a series of events that happen when one was preparing for something else entirely. The son of a carpenter composes a doctrine that the Roman Empire would eventually inherit. Columbus stumbles unexpectedly upon a continent that he did not calculate. An African American that no one had ever really taken into consideration becomes President of the United States....

In a nice volume edited by Franca Pinto Minerva, *Mediterraneo*, I read the response that a Tunisian man who lives in Palermo offers: "What is my country? It is the one that accepts me."

Today, can the Southerners truly say that they have a country? A future that is shared on a common land? Or can the complaint of the Muslim Slavs of the Balkans pertain to them as well: "We have been separated from our people without having been accepted by the others"?

A little over sixty years after the Unification, Tommaso Fiore, upon being asked by Piero Gobetti (who would later become a victim of Fascism) in Turin to describe the South, said that he did not believe it would be useful: "Our life has been." The South was considered an archaeological relic.

On the wall behind my desk I've had hanging, for years, two phrases by Paolo Borsellino. One is about Palermo, which he did not like, but loved for the same reason. The other phrase cost him his life: "One day, this land will be beautiful."

I believe that there is no other land in Europe today that has a more promising future, and as many riches to offer, than our South.

About the Author

Journalist and author of numerous books, PINO APRILE was born in Gioia del Colle, in Puglia. He currently resides in the Castelli Romani region of Lazio. He worked for many years in Milan. He was director of *Gente* and deputy director of *Oggi*. For television, he worked with Sergio Zavoli on the investigative series *Journey South*, and a weekly program for Tg1 (RAI News1): Tv7.

He is the author of numerous books translated into several languages. *Elogio dell'imbecille. Gli intelligenti hanno fatto il mondo, gli stupidi ci vivono alla grande* (Piemme, 2002); *Elogio dell'errore* (Piemme, 2003); *Il mare minore* (Magenes, 2004); *Il trionfo dell'apparenza* (Piemme, 2007); *A mari estremi* (Magenes, 2007); and *Mare Uomini Passioni* (Electa Mondadori, 2007). *Terroni* (Piemme, 2010) is his first book translated into English.

In August 2011, he was awarded honorary citizenship in San Bartolomeo in Galdo.

About the Translator

ILARIA MARRA ROSIGLIONI is Secretary to the Board of Directors and Special Events Coordinator for ILICA (Italian Language Inter-Cultural Alliance); she currently resides in Rome, Italy. She earned her B.A. in Italian Studies and Art History from Georgetown University.

RINGRAZIAMENTI • ACKNOWLEDGEMENTS

Questo fu il primo libro al quale cominciai a lavorare, più di trent'anni fa: non lo concludevo mai, ritenendolo sempre insufficiente, come il suo autore. Nel frattempo, ne ho scritti altri otto. Per tre volte la mia casa editrice mi inviò un anticipo e mi dette una scadenza, che divenne un affettuoso ordine nel 2009. Della pazienza e della decisione sono grato alla Piemme e a Maria Giulia Castagnone. E sarei falso se nascondessi l'emozione che ho provato nel ricevere il mio libro tradotto in inglese, per "gli americani."

L'ultimo mio parente emigrato a New York è morto qualche anno fa, eravamo coetanei. Il primo a mettervi piede fu Giuseppe Punzi, il 26 marzo 1914: aveva 34 anni, era di Laterza (Taranto), partito con la nave Europa, da Napoli. Quattro anni dopo, per tre notti sognò sua figlia Anna che gli diceva di essere morta. Scrisse alla moglie: "Ditemi la verità!" Era vero. Allora lui tornò. Un anno dopo, sua moglie partorì un'altra bambina e la chiamarono Anna: mia madre; e di nonno Giuseppe porto il nome. Lo scopro oggi, a 61 anni, il giorno prima che l'edizione americana di *Terroni* vada in stampa, e solo perché ne ho parlato con mia madre. Ho trovato il nome di mio nonno nel "manifesto" di Ellis Island del 26 marzo 1914, alla riga 0022.

Non potrò mai ringraziare per quanto meritano il professor Anthony Julian Tamburri, direttore del John Calandra Italian American Institute, Vincenzo Marra, fondatore di Ilica, e Ilaria Marra Rosiglioni, per avermi fatto recuperare un frammento perduto della storia della mia famiglia.

This was the first book I began to write more than thirty years ago; I was never able to finish, considering it always inadequate, as its author. In the meantime, I have written eight more. My publisher sent me an advance and gave me a deadline three times, which became an affectionate order in 2009. I am grateful to Piemme and to Maria Giulia Castagnone for their patience and decision to move forward. I would be dishonest if I hid the emotions I felt in seeing my book translated into English, for the "Americans."

My last relative to immigrate to New York died a few years ago; we were peers. The first to set foot there was Giuseppe Punzi, on March 26, 1914: he was 34 years old, from Laterza (Taranto), who left from Naples on the ship Europe. Four years later, for three nights he dreamed of his daughter Anna, who told him she was dead. He wrote to his wife: "Tell me the truth!" It was true. Then he returned. A year later, his wife gave birth to another girl, and they named her Anna, my mother, and I am named after my grandfather Giuseppe. I discovered this today, at age 61, the day before the American edition of *Terroni* goes to press, and only because I spoke with my mother about it. I found the name of my grandfather in the "Manifesto" of Ellis Island, dated March 26, 1914, row 0022.

I could never thank Professor Anthony Julian Tamburri, director of the John Calandra Italian American Institute, Vincenzo Marra, founder of ILICA, and Ilaria Marra Rosiglioni enough for allowing me to retrieve a lost fragment of my family's history.

Published by BORDIGHERA, INC., an independently owned not-for-profit scholarly organization that has no legal affiliation to the University of Central Florida or the John D. Calandra Italian American Institute, Queens College, City University of New York.